Circle of Grace

CIRCLE OF GRACE

*Praying with—and
for—Your Children*

GREGORY & SUZANNE M. WOLFE

BALLANTINE BOOKS · NEW YORK

A Ballantine Book
The Ballantine Publishing Group

Due to space limitations, the permissions and
acknowledgments can be found on pages 369–370.

www.randomhouse.com/BB/

Library of Congress Card Number: 00-105771

ISBN 0-345-41717-8

Text design by Debbie Glasserman

Manufactured in the United States of America

First Edition: October 2000

10   9   8   7   6   5   4   3   2   1

For Magdalen, Helena, Charles, and Benedict

He prayeth best, who loveth best
All things both great and small;
For the dear God who loveth us,
He made and loveth all.
—SAMUEL TAYLOR COLERIDGE

If you cannot pray in the synagogue, pray in your field. If you
cannot pray in your field, pray in your house. If you cannot
pray in your house, pray on your bed. If you cannot pray on
your bed, meditate in your heart.
—MIDRASH ON PSALM 4:9

What does it matter how I pray,
so long as my prayers are answered?
—SITTING BULL

Contents

Contents

PART 2: WITHIN THE CIRCLE—
THE PRAYERS

Acknowledgments

In writing this book, one of the lessons we've learned is that the act of giving thanks lies at the heart of prayer. And so we'd like to offer thanks for the many people who grace our lives and who have contributed to this book in myriad ways.

We'd like to thank our agent, Carol Mann, for her steadfast support, and our editor, Joanne Wyckoff, not only for her patience but also for the idea that launched this book into being.

The research and writing of this book were supported by a grant from the John Templeton Foundation.

We have benefited enormously from conversations about prayer with Kim Alexander, Robert Atwan, Leah Buturain, Scott Cairns, David Cullen, Richard Foster, Emilie and William Griffin, Jan Krist, Madeleine L'Engle, Paul Mariani, Michael Medved, Kathleen Norris, Eugene Peterson, Luci Shaw, Jeanne Murray Walker, and Walter Wangerin Jr. We're grateful to all of them.

We're also grateful to all those who have supported *Image: A Journal of the Arts and Religion*, the quarterly journal we founded a little over ten years ago. While *Image* is a journal for grown-ups, it has played a central role in our quest to understand the relationship between faith and imagination. The writers and artists we've come to know through *Image* have nourished us in countless ways.

For some crucial last-minute help, our thanks to Heather Vlach.

Our children—Magdalen, Helena, Charles, and Benedict—have been our best teachers and guides in the life of prayer. They are living proof that prayer doesn't have to make one prissy or stuck-up. Not by a long shot.

Finally, to the One who hears all prayers—from stuttered pleas for help to the adoration of the mystics—with equal attention, and whose wordless love sustains the universe, be all honor, glory, and praise, now and forever.

Introduction

Is there anything more pure, more full of wonder and hope for the future, than the prayer of a child? We find it difficult to imagine what that might be. For a child's heart, when it forms a prayer of thanks or praise or petition, has none of the self-consciousness and ambivalence of adulthood; it is a laser beam of light and love—focused, clear, and burning with urgency.

Prayer is natural to human beings, whether they are children or grown-ups. It takes place all the time, and not just in churches and synagogues. As Rabbi Hayim Halevy Donin has pointed out, we pray even when we don't realize we're praying. "Thank God!" we sigh in relief, on hearing that someone we love has begun to recover from a serious illness and is out of danger. Some prayers don't even invoke God's name: a gorgeous sunset might evoke a murmured response ("How glorious!") that is really an act of praise; a guilty conscience might bring us back to someone we've hurt ("Forgive me"), as our desire for reconciliation reaches upward as well as outward.

But prayer, like many other human capacities, will atrophy if it is not used and developed. Children possess an innate ability to pray, just as they have a built-in capacity to learn language. Most people wouldn't dream of being silent all the time around a child; we not only talk in the presence of our children but we devote a great deal of time to teaching them words and their proper meanings, pronunciations, and grammatical relationships. As parents, we help our children learn to name and thus understand the world around them.

Prayer is a particular form of language (though it often aspires to go beyond words) that children can pick up with the same ease as they do any other kind of speech. But the tragic reality is that those of us who live in the prosperous Western nations have largely failed, in recent generations, to teach our children the language of prayer. This failure, this neglect of our children's spiritual dimension, has had grave consequences for the moral and psychic health of our culture.

If you are reading this book, the odds are that you care deeply for children and want to find ways to enrich their lives and deepen their hearts through prayer. The moral decay that now permeates our culture places children at greater risk than ever before: violence, drugs, teenage pregnancy, and suicide loom like the Four Horsemen of the Apocalypse over our children's lives. The number of incidents where children commit violent, senseless crimes is on the rise. As we write, the horror of the Littleton, Colorado, high school massacre is still sending shock waves through America.

Even if the vast majority of our children will never directly experience the extremes of violence or criminal behavior, there is a widespread feeling that the innocence and idealism of youth cannot survive in such a cynical and materialistic society. We worry about a generation growing up whose emotions and moral sensibilities are blunted, and we say that something needs to be done.

But what *can* be done? Our first impulse—an impulse that is quickly taken up by politicians—is to restrict children's access to bad things. So we propose stricter gun control laws and install V-chips in our TV sets. There is much to be said for such measures, but most people recognize their limits. In the long run it is what lies *inside* children's hearts—rather than externals like guns and violent movies—that will determine their behavior and their future. Nurturing a child's heart is a task that takes years of love and attention; it's not a task that can be accomplished by legislation, however well intentioned.

That's why more and more parents are questioning the moral health of our culture. Now that they are parents themselves, recent generations—from boomers to Generation Xers—are rethinking the abandonment of traditional values and disciplines and are casting about for ways to instill moral values in their children without repeating the sins of smugness and narrow-mindedness committed by earlier generations.

Celebrating the virtues has rightly become an important element of character education. But too often discussion of the virtues remains abstract, as if classroom discussions about courage will make children courageous. We do need to talk more—particularly around the dinner table—about morality, but the limitation of talk is that it remains a thing of the head and not the heart.

The secret to your child's moral and spiritual development is this: your child should not simply *admire* goodness, but should actually *fall in love with* goodness. The Greek philosopher Plato believed that in order to live a full human existence we must develop a feeling of *eros* for the Good. Today we associate the word *eros* with "erotic," or merely sexual, love, but for the Greeks *eros* conveyed a passion that involved the whole of a person's character.

Traditionally, it was in reading—and listening to—stories, including the great epic tales of heroes, that children developed *eros* for the good, the true, and the beautiful. Storytelling anchors the virtues in the experience of believable characters. Through the miracle of imagination, a child can enter into a sympathetic relationship with the heroes of great literature, vicariously experiencing both their mistakes and their achievements. In previous books we have written on the relationship between storytelling and virtue, stressing the need to expose children to books and films that exemplify the moral imagination.

But in addition to storytelling, there is another path to a child's moral development: prayer. We have become convinced that prayer can become an essential part of a child's emotional and psychological growth—helping to bridge the gap between *knowing* what is good and *doing* what is good.

For most of the twentieth century—one of the most secular periods in human history—prayer was not something that one discussed in public. Even when prayer wasn't dismissed outright as a relic of primitive religion, it was reduced to something that was utterly private and individualistic. Of course, prayer *is* an intensely private experience in the soul of each human being, but so is romantic love, marriage, patriotism, and nearly every other affair of the heart. Yet in all these other realms we recognize that private experience intersects with universal truths, truths that we can and must address publicly.

At the dawn of the new millennium, prayer is no longer taboo. For the sake of our children and our future, it is time that we explore this ancient and hallowed means for reaching out beyond our human limitations to seek a higher power.

Of course, the first thing that many of us say to ourselves when we consider whether we should bring prayer into the life of our family is "How can I teach my kids to pray if I don't know how to pray myself?" There's the rub. It's at this point that many of us hesitate, perched on the knife-edge between good intentions and the challenge of putting them into practice.

Scientists have a phrase for the way human beings absorb new information: they call it the learning curve. In most cases the learning curve is steep at first, as we struggle to understand both the basic concepts and the finer points. But after a while the curve levels off and we become able to assimilate new ideas more quickly.

The learning curve for prayer can appear formidably steep and intimidating. But it is just at the moment of hesitation that grace lies in wait for us. When parents hesitate to teach children something they don't know themselves, they have already stepped out onto the right path, though they may not recognize it. Most of us sense that prayer is something that we must practice before we can preach it. This desire to avoid hypocrisy is in itself a step in the direction of spiritual authenticity. In the life of the spirit, wanting is often the same as having. The twentieth-century French novelist Georges Bernanos once said: "The wish to pray is a prayer in itself. . . . God can ask no more than that of us." And fifteen hundred years ago St. Augustine prayed: "We would not seek You if we had not already found You."

And that brings us to the purpose of this book. It is our hope that we can provide encouragement—and a little help with the learning curve—as you embark on the adventure of praying with your children.

Of course, it is possible to purchase one of the hundreds of collections of prayers for children on the market and give it to your children. But, to return to the analogy we used above, that would be a little like giving a two-year-old a dictionary and wishing her luck.

The central thesis of this book is that parents need to do more than simply give their kids prayers to say. Rather, parents should learn to pray themselves by praying *with* their children. This leads directly to the other conviction at the core of this book: that there is nothing wrong with making family prayer the springboard that helps you to develop your own interior life. The first thing that attentive parents discover when they teach their children to pray is that the children quickly become the teachers, reminding us of the innocence and wonder that we have lost, and restoring it to us with a grace and simplicity that can take our breath away.

In writing *Circle of Grace* we have tried to produce something that is more than just a manual of prayer. We've taken a few tentative steps in the direction of what we can only call the spirituality of family life. In the course of assembling this book we found— to our amazement—that very little has been written about the relationship between the ordinary, every-day experiences of living together as a family and the inner world of the spirit. Our emphasis, then, is not simply on the how-to of prayer but also on the moral and emotional *contexts* in which family prayer can take place.

Prayer is not a subject on which we consider ourselves authorities. Neither of us is ordained, nor do we have degrees in theology. Our credentials for writing on this subject are simply that we are the parents of four children ranging in age from pre-schooler to teenager and that we have been praying with them for over twelve years now. We've relied on our own experiences, a few good books, and a series of conversations with spiritual writers who have plumbed the depths of prayer.

We're not going to pretend that we're a Super Family—clean-cut, well adjusted, full of greeting-card sentiments. Not hardly. We snap at each other when we're tired. We try—and fail—to balance work and family time. We struggle on a daily basis with selfishness, resentment, and anxiety. To put it delicately, we are an *expressive* family, which sometimes means that all six of us are screaming at one another at the top of our lungs. On the other hand, we are also a physically demonstrative bunch—hugging, kissing, biting, wrestling, and so on. For better or worse, no emotion is repressed in the Wolfe household. And yet somehow we manage to hang in there, find the time to calm down, and even lift our voices in prayer. Slowly but surely, prayer has become an essential part of our cohesiveness as a family.

It is all too easy, when addressing the subject of children and prayer, to slip into sentimentality and a pious, otherworldly tone—what the poet Patricia Hampl calls the "eau de cologne language of spirituality." We've tried to avoid that mind-set like the plague it is. On the contrary, we'd like to think of ourselves as spiritual realists. As every parent knows quite well, family life is an exercise in barely contained chaos: babies crying, older kids rampaging, parents struggling with exhaustion and a day that is never long enough. Family prayer times are commonly beset by fidgeting, bickering kids, ringing phones, distractions galore. In these circumstances it isn't likely that we will find mystical illumination, or even emotional uplift.

That's why it is so important to remember that prayer is an art. Like any art, prayer requires us to overcome the powerful force of inertia. The life of the spirit requires time and discipline to grow; you can't just take a few prayers, add water, and expect instant holiness. The self-help industry has generated a lot of revenue by promising seven (or some other quasi-sacred number) "easy steps" to healing, wisdom, and prosperity. But the great spiritual masters know that the only effective steps are the small ones that we take every day of our lives—just like a one-year-old learning to walk.

The good news is that with discipline comes liberation. The obvious analogy here is with the musician who practices. After practicing innumerable scales and arpeggios, musicians can play with such freedom that they seem to be making up the music as they go along.

So it is with prayer. Somehow, by placing ourselves on a daily basis in the precincts of grace, the joy of heaven can suddenly irrupt into our lives. In our household, there are times when family prayers take place in the midst of giggles, good-natured wrestling matches, and the occasional naughty joke. Our family would certainly scandalize those who think that piety requires a long face and rigid posture. But there's no reason why prayer has to turn anyone into a prig. Many of the great saints and holy ones have possessed a mischievous sense of humor. In this regard St. Francis of Assisi springs to mind; he often indulged in playful irony. To take just one example, he loved to call his body, with all its embarrassments and complaints, "Brother Ass."

We've tried to write about prayer in the same vein of earthy humor and realism that characterized St. Francis's approach to life. If prayer has any meaning at all, it is about the way the divine penetrates the earthly, making ordinary things radiant and turning the chaos of our days into a joyful dance. As G. K. Chesterton once said, "Angels fly because they take themselves lightly."

There are other challenges that face those who try to write about prayer. For example, this book is addressed to a large and diverse readership, and yet prayer is a practice that often takes place within specific religious communities and traditions. What makes this even more difficult for us is that we have great respect for the differences and specific habits and rituals of the world's enduring religious traditions. Americans have a tendency to think that they can create their own personal systems of belief, but the attempt frequently leads to stagnation rather than freedom, eccentricity rather than wisdom. So we were faced with the question of how to show respect for specific traditions while also striving for breadth and variety in approaches.

In struggling to find the proper balance, we have followed two basic principles. First, both the prayers selected and our commentaries on them keep to the middle of the stream rather than paddling up the individual tributaries. In other words, we include many prayers from the Roman Catholic tradition, but not the Rosary or other prayers that involve a theology that is clearly unacceptable to non-Catholics. In a similar vein, we've gathered many Jewish prayers and blessings, but not entire Jewish ceremonies that properly belong to a specific, communal context. And so on. However, if you are offended by encountering the prayers of traditions other than your own, this book is not for you.

Second, we've borrowed an idea from C. S. Lewis's popular book *Mere Christianity*. In his preface, Lewis says that his exposition of Christian doctrine is intended to serve as a hallway—a meeting place where many different believers find common ground. But Lewis goes on to say that a hallway is not a dwelling place. Most of us need to find the door of the tradition that seems most welcoming to our spirits, and then to enter into that room to eat our meals and get warm by the fire. Some people prefer to move from room to room, sampling the goodness of several different traditions. The danger of this approach is that it becomes a sort of spiritual dabbling—an assortment of finger foods rather than a square meal. However, a serious interest in the diversity of religious expression around the world is an antidote to arrogant provincialism.

Our hope is that this book will also serve as a hallway, and that you will move on into the rooms where you can find nourishment and comfort. To that end, we've included an annotated bibliography that includes several classic and contemporary works from a variety of religious traditions.

Then there is the vital question of who it is that we are praying *to*. Some people would say that it doesn't matter to whom prayers are addressed because prayers have a therapeutic value in and of themselves. Prayer, to this way of thinking, has a calming effect and is simply a form of "personal expression." There's an element of truth to that. Prayer can bring deep inner peace and it is always colored by our unique personalities. But we consider it both ill-advised and self-defeating to think of prayer as merely a therapeutic device. If you approach prayer from a purely utilitarian point of view, as a stress-relieving technique, you're bound to be disappointed. There are many practices, ancient and modern, that are geared to calming body and soul, including meditation, deep breathing, and guided visualization. Prayer, however, requires us to *speak,* and even if we never hear an audible answer to our prayers, the whole process only makes sense if we are entering into a conversation with some*one*.

Here the witness of our children can infuse a healthy dose of common sense into the discussion. A child addresses his or her prayers to a *person* and seeks attention—and answers—from that transcendent figure. Children have a startling capacity for praying in a naturally conversational tone, as if they were talking to a beloved aunt or uncle. Modern psychology has brought much good to our world, but some of its more ideological strains have tended to caricature faith and spirituality as products of "childish delusion." We prefer to side with the Pulitzer Prize–winning child psychiatrist Robert Coles, who refuses to reduce faith to wish fulfillment. After a lifetime of work with children all over the world, Coles wrote *The Spiritual Life of Children,* in which he concluded that he sees children "as seekers, as young pilgrims well aware that life is a finite journey and as anxious to make sense of it as those of us who are farther along in the time allotted us."

We don't want to imply that prayer is incompatible with doubt or uncertainty about the existence and character of God. As most of the great spiritual writers attest, doubt is a close cousin to faith; healthy doubt, allied to an open mind and a curious heart, provides fertile ground for the inner life. Coles's analogy of the pilgrim is apt here. A pilgrim is not a mere wanderer; he has a goal, whether that be God or some form of enlightenment. But even the most ardent pilgrim knows that he is still on the road, that the journey is marked by moments where the path is sometimes clear and sometimes hard to discern. Just be careful that you don't let your adult uncertainties become a burden to your child. And by the same token, don't assume that your child's faith is merely naïve, that it cannot help you to recapture an intuitive knowledge that you've found difficult to hold on to.

Jesus rebuked his disciples for keeping children away from him. They had fallen into a trap not unlike that of some psychologists: they looked on spirituality as the serious business of grown-ups. But Jesus said: "Let the children come unto me, and do not hinder them; for to such belongs the kingdom of heaven" (Matthew 19:14).

So, with children as our guides and teachers, we write from the perspective that prayer is addressed to a personal God who created the world and who knows and loves each and every one of us in that world, and who answers our prayers in real, if mysterious, ways.

The first four chapters of *Circle of Grace* address the central features of prayer in the context of family life. Chapter 1 raises the question of why prayer is so urgently needed in family life today. Chapter 2 contains a sketch of what we call "a spirituality of family life" and the ways in which prayer can help us cope with conflict and stress. Chapter 3 focuses on the role that prayer can play in your child's moral, cognitive, and spiritual development. Chapter 4 responds to the many practical questions that occur to parents when seeking to introduce their children to prayer. When do I begin praying with my children? What if parents are of mixed faiths? Are there particular places or postures that are conducive to prayer? And so on. The remainder of the book is devoted to a collection of classic and contemporary prayers. Each chapter or section of prayers is introduced with anecdotes from our own family or from other families and contains practical suggestions for how to integrate the many different types of prayer into your family devotions.

It is our earnest hope that you will unlock your child's—and your own—potential for the divine conversation that is prayer. It is a well-known paradox of the spiritual life that when we gather together and focus our love and attention outward—on God's goodness and grace—we actually grow closer to one another. That is the secret of praying together as a family.

Part One

FORMING THE CIRCLE

Chapter 1

THE LOST LANGUAGE OF THE HEART:
Why You Should Pray with Your Children

A couple years ago, while we were browsing at an airport newsstand, our attention was caught by a headline on the cover of *Esquire*. The phrase went something like, "Yes, Virginia, there is a Jesus!" The facetious wording seemed appropriate to *Esquire*, a magazine that has always been sophisticated, literary, and thoroughly hip. But when we turned to the article to which the headline referred, we found something entirely unexpected: a serious and moving essay by the novelist Rick Moody entitled "Why I Pray."

Moody is a novelist who is perhaps best known for his book *The Ice Storm,* which was made into a film directed by Ang Lee. A painfully honest exploration of the moral, emotional, and social upheavals of the 1960s and 1970s, the novel traces the impact of these cultural changes in the lives of two prosperous couples in a Connecticut suburb.

Moody's essay in *Esquire* was autobiographical and

touched briefly on his own experience of living in the world depicted in *The Ice Storm*. He grew up in a wealthy Connecticut suburb, and like many privileged children in that world, he went to the best private schools and, eventually, to an Ivy League college, Brown University. And yet, despite all these advantages, Moody became a drug addict, beginning with marijuana and quickly running the gamut of illegal substances, from hash to LSD. After a ten-year-long binge he ended up in a ward of a Brooklyn psychiatric hospital with fellow addicts, alcoholics, and a group of other in-patients suffering from various forms of mental illness. There, for the first time in his life, he began to pray in earnest.

In attempting to trace what went wrong, Moody tells a story that many of us who are parents today can identify with. As a boy he found that Sundays in his mainline Protestant church were dull and lifeless. The adults in church, whom he looked on as "unclothed emperors," prayed for "the kinds of virtues that they rarely manifested in their own lives." He and his brother would sneak into their parents' bedroom and turn off the alarm clock, thus ensuring that they would miss Sunday school and church. That meant a whole morning in front of the television.

In high school and college, Moody sought alternative forms of bliss. "Belief wasn't something I, or my peers, believed in. At best, we felt strongly about ex-perimentation with drugs and about certain bombastic kinds of rock 'n' roll, and we believed that other people should leave us alone to pursue these interests without interference." But there came a day in the psychiatric ward when he found himself weeping for the hollowness he felt at the center of his being. Suddenly he found himself praying in desperation for rescue, and he has prayed ever since.

For a great many of us who were born into the baby boom generation or shortly thereafter, Moody's story has an eerie resonance. Whether we indulged in drugs or not, most of us grew up believing that we had cast off the hypocrisies and pretences of the older generations. We scorned the picture-perfect families depicted in black-and-white sitcoms, with their bland, comfortable lives and glib pieties. Our generation, we thought, was going to slough off the outdated moral conventions of the past. We would revel in our newfound freedom and allow ourselves and our children to develop in an organic, natural way.

We boomers have looked on our religious upbringings in various ways. Some of us felt traumatized by religious education that was harsh and inhuman, dedicated as it was to rules and regulations that seemed to deny our inner emotional life. Many others simply drifted away from the tasteless and odorless religion that Moody describes. In *The Cloister Walk*, poet and spiritual writer Kathleen Norris puts it this way:

> The confidence that faith requires is notoriously easier for small children than for adults. No matter what the circumstances of our upbringing, our capacity for trust, allegiance, and confidence is badly battered in the everyday process of growing up. I had a radiant faith as a child, mostly related to song and story. Like many people of my "baby boomer" generation, I drifted away from religion when catechism came to the fore, and the well-meaning adults who taught Sunday school and confirmation class seemed intent on putting the vastness of "God" into small boxes of their own devising.

Theirs was a scary vocabulary, not an inviting one. And religion came to seem just one more childhood folly that I had to set aside as an adult.

Somewhere on the road from our youth to our married-with-children maturity the idea of liberation from moral conventions led us away from the Summer of Love to the success-obsessed fin de siècle. Flower Power gave way to the Power Lunch. Perhaps, in the end, there wasn't much difference between these two ideas. Perhaps we just became a little more driven to earn the money and perks that we tell ourselves are the things that will make us happy.

The same phenomenon, it might be argued, has affected the way we raise our children. Where once the Montessori schools, with their emphasis on creativity and freedom, were popular, we now demand that our schools give children the skills that will make them "competitive in the world market." Nowadays we fret about how many computers are in each classroom and whether they have CD-ROMs or not. The old emphasis on education as a cultivation of the inner life—the process of reflecting on moral dilemmas illuminated by the arts, humanities, and civics courses—has given way to a pragmatic focus on science, technology, and business.

Both in our educational system and in the realm of public policy, we have stressed that morality and spirituality are *private* matters. What began as a healthy impulse—the need for authentic moral choice on the part of the individual, rather than passive acceptance of social conventions—has become a dangerous trend, the increasing loss of a shared moral order. So pervasive is this privatization of the inner life that we are no longer sure how to discuss morality with our children, or even whether we should engage in such discussions.

Don't get us wrong: it's not that parents today are less loving toward their children. We want to be generous with our children, but increasingly that generosity is defined on our own terms, rather than according to the immediate needs of our kids. As we pursue success and build our careers, we want our children to excel as well. We pay for music lessons, root for them at every soccer match, and try to help them win first prize at the regional science fair. As a society we have more wealth than ever before, and many parents lavish money on their children.

We're also a lot more conflicted about time, that scarcest of all commodities today. Even when we make the effort to take time off with our kids, our leisure can seem just as frenetic and driven as our work. Our quest for fun has a slight edge of desperation to it.

The frantic pace of modern life and the cultural atmosphere in which we live are not things that most of us can simply evade. There are larger economic, technological, and social forces at work that all of us must cope with in our own ways. And yet each of us has the responsibility to make the best of our circumstances, to resist the dangerous currents flowing through our culture by steering the little boats of our families into safe harbors.

There are occasions when we encounter terrible symbols of what can go wrong with our society and in particular with our relationships to children. The circumstances that surround such events are often complicated, but in recent years we have had reason to agonize collectively over the rights and wrongs of pushing our children to become beauty queens or record-setting pilots or championship athletes. Psychologists now have a technical term to describe this pathology; they call it the "hurried child syndrome."

But despite all these efforts with our children—the balanced, truly nurturing efforts as well as the dysfunctional ones—the fact remains that there are vast areas of childrens' lives in which we have essentially left them to their own devices. In particular, we have largely given up on any effort to form their moral and spiritual lives. This is the legacy of our own youthful ideas about the evils of one generation imposing its values on another. Our children should be free, as we sought to be free, to choose the values that are meaningful to them. It's a rationale that lies so deep in our generation's mind that it has become essentially instinctive.

Social critic Midge Decter, a trenchant analyst of our changing customs, is not impressed by this rationale. Decter's indictment is unsparing. Speaking as a parent to her children, Decter confesses the sins of her own generation.

It might sound a paradoxical thing to say—for surely never has a generation of children occupied more sheer hours of parental time—but the truth is that we neglected you. We allowed you a charade of trivial freedoms in order to avoid making those impositions on you that are in the end both the training ground and proving ground for true independence. We pronounced you strong when you were still weak in order to avoid the struggles with you that would have fed your true strength. We proclaimed you sound when you were foolish in order to avoid taking part in the long, slow, slogging effort that is the only route to genuine maturity of mind and feeling. Thus, it was no small anomaly of your growing up that while you were the most indulged generation, you were also in many ways the most abandoned to your own meager devices by those into whose safe-keeping you had been given.

If truth be told, very few people are satisfied with the results of this laissez-faire experiment with our children's lives. In the Western nations, and especially in America, there is a growing sense that something is missing from the child-rearing experience and that it probably has to do with the ways morality and spirituality contribute to the formation of character. As many opinion editorials have lamented in the wake of the Littleton, Colorado, high school massacre, many people today *have* children, but very few seem to be *raising* them.

We live in a world that is growing increasingly inhospitable to children. For all of the modern era's huge strides in the realms of health, technology, and material well-being, and for all our pride in being more advanced, tolerant, and frank about human experience, we are, nonetheless, witnessing the fraying of our social fabric. The most visible sign of this social disorder is violence perpetrated by and against children. But as terrible as overt acts of violence are, the darker and more insidious development is that violence, cynicism, selfishness, and apathy have crept into our children's *hearts*.

Over the past fifty years, the influence of parents and teachers on children has diminished while the impact of popular culture has vastly increased. As many social critics have pointed out, the rise of pop culture has gone hand in hand with the availability of hi-tech media— from movies, radio, television, and portable CD players to computers and the Internet—in our kids' lives. Debates rage, both in Congress and in our own homes, about explicit and violent lyrics in popular music and the easy availability of pornography on the Net. These are important, vital matters to discuss and address. But there is another matter that isn't as often considered: the impact of these media on the way our children think and feel. You don't have to be a technophobe to be concerned about the way modern media are changing the cognitive and emotional capacities of young people. An increasing reliance on visual media and the relative neglect of reading, the rise of what's known as attention deficit disorder, and similar problems have led experts to question whether children are able to make the kinds of distinctions that are necessary to a mature moral life. Most of us parents remain baffled by these technological and social changes, but our increasing concern for the moral education of children is evidence of our desire to respond.

The products of popular culture replace the need to use the imagination with special effects, character-building with a consumerist mentality, and the virtue of service with rampant narcissism. In an effort to stem this cultural drift, we seek solutions ranging from the installation of V-chips that allow parental control of the television to laws that restrict access to handguns. But even the most ardent proponents of such devices know that they are *external* to a child's soul and that they can do little to shape young hearts and minds.

In the last few years something of a reaction has started to take shape. Parents have begun to fear not only the extremes of violence, drug use, and promiscuous sex but also the more subtle ills that afflict children, including apathy, short attention spans, and a diminished sense of responsibility toward others. The enormous popularity of William J. Bennett's anthology *The Book of Virtues* attests to a widespread hunger for rediscovering the means by which we can give our children moral guideposts. Ironically, Bennett's book turned out to be a lot less compelling than many parents had hoped. Yet the impulse that led so many parents to buy the book is significant.

What is more, you don't have to be on the right-hand side of the political spectrum, as Decter and Bennett are, to be an advocate for a renewed commitment to moral education and the defense of the family. One of the most interesting developments in political and intellectual circles in recent years is the convergence of left and right on these issues. *The War against Parents,* by well-known liberal scholars Sylvia Ann Hewlett and Cornel West, is a book that made quite a splash when it was published in 1998. In it, Hewlett and West criticized both greedy capitalists *and* liberal intellectuals for creating a society that makes family life so difficult to sustain and nurture. "An important strand of liberal thinking," they write, "is deeply antagonistic to the parental role and function. Scratch the surface and you will find at least some folks on the left who don't particularly like marriage or children."

Another shining example of a political activist on the left who is an outspoken advocate of traditional moral principles and also prayer is Marian Wright Edelman, the director of the Children's Defense Fund. In the mid-1990s, Edelman set out to write a book about public policies relating to children and the family. But as soon as she began to write, "out tumbled prayers instead." The result was *Guide My Feet: Prayers and*

Meditations on Loving and Working for Children. In the preface to that book Edelman describes her childhood in the rural South, where she grew up as a preacher's daughter. Every Sunday morning at breakfast the children in her family had to recite a Bible verse by heart ("Jesus wept" was allowed only once!), and after church they would visit the sick and disabled members of the parish. Edelman is deeply concerned at our society's loss of the connection between morality and its grounding in religious faith.

> We Black children were wrapped up and rocked in a cradle of faith, song, prayer, ritual, and worship which immunized our spirits against some of the meanness and unfairness inflicted on our young psyches by racial discrimination and poverty in our segregated South and acquiescent nation. . . . We internalized the presence of God, personal as well as universal, who could open our earthly graves, snatch us from death's cold hands, lift us out of misery, and breathe a new spirit of life into us.

In her tenure as director of the Children's Defense Fund, Edelman has made prayer an integral part of her organization's activities, and we have included several of the prayers she composed in this book. "I worry in every fiber of my being," she concludes, "about our many children who, lacking a sense of the sacred or internal moral moorings, are trying to grow up in a society without boundaries, without respect, without enough positive role models . . . in a culture where almost anything goes. . . ."

If we really want to care for our children's souls we must cultivate their hearts in such a way that they learn charity, a passion for goodness, and generosity of spirit.

As Edelman reminds us, family life is the training ground where parents and children alike learn tolerance, forgiveness, responsibility, and service. The family has justly been called the "school of charity" because it presents us with a daunting, but wonderful, opportunity: to learn how to unite our individual wills and personalities into a loving—and lasting—community. It is the microcosm out of which emerge the virtues and gifts that make for a healthy, just society.

Of course, family life isn't easy under the best of circumstances: from newspapers to novels we encounter many heartbreaking stories about families in crisis. Add to this the massive social upheavals of the twentieth century that have strained the institution of the family to the breaking point. Economic pressures, changing social and sexual roles, and the massive increase in divorce rates have changed the definition of the family, perhaps forever.

Since this is a book about prayer and not social policy, it isn't within our scope to discuss the political status of the family. But we will venture this opinion: family life has been eroded by consumerism, the tendency to avoid problems by treating them as if they could be solved by store-bought quick fixes. So often today it seems that we treat the difficult challenges of life the way we use the remote control: we flip to a different channel, retreating into our own private worlds, or we just switch off. Too many families today seem to be arrangements of convenience— social and economic structures without the inward bonds of love.

Edelman's insight—that prayer helps children to make connections between knowing what is right and doing right—brings us back to the central thesis of this book. When parents and children pray together, we help to heal the divisions not only in our society but also within ourselves; in prayer we establish connections—between the head and the heart, between our beliefs and our actions, between family members, and between the little world of the family and the larger public realm. In the chapters that follow, we will explore these connections in detail.

Prayer invites us to slow down when we get caught up in the rush of modern life, to retreat from the noise and flickering imagery of the Information Age into peace and quiet, to move beyond the petty distractions of daily life so that we can learn to focus our attention on higher things, to turn outward from our self-centeredness and develop compassion for others. Perhaps these assertions sound grand and remote to you, particularly as you struggle to make time for your first steps on the road of prayer with your toddler or teenager. But who would ever set out on an arduous journey if the destination wasn't awe-inspiring?

The truth, however, is that most of us are daunted by steep slopes looming over us at the outset of the journey—the path that we have to blaze in order to be able to bring our children along with us. Morality is one thing, but spirituality is another. Many of the same parents who now feel comfortable talking about virtues are still hesitant to address the spiritual lives of their children. There's a natural shyness at work here. After all, few of us feel well-equipped to talk about God, prayer, forgiveness, and redemption—much less guardian angels—with our kids. Along with Rick Moody, we were too busy watching *Wonderama* and *Davey and Goliath* on Sunday mornings to become religiously literate. (Of course, by today's standards these were sweet, innocent programs—with plenty of moral and spiritual lessons—but not quite the same thing as praying and reading the Bible.)

Even those of us who take our children to church or synagogue are affected by this shyness about making prayer and spirituality the center of family life. The irony is that this is exactly where the problem began for Moody and so many others. If we take the family to church or synagogue for one hour on the weekend and then maintain total silence about faith for the rest of the week, can we blame our children for sensing that something doesn't add up?

Children are far more acute about these matters than we usually give them credit for. With their questing curiosity and passion for justice, children can pronounce swift and terrible judgments upon their parents when they sense the slightest disparity or hypocrisy. When young children sense a lack of consistency and sincerity, they tend to simply shut down their curiosity; they quickly learn to go through the motions and find something else to engage their wonder. Teenagers, as we all know, can be far more rebellious and critical of our failures.

With all the challenges that stand in the way of family prayer—from our feelings of ignorance and inadequacy to misguided ideas about leaving our kids to their own spiritual devices to the difficulty of finding the time and stillness for prayer in the frenzied pace of our media-saturated culture—it is easy to see why those initial slopes on the road to prayer are so steep. Nonetheless, we hope that you will "gird up your loins" (as the Bible puts it) and take heart. We believe that there is no more effective method for creating intimacy and mutual reliance in our families than daily prayer—prayer that is said not merely by children, but by the family as a whole. When a family joins together in prayer, it enables its members to escape their isolation and form a circle of grace.

Prayer has been defined in many ways, most commonly as a conversation with God. A conversation implies that one person speaks and then listens to what the other person says in response. In prayer we offer up our joys and pains, give thanks for the gifts and graces we have received, praise the Creator for the beauties of our world, beg for forgiveness and a deeper spirit of sacrificial love, and seek consolation for loss and separation. Prayer invites us to put aside our selfish preoccupations for a time and place ourselves in a larger context of meaning. Finally, prayer requires us to become childlike: filled with wonder, unselfconscious in opening our hearts and expressing our needs, and trusting that at the center of the universe is an unconditional, infinite love that seeks nothing but our good.

Prayer is not a magic bullet that solves all problems, nor should it become a veneer of piety that covers over issues and conflicts that remain unresolved. Prayer is an art, a discipline of the soul that requires honesty and humility, attention and concentration; it offers the opportunity to gather our scattered thoughts and anxieties and center ourselves.

If we truly want the best for our children, we must learn to care not just about their morality, but first and foremost about their spirituality. Because, in the end, children will do what is good only if they *love* what is good. Children have a sixth sense that tells them the difference between duty and love. They will do things out of duty, if they are told to do so, but acting out of mere duty uses up an enormous amount of what we might call a child's emotional capital. If that supply is not replenished it will simply run out, and that is a sad outcome indeed.

Suzanne learned the difference between love and duty at an early age. Her grandfather, John McEntee, was a devout and holy man. Because Suzanne's parents separated when she was only four months old, her grandfather became the paternal influence in her life. One of Suzanne's earliest memories is of his reading to her from a children's illustrated Bible, a practice that helped her to learn how to read at the precocious age of two.

John McEntee lived in Manchester, England, his whole life and came from Irish stock—he was a descendant of the people the English merchants brought across the Irish Sea in the nineteenth century to dig the Manchester Ship Canal. John McEntee's father was a drunk who was killed in an accident while working on the railroad; John became the man of the house at age thirteen. He had only one job his entire adult life: working in a printing plant for one of Manchester's daily newspapers. Though he had a poor education and never attended university, he joined the Catholic Truth Society, an organization that defended Catholicism against bias and prejudice. His particular specialty was the history of the popes, and as part of his work for the Society he would stand on a street corner and answer any questions that passersby had about the Catholic Church.

As a young girl, Suzanne would go to Mass with her grandfather, who was by then frail and elderly. Even though Vatican II had by that time eased the rule about fasting before receiving Holy Communion, reducing it from twelve hours to only one hour, John McEntee insisted on following the old rule (a rule that his age and illness exempted him from anyway). Because he hadn't eaten since dinner on Saturday night, he would get faint at Mass and Suzanne would lead him by the arm to get a breath of fresh air on the church porch. Suzanne recognized intuitively that her grandfather fasted not out of some neurotic masochism, but out of profound reverence.

After John McEntee died, Suzanne had an extremely rough adolescence (including a difficult struggle with anorexia nervosa, an eating disorder) and even a period of rebellion against the Church. But even in her worst moments of darkness and despair, her grandfather's love—his childlike purity of devotion—served as a lifeline. John McEntee was a dutiful man, but he performed his duties out of love. The radiance of that love became etched so deeply in Suzanne's heart that she scarcely knew it was there.

The miracle of prayer is that children need only the smallest amount of prompting to begin speaking its unique language. What comes haltingly, if at all, to the lips of so many adults comes streaming out of the mouths of children. And it is precisely here that another aspect of that miracle can be found: when you help your children to learn the lost language of prayer, they will in turn become your teachers and enable you to join the chorus.

Chapter 2

COMMUNION AND CHAOS:
An Earthy Spirituality of Family Life

If one person in a family is mindful, all the others will become more mindful. . . .
—THICH NHAT HANH

"The family that prays together, stays together." That was the motto of Father Peyton's "Rosary Crusade" in the 1950s and it became an instant cliché. For many of us that phrase evokes an image of the idealized Ozzie-and-Harriet family of the old black-and-white sitcoms—a picture-perfect family of two well-groomed parents and two docile children bowing their heads over a wholesome, red-meat-and-potatoes meal. Having lived through the social and cultural upheavals of the intervening decades, we tend to be cynical in our reactions to Father Peyton's slogan. That image of the family has little to do with current realities, we think, and it probably wasn't valid even back in the 1950s.

There's a reason for our cynicism. In those postwar years saying prayers and going to church often had more to do with middle-class notions of respectability than with a passion for the spiritual life. It was a time of prosperity and complacency about America's pre-eminent role in the world—haunted at the edges by

fears and uncertainties, no doubt, but always project-
ing an image of stability. To the extent that religion
became a matter of surfaces rather than the depths of
the spirit, a large percentage of baby boomers either
rebelled against it or simply drifted away.

Flash forward half a century and look at the way
television reflects our social habits today. More often
than not, the family dinner in our current TV sitcoms
consists of a couple of wisecracking teenagers (with
headphones on) waltzing into the kitchen, pausing to
make a joke at the expense of their single parent, and
then taking microwaved burritos to their bedrooms,
where they will immediately log on to an Internet chat
room. (Why doesn't it seem likely that those kids will
pause to say grace over their steaming packets of convenience food?)

The image of a family praying together seems impossibly quaint these days. After all, the 1950s-style
family is long gone as the social norm. Today it is just
as likely that the family will have two working parents,
or a single parent trying to attend night school in order
to get a better job. Then there's soccer and choir practice, piano and karate lessons, trips to the health club
and the grocery store, community meetings—all the
comings and goings that can make a kitchen look a lot
like Penn Station. Add to this the increasing amount of
time parents spend on the daily commute, working late
at the office, and on business trips.

You don't have to be a self-righteous conservative
to feel ambivalent about just how far we have come in
recent decades. This era has witnessed an enormous
extension of personal freedom—in terms of sexuality,
marriage and divorce, career options, and more. As
the older social and moral restrictions on choice were

left behind, our options multiplied. While we can legitimately disagree about the relative merit of these newfound freedoms, there is a growing consensus that such freedoms take a toll on our children. This much is clear: in order to enjoy greater personal liberty, most of us work harder than ever before. The pace of life is faster and the world of work is more competitive.

As parents we have become concerned about whether our kids will be prepared to enter such a competitive workplace, and so we buy them computers and push them to excel in sports, music, and other endeavors. And so the cycle is perpetuated.

Time is the scarcest commodity in the home today. Perhaps that's why many of us are secretly nostalgic about the world of Ozzie and Harriet—they had the time for family meals and for conversations in the living room. Now we move about the house, sunk in what are becoming increasingly private experiences.

Under such conditions, the pressures on the family unit today are immense. Our collective fears and anxieties about this state of affairs are dramatized not so much on television as in the movies. Think of all the comedies that revolve around the theme of adults becoming so wrapped up in their work and personal preoccupations that they neglect their children, only to be redeemed by those children in the end. To take just one archetypal film, consider Steven Spielberg's *Hook*, based on J. M. Barrie's classic play, *Peter Pan*. In *Hook*, Peter Pan (played by Robin Williams) has grown up and forgotten his youthful adventures with Wendy in Never-Never Land. In fact, he has become a high-flying corporate executive who has a cell phone permanently glued to his ear. He is an abject slave to time—working so late that he always misses his son's

Little League games, which he has videotaped for him. Only when the nefarious Captain Hook (played by Dustin Hoffman) kidnaps his children does Peter return to Never-Never Land. There the Lost Boys seek to reeducate him, helping Peter to regain his childlike spirit and remember his true identity.

Perhaps the most delightful scene in *Hook* is when the Lost Boys sit down to a pretend meal. Sitting down at a table filled with empty bowls and plates, they begin to imagine a glorious feast. The grown-up Peter is, alas, a literalist; he complains that he can't see any food. But as the children chow down on their make-believe feast, he is slowly drawn into the childish feat of imagination that magically *makes* the food appear. And this, in turn, leads to the mother of all food fights. In their childish, intuitive way, the Lost Boys know that at the heart of any meal is *festivity*—a joyful celebration of our common need for nourishment. They have not forgotten the sheer earthy sensuality of the feast. As grown-ups we tend to worry about body odors and cleanliness, but children happily walk around smeared with mud and sticky to the touch from the candy and soft drinks they consume.

Hook, for all its swashbuckling theatricality and star power, is not a great film: it works with many of the archetypal themes of childhood, but the script isn't up to the profundity of those themes. On the other hand, *Hook* is very instructive, because it accurately reflects the anxieties and yearnings of contemporary parents. More important, it points to what we consider to be four essential elements in the spiritual life of a family. As *Hook* reminds us, what families need most are the ability to slow down the rush of time; an earthy, "sacramental" vision of the world; a spirit of playfulness; and the capacity for true intimacy. The family that prays together nurtures these four capacities.

The word "capacity," however, is far too dry and abstract to convey what we mean here. The novelist Flannery O'Connor once used the phrase "the habit of being" to describe a fundamental orientation of the human heart toward the transcendent. In the discussion that follows, we will explore these four habits of being—habits that can help carry us through the chaos, stress, and emotional roller-coaster ride that is family life. We've come to believe that these habits of being can best be developed through prayer; they are, in essence, facets of prayer itself. Through prayer, these habits enable the love of parents and children for one another to grow into something precious—into the mutual love we call communion.

Entering into Sacred Time

As we've already suggested, our culture has a dysfunctional relationship to time. Obsessive-compulsives that we are, we are well aware that something is wrong, but we can't help ourselves. Perhaps that accounts for the tremendous craving in our society for timelessness, for oases of rest and refreshment on our relentless treks from one point to another. The recent surge of interest not only in Eastern forms of meditation but also in the ancient monastic traditions of the West testifies to this desire to slow down and seek meaning.

America's most highly trained practitioner of the Tibetan Buddhist tradition, Lama Surya Das, recently wrote an op-ed column on this subject. Our deeply ingrained work ethic, he suggests, has never been tempered by an emphasis on the values of "balance and relaxation." He continues:

> Commercial pitches today show an American that is always "connected." Whether on an airplane, on the road, or on the beach, we are always at work.
>
> And there's nothing wrong with living the high-paced, high-energy life that Americans lead. It's like surfing: Either you drown, or you have a great ride. And if you can manage not to get carried away, then you can ride that wave.

But people are drowning, as Lama Surya Das well knows, and family life is one of the first things to get swamped by these endless waves of work. In the midst of our research for this book, we came across a shocking statistic: average working parents spend less than six minutes per day in genuine conversation with their children. And as you might expect, fathers speak to their children less than mothers do.

When we interviewed the novelist and spiritual writer Walter Wangerin Jr. on the subject of prayer, he began by reminding us that the one thing that always shocks children is when we fail to listen to them. That comment made us think back to the many times when we have been sitting on the couch, dead tired or preoccupied with some concern, only to realize that one of our small children has taken one of us by the chin and tried to swivel our head in his direction—sometimes half a dozen times before we finally get the message. Yes, children can be incredibly demanding—demanding enough to be told to relent—but how often do we fail to give them the personal attention they need?

Even when our family is all in one room, we find it hard to summon the energy to face one another and talk. It's so much easier to eat our dinner on trays in front of the television, and then to head off in separate directions. Eating dinner at the dining room table is one solution—we keep pledging to make that happen. But on the days when we don't sit down to dinner across the table, we at least gather for evening prayer, the one moment of the day when we always stop what we are doing to gather our thoughts and direct them to God.

Prayer cannot stop time, but it can allow us to step into a different sort of time. When we cease our normal "worldly" activities to pray, we move from the horizontal to the vertical dimension. Instead of driving forward, we look "up." The theologians and mystics speak of worship as sacred time. When prayer becomes a daily part of life, those moments of devotion seem to be linked together, almost as if prayer were a special *place* in our lives. That is the paradox of sacred time, that it puts us into a mode of existence that is simultaneously *set apart* and yet, in a mysterious way, truly our *home*.

Another way of putting the paradox is that when we look up to heaven we are able to delight more fully in our life on earth. Saying grace before a meal makes that meal taste better. Does that sound odd or irreverent? It shouldn't. If we pray with real gratitude before a meal, we slow down just a bit and remind ourselves that every meal, however humble and quickly consumed, is a feast. A grace that our kids occasionally blurt out is: "Good food, good meat, good God, let's eat!" The very speed of the prayer acknowledges our hunger, and yet even this jokey grace constitutes a tip of the hat to God, the giver of every good thing.

Saying grace over a meal is only one way for us to enter into sacred time. Because our evening prayers combine formal and spontaneous language, we have become able to share our concerns, anxieties, and hopes with one another. God may be our witness, but we are still sharing with one another in prayer. Perhaps this is the truth that Jesus was trying to communicate when he said that "when two or three are gathered in my name, there I am also." We'll come back to this point later.

For now, let's just say that we make a very grown-up mistake (of pride and condescension) if we think that children don't sense the worth of prayer as sacred time. That doesn't mean that there won't be complaints about prayer—or at least pleas for postponement! Our family is as human as any in this regard. But as with so many good things, once we are drawn in and our restless hearts are stilled, something unique and infinitely valuable takes place. Time slows down. We look at one another. We are home.

Splendor in the Ordinary: A Sacramental Vision

"The world is too much with us," as the poet Wordsworth famously wrote. But what, exactly, did he mean by "the world"? Well, in part, he meant the mall. His poem continues: "Getting and spending, we lay waste our powers." Lama Surya Das concurs: "Instead of living, we are shopping."

Most of us need to make and spend money, but when this process becomes an end in itself, as it often can these days, our emotional and spiritual powers are wasted. Another old-fashioned term for this realm of material concerns was "the profane." It's from the same root that gives us the word "profanity" (a quaint concept, to be sure, in the age of *South Park*). According to ancient philosophers and theologians, the opposite of the profane is the sacred. Sacred things are not merely material but have somehow been hallowed by a spiritual purpose. A church, synagogue, or mosque, for example, is a "sacred space" because it has been set aside for worship of the divine, even though it may be made of the same bricks and mortar as the supermarket next door.

We are so continually plunged into the realm of the profane—work, shopping, popular entertainment—that the peace of the sacred eludes us. The profane dimension often promises a form of peace, but what it really offers us is not peace but distraction. We need to be distracted from our fears and uncertainties by myriad forms of amusement, and by commercial messages that constantly promise sexual fulfillment, the luxuries of wealth, and the allure of power. Money, sex, and power have always advertised themselves as forms of ecstasy, and despite thousands of years of human experience to the contrary, we are tempted to think of them as quasi-sacred things. But they aren't sacred, as all of us know at some level of our being.

But where are the sacred, higher things to be found? How can we extricate ourselves from the materiality of daily life? As parents, how do we protect our children from the worst excesses of the profane? Must we throw out the television and stop going to the mall?

When thinking about spirituality the first mistake that most people make is to assume that the sacred exists on some transcendent plane that is remote from daily life. But we don't have to go to monasteries on mountaintops to draw close to God. All the world's great religious traditions teach that if we are to encounter the sacred, we must find it in the mundane routines of eating and drinking, waking and sleeping, traveling and resting.

In a similar fashion, prayer should be understood not so much as a retreat from the ordinary as it is a hallowing, or consecrating, of the ordinary. As we said, a sacred space is built out of the same materials as any other building. Indeed, to shift to another example, we should remember that the holiest rituals of the world's faiths all center on the most mundane need of all—our need to eat and drink. And so the great religious traditions make rituals out of meals: the seder, the Eucharist, the tea ceremony. To break bread as a family is always an opportunity to consecrate the material goods we need for our bodies to a higher purpose—the love that ought to bind us closer to one another. We think it's safe to say that if you cannot glimpse the sacred in a simple family meal you will not find it on mountaintops or in deserts.

In *Prayers for the Domestic Church*, Edward Hays writes:

> The first altar around which primitive people worshipped was the hearth, whose open-fire burned in the center of the home. The next altar-shrine was the family table where meals were celebrated and great events in the personal history of the family were remembered. The priests and priestesses of these first rituals were the fathers and mothers of families. . . . Each home had a shrine, its special sacred spot, where family members gathered in

times of trouble and in times of rejoicing and remembering, there to bless their God with song and
praise.

One of the few times when we experience a faint
echo of the ancient family altar is on one of the major
holidays—if that echo isn't drowned out by the relentless noise of the profane world of getting and spending. (Every year we bemoan the commercialization of
Halloween, Christmas, and Hanukkah, then speed off
to the toy store.)

The ability to see the sacred in the everyday is what
we call sacramental vision. You don't have to belong
to a church that officially believes in sacraments to appreciate the deeper metaphorical value of the word.
Simply put, a sacrament is an outward and physical
sign of an inward and spiritual grace. Bread, wine,
water, oil, candlelight—these and an infinite number
of other things can become vessels of grace and truth
for us.

Children are born with sacramental vision; it's standard equipment for them. Their imaginations are always seeing the humble stuff of life—from tattered
dolls to grubby building blocks—as standing for glorious realities that transcend mere appearances. So powerful is a child's imagination that it can make the
invisible visible, as in the thoroughly sacramental meal
that the Lost Boys create in *Hook*. The sad truth is that
as we grow up, we lose our sacramental vision and become cynical literalists.

Prayer can help everyone—children and grown-ups
alike—close the gap between the sacred and the ordinary, evoking a deeper sense of gratitude, love, and intimacy. In our own spiritual journey we've been inspired

to develop our sacramental vision by the writings of the Hasidic masters. Hasidism began in the eighteenth century with the teachings of Israel Ben Eliezer, known as the Baal Shem Tov. The Hasidim had a marvelous capacity to move effortlessly from the rigors of prayer and religious observance to the joy and freedom of mystical vision. Our favorite story from *Tales of the Hasidim* (edited by Martin Buber) reflects what we can only call their earthy spirituality.

> At the festival of Simhat Torah, the day of re-joicing in the law, the Baal Shem's disciples made merry in his house. They danced and drank and had more and more wine brought up from the cel-lar. After some hours, the Baal Shem's wife went to his room and said: "If they don't stop drinking, we soon won't have any wine left for the rites of the sabbath, for Kiddush and Havdalah."
>
> He laughed and replied: "You are right. So go and tell them to stop."
>
> When she opened the door to the big room, this is what she saw: The disciples were dancing around in a circle, and around the dancing circle was a blazing ring of blue fire. Then she herself took a jug in her right hand and a jug in her left and—motioning the servant away—went into the cellar. Soon after she returned with the vessels full to the brim.

As our children have grown and our family prayers have become woven into the fabric of our days—days that are filled with leaking diapers and crayon doodles on the walls, burnt toast and scraped knees—there have been times when, in the midst of it all, we've ex-perienced the equivalent of that blue fire. Those are mystical moments that none of us is likely to forget.

Playing with God

Most of the prayers we've gathered in this book relate to the rhythms of life—rhythms of the day, of the year, and of the transitions and phases of childhood. As Zen masters like Thich Nhat Hanh have written, the greatest enemy to the spiritual life is the human tendency to take things for granted, to sleepwalk through life. Prayer calls us to wakefulness or "mindfulness."

When we say grace over a meal, pray before bedtime, celebrate a holiday, mourn a deceased relative, we enact a ritual. Down through the centuries there have been critics of ritual who fear that it can become a form of magic or an end in itself. But seen in the proper light, rituals are nothing more than heightened or stylized forms of the acts we perform every day. Through prayer and ritual we enter into a moment of sacred space/time, but only because we are *underlining*, as it were, our ordinary experiences. The rites we practice enable us to pause for a moment and seek meaning. Without such moments we plunge breathlessly through time, too harried and distracted to know inner peace.

Children love rituals with the same passion they bring to games, and it is not sacrilegious to say that at the heart of all sacred rites is a form of play. In play there is a paradoxical relationship between the rules (often elaborate and byzantine in complexity) and the feeling of joyful liberation brought about by following those rules. Learning the rules and playing by them isn't always easy, but they make the game possible.

Similarly, children love repetition, and games are nothing if not repetitious. Grown-ups frequently experience a child's love of repetition as something akin to Chinese water torture ("Stop saying that a million times!" "Will you please stop banging on the table!" Etc., etc.) But think about it for a moment. Aren't most games that adults love equally repetitious? A baseball game has the same field, the same nine innings, the same rules every time out, 162 times per year. And yet for the sports fan all that repetition allows for an infinite number of variations. No two games are alike; no two home runs, double plays, or pitching duels are quite alike. The same can be said of every sport, from badminton to professional wrestling.

Saying our prayers is no different. The rules and the repetition become gateways to spiritual liberation, just as in jazz, when musicians begin with an old melody and play a series of improvisations on it. Of course, routines of any kind can become ruts, hollow and lifeless. But once we are hooked on baseball or jazz or prayer, we sense the infinite possibilities within the game and boredom becomes the exception, not the norm.

Consider another dimension of childish play. How many children's games are stylized reenactments of everyday experience? In its most basic forms (sans electronic gadgets), play is a powerful extension of the imagination. Though there is a strong element of escapism in play, a surprising amount of it enables children, through imagination, to participate in the roles and responsibilities of adult life. To "make believe" is a process that often allows children to reenter the real world as though through a magic doorway. Don't we adults treat sports in a similar manner— as a metaphor for life's triumphs and tragedies, its underdogs-overcoming-incredible-odds and its unlikely comebacks?

Prayer is never far from this type of metaphorical

play. Many of our prayers are ritualized reenactments of ordinary activities. This is obvious in the case of the ceremonies we alluded to earlier—the seder, the Eucharist, the tea ceremony—which are based on the daily necessities of eating and drinking. But every time we light a candle, place a hand on a child's head, bow, kneel, or hold hands during prayer, we are taking ordinary acts—seeking light to see by, or reaching out for the reassuring, protective touch of a loved one— and making them extraordinary. In the next chapter, we will argue that family prayer is in some ways a ritualized conversation, a dramatic way of placing our immediate concerns not only before God but before one another. The fundamental purpose of these rituals is not to send us away to some remote fantasy world but to remind us of the glory and beauty we experience in the here and now.

G. K. Chesterton once wrote a novel in which the main character walks all the way around the world in order to find his own home and appreciate it for what it is. The poet T. S. Eliot wrote of our need to return home and know it as if for the first time. In the same way, prayer brings us back to ourselves. When we gather together in family prayer to play out our needs and desires, our feelings of fear and gratitude, we all become like children playing in the fields of the Lord.

Intimacy and Communion: The Virtue of Showing Up

All too often these days the family seems to be little more than an arrangement of convenience, a collection of individuals in pursuit of different interests and agendas. One of the central purposes of the family is to create a supportive environment in which each of its members can flourish as an individual. The question that begs to be asked, however, is whether true individuality can be nurtured in the absence of community. Historians and cultural critics point out that when a society is too individualistic it lacks the common values and understandings that bind people together and that provide the groundwork for individual freedom and self-determination.

If the same principle can be applied to the family—and we think it can—then parents have to work at building the family into a small but loving community. Prayer can play an important role in that process. After all, prayer gives *all* of us the chance to be childlike, to recognize our common lot in this world and our dependence on God's loving-kindness. That is why parents need to pray *with* their children. If we are merely present when our children pray, then we step outside the circle of grace—something our children will notice, sooner or later. The essence of the prayer experience is blessedly democratic: parent and child both stand before God as needy, imperfect creatures, joined in love to seek peace and strength.

Praying together as a family provides a healthy context in which family members can develop their personal prayer life. In our hyperindividualistic culture, there is often a tendency to think of prayer largely in terms of the soul's solitary struggle with God. But there is a natural rhythm that develops among those who take time to pray every day; it impels us to join our voices with others. Many of the great spiritual writers have warned that the pursuit of a more reflective, spiritual existence can sometimes cause us to become too self-conscious, too wrapped up in our immediate problems and anxieties. It is possible to lose perspective if we get trapped up in the hothouse of the self. A particular application of this principle relates to children: one of the dangers of leaving them to explore the spiritual life on their own is that they will lack guidance and context for their search. Children can be brutal self-critics; if they feel too isolated, they can develop an unhealthy feeling of inadequacy.

In her best-selling books, *Dakota* and *The Cloister Walk*, the poet Kathleen Norris explains that she was drawn to Benedictine spirituality in part because of the order's wisdom in balancing the needs of the individual and the community. A Benedictine monastery, Norris notes, is like an extended family—a disparate group of individuals who are thrown together and who have to learn how to live in peace and harmony. The Benedictine emphasis on praying in community acts as a constant reminder of our interdependence, our common sins and weaknesses, and our need for forgiveness and forbearance.

There's another simple but extremely valuable lesson that families can learn from the monastery: the monks and nuns *show up*. They pray at regular times, whether they happen to be in a prayerful mood or not. As Rabbi Hayim Halevy Donin puts it, "If I did not regularly pray out of a sense of obligation to pray, I do not think that I could really pray at those times when I truly want to do so."

This may seem like a rather grim virtue, but we happen to think it is another example of the monastic wisdom about human nature. Our culture is saturated with advertising and a stream of other messages that constantly invite us to seek immediate gratification. The slogan "If it feels good, do it" may seem a little dated, but we believe that it remains just beneath the surface of our culture. Prayer, however, is not something we can do only when we're in the mood. Those who approach prayer in that spirit will soon stop praying.

The truth is that prayer, like a good diet or an exercise program, has to be performed on a regular basis or it will simply join the other enthusiasms that come and go in our lives. This may seem to contradict what we wrote in chapter 1, where we argued that prayer should proceed out of a spirit of love rather than duty. But the human heart is a fragile thing: when we make our immediate desires and emotions the measure of our actions, the world rapidly contracts. To pray is to acknowledge a higher power, to place ourselves in the presence of the love that created the spinning galaxies and every one of us. If prayer is a relationship with God, it requires the same effort and stamina that any intimate human relationship needs. When a husband and wife fail to say "I love you" to one another, the relationship falters; so, too, children's hearts wilt unless they receive daily expressions of love from their parents.

Prayer is a discipline: it requires that we show up. Sometimes we will experience what the great sages and mystics have called spiritual dryness. But those same wise men and women also tell us that by placing ourselves in God's presence every day, we will have moments when our tiredness or fear or hurt will suddenly fall away and be replaced by peace, illumination, joy. The spirit of God is not something that we can summon by an act of will; rather, it is an ever-present reality—a "still, small voice"—to which we must become attuned. But we've got to show up and then quiet down if we hope to hear that voice. We parents can get impatient with children who tell us that they don't feel like eating their vegetables or brushing their teeth or picking up their rooms. And yet we have our own grown-up bad habits, don't we?

To gather each day to pray as a family is to relinquish our individual preoccupations and to place our little community in God's hands. The words that we address to God rise up like incense, bearing our pleas for forgiveness and shouts of praise, our sighs of gratitude and moans of pain. Prayer is consecrated speech: language that is dedicated to a higher purpose.

Now that the two of us have been praying with our children for over a decade, we've begun to sense the way our prayers have been woven into the tapestry of our family history. It takes only a few golden threads to provide the highlights that give richness and texture to a tapestry. Through bedtimes and mealtimes, baptisms and confirmations, infancy and adolescence, prayer has helped us to celebrate the love that binds us to one another.

Has prayer helped our family to stay together? Absolutely. But it has done more than that. It has enabled us to go from a mere union of individuals to something much richer and more meaningful—a *communion* of souls making a common pilgrimage through this life.

Chapter 3

THE SOUL IN PARAPHRASE:
Stages in Your Child's Prayer Life (and Yours)

There is a paradox at the heart of a child's spiritual life that often goes unresolved, and it is this: in order for a child to experience the fullest growth, parents need to make the first move. It's true that children can develop a profound spirituality even without help from their parents and even in the most dysfunctional and adverse circumstances. But the responsibility for nurturing the souls of our children rests squarely with parents. Just as a child's educational performance and moral behavior depend to a great extent on the quality of his or her home life, so too does a child's progress in the realm of the spirit. If the school health class is no substitute for talking to your children about sex, why should anyone imagine that Sunday school is sufficient to nourish a child's spirituality?

In order to make prayer a living part of family life, there are two major hurdles that most of us have to get over. The first is a lingering sense that to pray with our children is somehow to impose something on them—

the legacy of past generations' myths about freedom and self-determination. The second is the feeling that we are spiritually inadequate, that we cannot nurture our children's inner life because our own is not good enough. It's only natural to feel that these hurdles are impossibly high, that leaping over them will end in an embarrassing fall. But we tend to make them—like so many things that we fear—larger and more ominous than they really are. Because both of these hurdles are based on misconceptions.

In *The Book of Virtues*, William J. Bennett responds to the notion that we don't have the right to impose our values on others by quoting an anecdote from the *Table Talk* of nineteenth-century poet Samuel Taylor Coleridge. In Coleridge's day, the English freethinker John Thelwall had written that it was "unfair to influence a child's mind by inculcating any opinions before it should have come to years of discretion, and be able to choose for itself." When Thelwall later paid a visit to Coleridge's cottage, the poet took him outside. "I showed [Thelwall] my garden," Coleridge wrote, "and told him it was my botanical garden. 'How so?' said he, 'it is covered with weeds.'—'Oh,' I replied, '*that* is only because it has not yet come to its age of discretion and choice. The weeds, you see, have taken the liberty to grow, and I thought it unfair in me to prejudice the soil towards roses and strawberries.' "

If we pray with our children in a spirit of love, there is little or no chance that they will be traumatized, even if they choose not to share all of our convictions when they grow up. Do we as adults resent our parents simply because our politics or professional choices are different from theirs? Only if parents act in a spirit of coercion can prayer or any aspect of faith become a source of injury. But the very essence of prayer is opposed to coercion. Children's hearts, to return to Coleridge's metaphor, are like soil that needs only weeding and planting; the soil itself gives the growth.

It's true that many children will resist the introduction of prayer into their lives. Kids are fairly conservative; they like routines and resist change. But it is vital that we distinguish between the need to get over a child's initial resistance to a new practice and the danger of parents becoming overbearing and coercive.

There is a right way and a wrong way to introduce prayer into family life, and it would be unwise for parents to ignore the dangers of the wrong way. In researching this book, we've certainly come across people who had negative childhood experiences with family prayer. We've talked to some people who hated "family devotions" when they were children, not because they were rebelling against religion, but because they felt excluded—they were simply bored spectators rather than participants. "When I was a kid," our friend Jeanne told us, "we had family devotions after dinner. First we read from the Bible, then each of us kneeled down by our chairs while our parents prayed. My favorite possession during those years was a Cinderella watch, which I took apart so I could study the moving gears while everyone else closed his/her eyes. Back then, I think I associated prayer with a mechanistic universe."

Prayers become mechanical when a child feels cut off from what is going on around him. That's why our focus in this book is on the need for parents and children to pray together, to make prayer a shared adventure. As with so many habits and disciplines, prayer is easier to introduce when a child is quite young. Anyone who has prayed with small children knows that they need only the barest hint about what prayer is before they demonstrate a natural proficiency in talking to God. Teaching young children to pray is more like unlocking a gate than imposing an alien point of view. In chapter 4 we deal more directly with the issue of a child's resistance to prayer and the challenges of introducing prayer to older children.

The more serious obstacle to praying with our children is our own sense of spiritual insufficiency. "How can I give my children what I don't possess myself?" At some point nearly every parent asks this question, consciously or unconsciously. The question has a sound instinct at its heart, but it can also serve as an excuse. If you postpone praying until your motives are pure and you've become an expert in theology, you'll never begin to pray.

Richard J. Foster, in his book *Prayer: Finding the Heart's True Home*, addresses the issue of the mixed motives we bring to prayer.

> The truth of the matter is, we all come to prayer with a tangled mass of motives—altruistic *and* selfish, merciful *and* hateful, loving *and* bitter. Frankly, this side of eternity we will *never* unravel the good from the bad, the pure from the impure. But what I have come to see is that God is big enough to receive us with all our mixture. We do not have to be bright, or pure, or filled with faith, or anything. That is what grace means, and not only are we saved by grace, we live by it as well. And we pray by it.

We've already quoted Georges Bernanos to the effect that the desire to pray is already a prayer. Perhaps that's evidence of the grace that Foster describes.

The notion that we need to possess a theological education before we can pray is another misplaced concern. The glory of prayer is that it accommodates almost any kind of human expression, from a single word ("Help!") to the most erudite composition of a religious sage. Prayer is not a sequence of words or pious thoughts but the act of opening one's heart to God. In our fear and insecurity we think that we are unworthy, incapable of uttering the right words. But what does that say of our concept of God? None of the world's great religious traditions depicts a God who is so finicky that he refuses to accept our stuttered pleas, our mixed motives, our recurrent anxieties.

There is a wise old saying that "faith follows action." This means that we often have to act on our faith before we can feel the emotional reality of that faith. To use an image straight out of pop culture, we have to become like Indiana Jones in his quest for the Holy Grail: we have to step out into what sometimes seems like an infinite abyss in the hope that our feet will find solid ground. Prayer is the single most effective action that we can take to live out our faith, to bring that faith to life.

The faith that comes so naturally to children can renew our spiritual life. Living in faith is, after all, the very essence of childhood. Nearly every aspect of a child's life requires faith—a trust that food, shelter, clothing, and love will always be there. Children are utterly dependent on their parents, but unless they are living in an abusive situation, children wear this dependence lightly and even joyfully. Paradoxical as it might seem, children have an amazing capacity for *confident dependence*, which is perhaps the most concise definition of faith we know.

The tragedy of the fallen world in which we live is that, somewhere along the line, we lose that sense of confident dependence. At some point we seek to live out of our own will, to become masters of our own destinies. The result is fear, insecurity, and a restless heart. That's why praying with our children can become such a powerful source of personal, spiritual renewal. To pray with our kids, to nurture their spiritual lives and witness their faith, is to come full circle, to replace cynicism and despair with a transfusion of child-like innocence. Only when we overcome the excuses and all the inertia of our recalcitrant hearts—only when we say our prayers on a daily basis with our children—will we find the healing we need.

In the short introductions to the chapters and sections of prayers included in this book we discuss many of the specific types and occasions of prayer. In this chapter, we'd like to step back and see in larger perspective the stages of your child's spiritual life and the prayers that are appropriate to these phases of development.

When should a child's prayer life begin? Ideally, it would begin before he or she is even born—or ready for adoption. What better way to give expression to all the hopes and longings of expectant parents than through the medium of prayer? Mothers talk and sing to babies in the womb, and the underlying love that they are communicating is as close to prayer as anything they will ever say or do.

Of course, preparing for the arrival of a new life brings worries as well as surges of joy. But prayer can help to place the emotional ups and downs of expectant parents in the context of loving concern. The responsibility of caring for a fragile new life is an awesome thing, yet too often the pressing demands of the daily grind cause us to lose sight of what's at stake. At some point in every parent's life, however, there comes the recognition that we can only be guardians of this new life, that we are stewards rather than creators or possessors. To pray for our children reminds us that we share in the responsibility of parenthood with God, who is the father and mother of us all. We have often found that in praying for our kids we experience a sensation as of a burden being lifted: for a brief moment, we recognize that our own power is insufficient and that we don't have to be Superman and Superwoman. Prayer helps all of us to take off the capes and tights and acknowledge that God's love and care encompass parents and children alike. What better time to begin learning this lesson than in the weeks and months before our new child arrives?

For the first two to three years of life, before we can expect a child to comprehend enough to say his or her own prayers, parents can continue to wrap the child in a mantle of devotion. There are many spiritual writers today who point out the intimate relationship that can develop between the body's movements and postures and the inner disposition of the soul. Just as it is possible to learn how to pray while taking a daily walk (what's known as "prayer-walking"), so too can we make bathing, cuddling, and singing to a child physical incarnations of prayer—with or without words to accompany these actions.

In fact, we would argue (with a goodly amount of scientific evidence to back us up) that both babies in the womb and very young children have the capacity to know and respond to the type of love that is being communicated to them. An example of this from our own experience involves the parental blessing. We

have followed the ancient practice of blessing our children each night from the day that they were born.
Placing a hand on each one's head, we pronounce the
words of blessing. Then we make the sign of the cross
on their foreheads. We've found that all of our kids,
even if they're restless, whiny, and unwilling to go to
sleep, will quiet down and receive the blessing with
an expression that we can only call solemn. Our youngest child, Benedict, has taken to stroking Dad's outstretched forearm during the blessing—a gesture of
indescribable tenderness. We're convinced that our
kids recognize something special, something that has
the sacred character of a religious ritual, when we give
them these blessings—and that they receive these
blessings as gifts. Lest this sound a little too mystical,
we have to report that our kids frequently return, immediately after their blessings, to their gripes and
protests. (No one ever said that prayer was *magic*.)

A practice that can start when your children are very
young, but that can continue almost indefinitely, is
praying *over* them. This sort of prayer is not for everyone, since it involves the kind of spontaneous prayer
that makes some people self-conscious, but it can be
among the most moving and comforting of any prayers
said by a parent. Praying over a child is just another
way of wrapping the child in a blanket of love and protection. Simple, heartfelt words rather than eloquence
are the essence of such prayers. We provide some models for this sort of prayer in the section on prayers for
parents, grandparents, and others who love children.

In attempting to sketch out the stages of a child's
evolving prayer life, we have found it helpful to think
in terms of four broadly defined concepts, which par-
allel, to a great extent, the chronological development

of a child's spirituality from toddlerhood to adolescence. We don't claim scientific or clinical authority for these concepts, but they have helped us to think about the interaction between prayer, spirituality, and the emotional and mental growth of children. The four concepts we have singled out are prayer as relationship, prayer as attention, prayer as participation, and prayer as transformation. For many reasons, including differing personalities and the ages of children when they are first introduced to prayer, it is impossible to assign specific ages for this widening progression of prayer-consciousness. We can say this much: the first stage—prayer as relationship—can begin when your child is still a toddler, while the last stage—prayer as transformation—will probably develop fully only when your child has become a teenager. That each of these stages contains powerful, direct lessons for us grown-ups is a fact that never ceases to amaze us.

Prayer as Relationship

Small children have a natural talent for empathy. Anyone who has been around children knows that they will often look into your face and change their expression to match yours. It can be quite startling to be confronted with a little empathetic mirror whose face suddenly takes on a look of adult worry or sadness. A child's gaze can be so filled with wonder, love, and a hunger for knowledge that adults, who have learned to be more guarded and emotionally defensive, can find themselves becoming uncomfortable. Our response to the gaze of a child will determine to a great extent what that child learns about the world: trust or fear, love or selfishness. Since the heart of prayer is our ability to become transparent before God, to open ourselves and our needs to the One who loves us and seeks our well-being, the vulnerability and openness of children is a powerful example to *us*.

Young children think in terms of relationships rather than abstractions; they look for role models rather than ideas to guide them. The same phenomenon applies to their understanding of God. As the child psychiatrist Robert Coles puts it, "In the lives of children, God joins company with kings, superheroes, witches, friends, brothers and sisters, parents, teachers, police, firefighters, and on and on." It takes time for children to begin to separate God from superheroes and firefighters, but their assumption that God is a *person*, someone to whom they can talk and relate, seems to us to be just the kind of wisdom that adults tend to forget—or avoid.

Parents themselves are perhaps the single most important image for a child's understanding of God. A recent study, entitled "Parent-Child Relationships and Children's Images of God," by psychologist Jane R. Dickie and a team of researchers, broke new ground in this area. In particular, Dickie and her team sought to discover how children perceived images of God as a "powerful, just authority and/or as a nurturing, compassionate care-giver." After studying two sample groups of children between the ages of four and eleven, Dickie and her team concluded:

> Despite differences between the two samples in race, socioeconomic status, and religious affiliations, remarkably consistent findings were demonstrated. When parents were perceived as nurturing and powerful (especially when mother was perceived as powerful and father was perceived as nurturing), children

perceived God as both nurturing and powerful; more like father in early childhood and more like mother or both parents in middle childhood.

Dickie's study offers some fascinating insights into the way fathers and mothers can break down sexual stereotypes and embody the virtues of authority and compassion in profound ways. But the bottom line of this study is clear—the more deeply parents are involved in their children's lives, the more balanced and profound is the image of God held by those children.

The prayers of a young child have a refreshing simplicity, even when they seem to be theologically or morally "wrong." Our children have prayed in one breath for God to bless Mommy, Daddy, and everyone else in the family (especially our pets), and then proceeded to ask God for a variety of toys and candy (using specific brand names). If we are honest, we'll recognize the same configuration of mixed motives that may attend our own prayers, and our attempts to correct our children's prayers will be correspondingly gentle. In these sweet, unself-conscious prayers, a child is learning to see God as protector and provider, the source of blessing and bounty.

A relationship involves a conversation, or at least a sense of companionship. Children often testify with remarkable confidence that God has spoken to them and been present in their lives in various ways, both in times of joy and in times of sorrow.

As a child grows, there comes a recognition that a relationship with God entails an appropriate balancing of give and take; they realize that you don't ask a friend for something that is utterly self-centered or that would violate the friend's love and trust. When our daughter Helena, who was eleven at the time, received a nasty gash from a piece of broken glass, she went to the emergency room to get her arm stitched up. We asked her if she prayed in the hospital. She responded: "When I got my stitches, I said: Dear Father, thank you that I didn't get anything worse than I already have, and I hope that I can get better. Jesus, I know these stitches are for my own good and I know I am going to take them because if I don't my arm is going to hurt even more." Helena did not ask for the pain to be taken away, but only for the strength and courage to endure it, because God wanted her wound to be healed in the right way.

Another simple but affecting story is recounted by the poet David Brendan Hopes in his memoir, *A Childhood in the Milky Way*. One night the young Hopes was haunted by fears that Godzilla would attack his house.

> That particular night, Mother and Father are going out. Mother is dressing by the pink glass lamps in her room, putting on the perfume I smell now in memory as I type. I am crying. She asks me why, and I overcome my deep inclination to say, "Oh, nothing." I tell her I am afraid.
>
> "Of what?"
>
> "Of monsters."
>
> I think I expected her to make fun of me, but instead she says an amazing thing. "Why don't you pray? Ask Jesus to take the fear away."
>
> I did, and He did. That was the beginning of a life that has been an almost uninterrupted dialogue between me and the long-suffering deity.

There have been caricatures of religious faith that treat it as nothing more than wish fulfillment or an indulgence in "magical thinking." But we have found that in prayer a child looks to God not simply as a magician waving a wand, but as a friend. A friend, even one with great power and resources, does not simply dole out quick and easy solutions; rather, friends help us work through our problems. Prayer, when it emerges out of a sense of a relationship with God, is grounded in moral realism—the kind of realism we noticed in Helena's account of getting her stitches. That's why we're convinced that prayer constitutes a profound engagement with reality, rather than a withdrawal from it.

Prayer as Attention

Relationships are a two-way street: in them both people share their needs and pay attention to the needs of the other. Though most young children have remarkable powers of empathy, they tend (naturally enough) to dwell on their own thoughts and emotions. But as children mature, their capacity for an imaginative grasp of the world around them increases dramatically. The world expands with their growing minds and hearts.

One of the tragedies of our times is that our children's natural curiosity is stunted. A curious mind is one that can concentrate its regard on an object for a sustained period of time. But today popular culture and high-tech gadgets provide kids with endless distractions based on ever-increasing volumes of noise, special effects, and violence. The restless, flickering images of music videos flash across TV screens for an average of a couple seconds at a time. Is it any wonder that attention spans are dwindling?

Though it's not likely that these trends are going to change in the foreseeable future, there are ways that parents can help to nurture their children's powers of concentration. Reading aloud to children is one method that has been championed in recent years by educators like Jim Trelease. In listening to a story, a child learns to comprehend plot, build vocabulary, evaluate character and motive, and create mental pictures of settings that may be exotic or set in the distant past.

Prayer is another means by which children (and adults) can develop their ability to attend to the world around them. The great twentieth-century poet W. H. Auden put it this way:

> To pray is to pay attention to something or someone other than oneself. Whenever a man so concentrates his attention—on a landscape, a poem, a geometrical problem, an idol, or the True God—that he completely forgets his own ego and desires, he is praying. . . . The primary task of the schoolteacher is to teach children, in a secular context, the technique of prayer.

When we pray, we develop mindfulness, a heightened state of awareness of the wonders of creation and our place in that creation. In prayer, children direct their gaze outward—toward God, family, and friends. When children praise or thank God, or ask for protection over loved ones, they are attending to realities that are beyond themselves.

As your children grow in the life of faith, you will notice yet another facet of their attention to the world. They will become more aware of themselves—of their actions and the impact of those actions on those around them. When a child confesses faults and pleads for help, something profoundly significant has taken place: the birth of the child's moral life, the first stir-rings of that most precious of human capacities, the conscience. In our own family experience, we found that our kids needed a little prompting before they would confront their failings during family prayers. But soon this "examination of conscience" became a natural part of their spontaneous prayers at night.

This leads us to one of the central paradoxes of faith, as attested by nearly all of the great religious tra-ditions: those who turn outward in prayer become far more vibrant individuals, more "in touch with them-selves" than if they had turned their gaze inward. When your children begin to attend to the divine, they will become more deeply and fully human.

To pay attention to the world inevitably means to become more curious about it. When children begin to pray you can expect a steady stream of mind-boggling questions. Unlike so many of us jaded grown-ups, kids are interested in wanting to know the reason "why" things are the way they are. How many parents down through the ages have noticed that the ques-tions children ask quickly become theological—even when prayer isn't a daily part of family life? Who made the world? Did God make Pepsi?—a question our son Charles once asked. What came before God? Does God know what we are thinking? Why does God allow people to suffer? As a parent, you will probably find yourself feeling "theologically challenged" by all these questions. Which of us hasn't given in to the tempta-tion to shut down our children's endless questioning? But there's no need to panic. In our experience chil-dren will not be shocked if you admit that you're not sure of all the answers. What they *will* look for, however, is some sign that you, too, are struggling to understand, that you're willing to try to articulate some response to them. For most children, we suspect, it is enough that you are accompanying them on a journey of faith. Prayer, scripture reading, and conversation can become powerful means by which we can probe into the realm of the spirit. What else is this probing but a serious form of attention?

One of the most moving illustrations we have found of a child's ability to "lose" herself in prayer, only to vividly "find" herself in the process, comes from Robert Coles's book *The Spiritual Life of Children*. In a chapter entitled "Representations," Coles includes religious pictures drawn by children along with his commentary. One of the simplest and most affecting of those pictures shows a black girl on her knees with her back to us, facing a large pink bed. Coles explains that the picture was drawn by Leola, a twelve-year-old from a "broken-down" Georgia neighborhood. The lack of feet in Leola's picture comes not from any defect in her drawing, but because she lost her legs below the knee in a car accident that killed her father.

Prayer is central to Leola's life. It is the time when she can hum and sing to God, to come to Him when she feels the "down and out blues." "I tries to be grateful that He sent me here," she explained, "and if He can see that Leola is 'deceptifyin,' then He'll forgive me, because if you try to be good, and you can't get there, not all the way, then that's only making you one of His folks, and He can't expect more of you than He gave you. . . . Oh, I talk to my legs. I tell them I'm sorry it happened to them, I'm real sorry! I tell them I won't forget them! I tell them we'll take up the slack—my arms and all I can get me to do from the waist up!" Coles watched Leola draw her picture and his comment on it captures the fierce attention this girl brings to her prayers:

> Then she looked at what she had drawn—the colors, her colors, her color, her body, both halved and suggestively complete in its intense and committed holding, its mix of self-affirmation and self-effacement . . . its back turned in a goodbye to itself, a hello to the Other One, who is . . . the great blank of the infinite receiving one child's picture of devotion: a rendering of the austere aloneness of meeting God, the transport of prayer, the call to the world beyond worlds, the name beyond names.

One can only call Leola's faith heroic, a force that has been refined and strengthened in the fires of tragedy and adversity. Her powers of attention and her search for meaning are fierce; in prayer she asks questions and finds answers. Even if most of us—children and parents alike—can't aspire to that type of heroism, Leola's faith enables us to catch a glimpse into a heart made wise through prayer.

Finally, it should also be remembered that prayer involves listening as well as looking, the attempt to hear God's response to our petitions and hopes and praise. This, too, is a form of attention, one that searches for meaning and the mysterious ways in which God's grace touches our lives.

Prayer as Participation

Whenever the topic of the "youth generation" surfaces on the op-ed pages of newspapers and magazines, it tends to evoke strong emotions. Are today's youth more decadent than those from previous generations, or are they imbued with special qualities that will help bring about social renewal? There are merits to both sides in this debate, we suspect, but there is one question that is perennially valid: do young people believe that they are vital participants in society or are they apathetic and disconnected from political and cultural institutions? In a media-dominated time, our children may be in danger of becoming couch potatoes before they even reach adolescence. The many complex problems that confront us, both at home and abroad, won't be solved by a generation of bystanders.

Now, prayer may seem like the last thing that would encourage children to participate more fully in the world around them. After all, most of us have been conditioned by decades of second-rate Freudianism to think that prayer is little more than a passing of the buck to God. To be fair to the critics, it has to be said that there is a grain of truth in this assertion—prayer *can* at times become a substitute for action. In his book *Letters to Malcolm: Chiefly on Prayer*, the great spiritual writer C. S. Lewis confessed: "I am often praying for others when I should be doing something for them."

However, we are convinced that prayer, when it is practiced in the right spirit, is a powerful means through which children can learn responsibility and a sense of engagement with the world around them. As we suggested in the previous chapter, this is one of the central paradoxes of the spiritual life: that when we pursue heaven with true passion we find ourselves caring more deeply for earth than we had ever imagined possible.

The question of whether our prayers can directly

influence the course of events, though, lands us quickly in a tangle of complicated and mysterious issues. Countless people pray every day for things that don't come to pass—from the healing of illnesses to peace on earth. It is one thing to say that our prayers are always subject to God's approval, but it is another for us to find emotional satisfaction in that idea, particularly when we suffer loss and disappointment.

Nonetheless, some intuition, buried deep in our hearts, leads most of us to believe that our prayers matter, that in the divine economy our petitions add to the balance of goodness in the universe. The Bible is full of instances when men and women bargain—often successfully—with God, obtaining clemencies and blessings. The seventeenth-century poet George Herbert described prayer as an "engine against th'Almighty," meaning by "engine" something like a catapult that hurls weapons against the fortress walls of an adversary. Prayer invites us into a passionate embrace of the world, not a withdrawal from it.

As long as children do not equate prayer with magic or instant solutions, they will continue to join the worldwide chorus of petitions to God. In the process, they will begin to understand that they are not merely spectators of life, but agents of change.

How is this so? As parents we've been reminded again and again that school and family life are the twin stages on which the dramas of childhood are played out; they are the microcosms where children learn the virtues and manners that will prepare them to enter society as adults. What we've discovered during family prayer times is that our children, in sharing the hurts and anxieties they experience at home and school, develop a strong awareness of the roles they play on these stages.

Our friend Kim's eldest son recently started junior high school. One of the first school-related experiences of the year came about after he signed up for seventh-grade football. With one hundred kids on the team, he was plunged into a chaos, what Kim calls a "*Lord of the Flies* scenario." There were plenty of swaggering bullies who would mercilessly mock anyone who seemed vulnerable. Kim's son had spent the previous summer reading Jack London novels, so he quickly recognized the dog-eat-dog environment. At one point he got his schedule mixed up and missed the beginning of a practice. Since thirty boys had already dropped out of the team—victims of two-hour practices in the heat of a Texas August—some of the boys still on the team thought his late arrival meant that he too had quit. So they locked him out of the locker room and called him a girl. He came home terribly upset.

The pattern that Kim follows in such moments is to begin by speaking seriously with her son about the experience, then they make jokes about it, and finally she will pray over him. This particular incident came and went quickly—kids can be casually cruel one moment and friendly the next—but it was crucial that Kim was there for her son while the pain was still fresh.

Though Kim prays out loud *for* her son, he is also immersed in the spiritual/emotional context of prayer, which forms his whole outlook on life. Prayer gives him the courage to resist the temptations of vulgarity and brutality that surround him; it enables him to pity and forgive—and to laugh at human folly. Of course, he and his siblings have asked Kim what prayer actually accomplishes, since the class bullies are not instantly converted every time they are prayed for. Kim's reply to this question is straightforward. Suppose I walked into a classroom and asked for ten volunteers, she says. You don't have to volunteer, but the job is going to get done, with you or without you. So why not volunteer and help complete the task? When you pray, she concludes, you are participating in the work of reconciliation and healing that God is carrying out. This may not answer every doubt in her children's minds, but it becomes a part of their reflection on their role in the small society in which they live.

There is another sense in which prayer can increase a child's feeling of active engagement with the world around him or her. In prayer we have the opportunity to admit our faults, ask forgiveness, and seek reconciliation with others. Prayer clears a space in which we can put aside our egos and reflect on the consequences of our actions. We asked our daughter Magdalen about this when she was thirteen. "When I have to apologize," she said, "sometimes I don't want to become vulnerable, because that can make me just get into another fight. You don't fight during family prayers, so I can open up and know that it's not going to hurt me." We've also found that during family prayers we can admit to each other the times when we failed to contribute to the daily work of the household.

When we asked the poet Scott Cairns to share his family prayer experiences with us, his response echoed Magdalen's. Family prayers in the Cairns household, he told us, "are more like indirect conversations with each other; prayer of this sort is a useful convention for expressing love, gratitude, fear, and various other anxieties to one another in a way that does not demand direct response from spouse or child. These prayers have been, and remain, powerful moments of familial confession."

Charity begins at home, as the old saying goes. From the microcosms of home and school, a child's circle of awareness expands to the larger stages of community, nation, and "global village." The big question is whether the child's understanding and compassion will also widen. In our own household, we have noticed that by the time our kids reached the age of ten or eleven, they became more aware of the various crises and catastrophes reported in the news. Gradually, these events began to enter our evening prayers. Whether it be the plight of refugees fleeing from "ethnic cleansing" or the death of a child in a fire, corresponding pleas for healing, wisdom, and consolation now rise from our home in southeastern Pennsylvania.

This interest in wanting to move from prayer to directly helping others can start in the smallest, most humble of ways. When our friends William and Emilie Griffin first gave one of their daughters an allowance, they were surprised when she put the entire amount into the collection basket at church. "But that's your *entire* allowance for the week," Bill Griffin remonstrated. "Well, I just gave it to God," she said. And that was that.

Prayer as Transformation

Our teenage daughter Magdalen's understanding of prayer—that it provides for her something like a consecrated space where she can work out problems—helped us to see prayer in a new light. As our children have grown, prayer has come to play a vital role in the way they process the emotional and moral challenges of daily life.

That's why prayer is the ultimate antidote to violence, one of the worst menaces plaguing our children today. If violence is an inability to work out conflicts constructively, then prayer offers a profound and life-changing alternative.

It would be misleading to say that prayer merely offers us emotional release, as if it were little more than a sanctified form of venting. Because prayer is said in the presence of God, and is addressed *to* God, it is shaped and conditioned by our relationship with God. To be sure, there are times when in moments of frustration and pain we may hurl our prayers at God, as in Herbert's image of the besieger's "engine." But if we open our hearts to a loving and good God, then we become like wayward children who have the opportunity to repair and deepen a relationship with a parent. God is the silent listener who encourages us to reveal our vulnerabilities in the context of love and trust.

There is an old cliché that compares the practice of psychological counseling and therapy to the Catholic practice of confession. Of course, an intermediary like a priest isn't a requirement for prayer. But the cliché contains a profound truth: in order to work through our problems, we need a sympathetic ear, an ear that allows us to explore and resolve what is inside us. To quote the poet George Herbert again, prayer invites us to offer up our "soul in paraphrase."

Most people today sense that the image of God as a vengeful and judgmental listener does not represent the heart of the biblical tradition, despite the caricatures that have been drawn by both extreme secularists and fundamentalists. In the Old Testament, one of the most frequent refrains tells us that God is "slow to anger, and abounding in steadfast love." And in the New Testament, Jesus clearly prefers to let others reveal what is inside them, for better or worse. When Jesus tells those who are prepared to stone the adulterous woman that the person without sin must cast the first stone, he is not arguing for moral relativism. Rather, he is reminding us that God's righteousness and compassion are greater than brittle human judgments.

One reason that we believe parents and children should pray together is that they can experience in prayer this hallowed process of transformation, this laying open of hearts before the divine listener. Flannery O'Connor, whose stories and novels have been recognized as ingenious spiritual parables, was fond of the phrase "Everything that rises must converge." When we pray together, our hearts rise above petty sins and fears and converge in the heart of God.

Prayer is also a time for revelations and surprises, most of them quite pleasant. Our son Charles, who is now eleven years old, spends much of his time assiduously cultivating the image of the young slacker—slouchy walk, baggy pants, reversed baseball cap, the works. (His one passion is practicing martial arts.) And yet, when it is Charles's turn to offer up some spontaneous prayers in the evening, he will speak with what we can only describe as an astonishingly supple, deeply spiritual intelligence. It is at moments like these that we realize how observant he is, both of himself and of the world around him, and we become aware of his ability to put those observations in a prayerful context. So we are reminded, in a particularly vivid way, of how easy it is for us as parents to stereotype our own children, to make assumptions about them that fail to do them justice. To experience such moments in prayer is both chastening and exhilarating.

The spiritual writer Richard Foster has said that "to pray is to change." Once this prayerful process of transformation begins, you may find that your children are not the only ones who are changing, but that you too are being changed—slowly, imperceptibly—by the invisible power of God's grace.

Chapter 4

PRAYING TOGETHER AS A FAMILY:
A How-to Guide

The family is the country of the heart.
—GIUSEPPE MAZZINI

Because this book is not just about the theory of prayer but about the need to pray on a daily basis with your children, it's time to get practical. This is the hard part—moving from the desire to pray to prayer itself. A thousand different things can—and do—hold us back. And even if we do begin to pray, this "habit of being" is not an easy one to maintain, at least for us grown-ups. The sheer inertia of our existing habits, our immersion in "the profane," makes it difficult for us to persevere in prayer.

As we agonized over what kind of advice we could offer at the beginning of this most practical of chapters, something odd happened. Just as we were about to set forth a list of carefully reasoned recommendations, out popped a fairy tale instead. At first we reacted to the sudden existence of this fairy tale with a mixture of horror and curiosity. It seemed out of place. We were writing a nonfiction book, weren't we? But then it occurred to us that fairy tales are among the most practical literary forms ever invented. As thinkers like Bruno Bettelheim have pointed out, fairy tales are ultimately about the human need to face our fears and temptations and then make the right choices; that's why these narratives are such a strong source of consolation and encouragement. Perhaps this little story, "Orana's Quest," was written precisely because we know, from firsthand experience, just how daunting the life of prayer can be. Our hope is that you will find this story mysterious and appealing enough that it doesn't read like a preachy allegory. We suspect that there is quite a bit of Orana in all of us. In short, this story touches on some of the longings, fears, and dreams that you feel as parents and caregivers for the children in your life.

Orana's Quest: A Fairy Tale

Once upon a time, a peasant woman named Orana lived in a small cottage at the edge of a forest. Her husband, a blacksmith, had died a few years before in an unfortunate accident with an overheated forge, but Orana found consolation for her grief in the love she had for her young children—a son, Roland, and a daughter, Gemma.

Orana supported her family as best she could by working as a blacksmith, for she was also the only child of a blacksmith—a kindly man who had indulged his daughter in everything, including her desire to learn the trade. After years of labor in the smithy, Orana had developed a sinewy strength, and she loved nothing better than hammering out red-hot iron on her anvil. But the villagers were outraged that this woman should dare to be a blacksmith and only a few kindly souls brought her work (and they came mostly at night). She began to worry that as her children grew she would not have the means to feed them.

"It's not FAIR!" Orana would say as she flattened a bar of glowing iron into a horseshoe. (She had a way of speaking certain words in time with her hammering.) "I do good WORK!" she said, as sparks flew about the room. "But what can I DO?"

Her children, who would often watch her work (from a safe distance), would shout back over the din made by their mother's hammering: "Don't worry, MOTHER. We'll be just FINE." Orana would pause for a moment, smile at her children, and then wipe the sweat from her brow and go on pounding.

One day a passing stranger stopped by Orana's house and asked for a cup of water. The stranger was an observant fellow and, after asking a few tactful questions, sensed the nature of Orana's plight. "You know," the stranger said, "you really should go to the castle. Once a year the king and queen take some peasant children into their service. Go and plead your case. Perhaps you'll get lucky."

Orana thought about it. She had no idea how to approach the king and queen or what words to use. Why would the king listen to a poor, ill-educated peasant woman, much less a woman blacksmith? And the queen? How could a creature of such splendor take notice of a soot-stained peasant? But several dozen horseshoes, a pair of stirrups, and a set of kitchen knives later, Orana overcame her reluctance and determined to make the attempt.

The next day she walked to the castle, which was just on the other side of the forest. When the magnificent towers and battlements of the castle came into view, Orana froze with wonder and terror. The scarlet-and-gold banners atop the castle snapped in the wind and the sun glinted off the windowpanes. Orana stood there for a long time, gazing up at the castle. Then she turned and went home.

The sparks flew fast and furious from her anvil that night.

As you can imagine, Orana's failure of nerve brought on a bout of melancholy. She felt she was failing her children, but the last thing she wanted to do was to burden them with her worries. One evening, when she caught Roland and Gemma looking at her with even more anxiety than usual, she decided to take them out for a picnic. She asked them to pack some food into a sack and led them off into the forest, not paying much attention to where she was going.

After passing through a rather dense part of the forest, they suddenly came upon a grove of birch trees. On entering the grove Orana gasped.

"What is it, Mother?" Gemma asked.

"This is a place I knew and loved as a child, but I haven't been here for years and years."

"It's beautiful," said her son. "Why have you never taken us here before?"

"Your father and I used to play here when we were children. He always wanted to bring you here, but the villagers gave him so much work and, well, after so many years, we just forgot the way. . . ."

"Let's eat," Roland suggested. They sat down in a small meadow at the center of the grove. On either side of the meadow, the trees soared up like the columns of a cathedral. As they ate their simple meal in the cool of the evening, Orana looked at her children and said: "You know how much I love you, don't you?"

"Yes, Mother," the children said in unison, a little self-consciously. But Orana, who knew she was embarrassing her children, could see the love in their eyes.

Just then there was a rustling sound in the trees not far away. "Did you hear something?" Orana said.

"It's just the wind," said Gemma, chewing on a crust of bread. "Mother, can I stoke the forge tomorrow?"

"Yes, child, but only under my supervision. Don't forget what happened to your father." Orana paused for a moment, lost in thought. Then she said: "What a wondrous evening it is. Look at the moon. It's always been a mystery to me. It seems so far away, but also as familiar as our oldest friend. So cold, and yet so lovely."

They all gazed at the moon for a while until the first stars of the evening began to gleam. Then they went home before darkness fell.

The following day Orana determined to go to the castle again. This time she made it as far as the castle gate, where she was confronted by a knight standing guard at his post. He held a tall, razor-sharp pike in one hand and stared straight ahead. Orana cleared her throat to gain his attention and took a deep breath. But when she tried to speak, her tongue seemed glued to the roof of her mouth. She managed a few odd gestures, but, alas, no words emerged from her lips.

The knight was clearly becoming impatient and was about to dismiss her when she blurted out: "Those are some nasty dents in your helmet, good sir. I could fix them for you."

"Be off with you, woman. Are you stark, raving mad?"

And so she turned back and went home.

Later that day, back at the cottage, the forge

glowed dangerously hot and clouds of red and yellow sparks flew across the room. Despite, or perhaps because of, her mounting frustration, Orana asked her children that evening if they would like to go back to the grove again. Without answering they ran to the larder and filled a small sack with food. Then they took their mother by the hand and led her straight to the grove, which they had no trouble finding. There Orana felt her spirit grow easy again. The wind gently rustled the leaves and the moon waxed brighter.

Daunting as her setbacks at the castle were, Orana was not deterred. She wanted the best for her children and she decided that she would go back to the castle until she could hammer out some words that would please the king and queen. On her next attempt she made it past the knight but soon after entering the castle she came across an old washerwoman—a peasant like herself.

The woman glared at her. "What do you want?" she demanded.

"I've come to speak to the king and queen, to see if they will take my children into the royal household."

"Bah!" said the washerwoman, "I tried that long ago and it never came to anything. A lot of hot air and for what? I could never get close to their Royal Highnesses." Having said this, the old crone stumped off into the castle's depths.

The bitterness of the woman assaulted Orana like a blow in the face, but it did not end her quest. Perhaps because Orana sensed something suspect about the old woman's bitterness, she decided to persevere.

Still, she made little progress. One day she confronted a scholar in the castle whose haughty looks made her feel as cold as a bar of iron in a bucket of water. On other days Orana found herself blocked by unsuccessful conversations with other inhabitants of the castle. There was a sweet-but-extremely-vague lady-in-waiting, who counseled Orana to get in touch with her feelings before trying to meet the royal couple. Then there was a clerk who offered her seven easy steps to gaining a successful audience with the king and queen; he even gave her a scroll with each of the steps clearly explained.

Each afternoon Orana would return home and the sparks would fly from her anvil, and each evening the beautiful grove would be the site of her family's humble meal.

But Orana kept going back to the castle. Finally she made it all the way into the private chamber of the Lord Chancellor.

He looked up from the pile of parchment sheets on the table, brushed a fleck of soot from his chain of office, and simply said, "Yes?"

For the first time, Orana found the gift of speech. Words poured out of her like molten gold, passionate and eloquent. She told the Lord Chancellor about her life, her love for her late husband, her delight in her work as a blacksmith, and the pain she felt when she encountered rejection and misunderstanding. Above all, she spoke of the hopes and dreams she had for her children. She begged that her children be taken into the service of the royal family.

When she was finished, the Lord Chancellor looked at her for a moment, shuffled the parchment around his desk, and cleared his throat.

"Yes, well, that's very well put, I must say. But I'm afraid the king has filled his quota for the year. Come back again in twelve months."

On hearing this reply, Orana, I am sorry to say, made a rather colorful gesture at the chancellor and stormed out of the castle. Back at the cottage that afternoon the forge became a white-hot inferno. Only the timely arrival of Roland and Gemma prevented the forge from exploding. They quickly saw how overheated the forge was and ran to douse it with buckets of water.

The children dragged their despairing mother out from the billowing clouds of steam and soot. Then they gently guided her out to the forest grove. Orana sat down in the meadow, dazed and spent. Roland and Gemma embraced her.

After what seemed like a long time, the trees began to rustle again, as if a strong wind were sweeping through the grove. Suddenly, from behind a stand of trees, a man and a woman emerged. The man was dressed in sumptuous robes and a small gold circlet rested on his head. The woman wore a long gown and an elaborate headdress, from which hung a sheer veil.

"Your Majesties!" the children said and knelt before them. Orana merely looked up at the royal couple and said nothing.

"Children, what's wrong with your mother?" the king asked.

The children explained, in their simple way, their mother's quest. Both the king and the queen listened carefully, nodding their heads from time to time.

After telling the story, Gemma turned to the king and said: "Sire, each night we come out to this grove to eat our supper, and each night we have heard a rustling in the trees. Were you and Her Majesty there all the time?"

The king gazed intently into the girl's eyes. "Yes, we were. You see, we love this particular grove of trees very much and come here every night."

The queen pulled the veil back from her face and said to the girl: "Dear child, you can't imagine how desperate we are to come here. By the end of each day we simply have to get out of that castle. It's always damp and stuffy in there—in more ways than one. So, many years ago, we had an underground passage dug that enables us to come directly to this grove. We love to come out here and gaze at the moon."

Orana turned to the queen. "Then you've heard everything we've said out here."

"Well, yes, we have, actually. That was rather rude and we're very sorry. But we didn't want to barge in on you. You're a very loving mother and your children are truly kind and generous."

"The Lord Chancellor turned down my petition that you take my children into your service. He said you'd filled your quota."

The king sighed. "I apologize for that, too," he said. "No matter how many times I tell my servants that there is no quota, they end up getting self-important and turning the castle into something of a club—"

The queen interrupted him. "How many times have I told you to dismiss that pompous old toad?"

"I've dismissed a legion of chancellors in my time," the king said, a trifle defensively. "It's not easy to find good help, you know."

The queen took Orana's hand. "Rest assured that the chancellor will be searching for new employment in the morning."

Orana was not so easily consoled. She narrowed her

eyes slightly and said: "I don't know what I did wrong. Every day I tried to get into the castle to see you, right into the heart of your kingdom. At first I had no words. But even when I found the words I still couldn't reach you."

The king bowed slightly, as if conceding that Orana had a point. "There are many things and many people that come in between us and our subjects. There are times, I am sure, when we must seem impossibly distant to you. But never forget that the kingdom is always where *we* are. Each night you've come to this grove and we have been here too. When you speak to your children with love and describe the beauty of the moon, your words ring true—they are music to our ears. So you *have* been in the heart of the kingdom all along and your words have found a hearing."

Orana nodded and looked steadily at both the king and the queen. "Then you'll take my children?"

"Of course we will."

At that moment, Gemma interjected. "I won't go unless I can work for the royal blacksmith."

"My dear," said the queen, "you shall be the apprentice for our *new* royal blacksmith." She turned to Orana and smiled. "That position also happens to be open at the moment."

"But I don't want to leave our home," Roland said.

"You don't have to," said the king. "Every day you can come to the castle through the grove and the secret passageway."

This solution satisfied everyone.

Then they all walked into the center of the grove to gaze at the moon.

Postscript

Orana's quest is not unlike that of any parent who is considering making daily prayer a part of family life. Though the obstacles are formidable, Orana perseveres in her journey. Another important detail worth noting is that she remains true to her inmost self. Prayer may bring about change in our lives, but that change takes place within the core of our existing personality, within the identity that we receive as a gift from God. Perhaps that's why so many readers in recent years have gravitated to the spiritual autobiographies of writers like Anne Lamott and Kathleen Norris. Though these writers undergo life-changing conversion experiences, they retain the same sense of humor, passions, and traits that they always had. Prayer simply animates our inner selves; it doesn't require us to become someone else. That, in a nutshell, is the best advice we can give anyone setting out on a spiritual adventure.

In the remainder of this chapter we will deal with questions about the *how* of family prayer. Keep in mind that our thoughts about the particular *types* of prayer you can use are in the brief introductions to each section of prayers in the second part of this book.

Getting Started: Baby Steps

Where to begin? How can we move out of the powerful currents that flow through our lives in order to find the "still waters" where prayer is possible? How, in short, do we gather together as a family to break the ice with God?

The answers to these questions may vary, depending on many factors, including the ages of your children, your schedule, and your religious and cultural background. But we think it is safe to say that there are two opportunities for family prayer that nearly everyone can make a part of the daily routine: grace before meals and evening (or morning) prayer. In fact, these two forms of prayer are not only the best places to start, but they may also become the principal prayers in your family life. A family that says grace and morning or evening prayers every day will have all the time they will ever need to grow together in grace and love.

The great advantage of these two types of prayer is that they are eminently *natural*. Prayer on such occasions is not imposed or artificial, but something that grows out of our deepest human instincts and aspirations. Because children have not acquired adult cynicism or a jaded approach to the world, they retain a strong intuitive connection to these instincts. And because they are so dependent on others, children are less tempted than adults to believe that they can either earn or create the blessings they enjoy.

Hunger is perhaps the most vivid reminder human beings have of the fact that we are fragile creatures who depend on nourishment for our very existence. Our kids have no inhibitions about telling us when their bodies are needy or thanking us when they are satisfied. To ask a blessing before (or after) eating a meal is to acknowledge that human fragility and to celebrate the bounty of God's creation.

So it is with morning and evening prayer. When we salute the new day we pause to take note of our rising from the symbolic death of sleep into new life and new possibilities. At the same time we can use this quiet moment before the day's activities are upon us to commit those activities to God's hands. To make such an offering at break of day is to summon a spirit of peace that can help us—and our children—through the anxieties of the day.

As darkness falls in the evening we may look back over the day's experiences, expressing gratitude for the good things we achieved and sorrow and regret for the bad things we have said or done. At night our fears tend to emerge—from the child's fear of monsters lurking in the dark to the parent's insomniac worries about money, work, and personal relationships. To pray at close of day allows us not only to examine our hearts but also to seek comfort in God's encompassing love.

We'll delve into these ideas more fully in the introductions to these types of prayer. But the point we want to make here is that grace and morning or evening prayer are the most natural places to begin family prayer. For a family that has never prayed together at all, why not begin simply by saying grace for the first few weeks or months? Most traditional, written graces are short and sweet. Even if you prefer to say a spontaneous prayer, it does not have to be long or elaborate to have a profound impact on your family.

Unless your family is made up of all "morning people," the most likely time for daily prayer will be in the evening. When your children are quite small, the most natural time is just before sleep. Prayer, lullabies, and reading aloud are activities that simultaneously calm children down and stimulate their hearts and imaginations. Here, too, one can begin quite modestly, with a couple short prayers and an opportunity for your child to ask God's blessing on family and friends.

Though prayer is natural to human beings, prayer is

also an art. Just as a child starts by banging out random notes on the piano, and then begins formal lessons with scales and arpeggios, so the art of prayer must begin modestly and progress slowly to the more ambitious and complex. However, the goal we seek in mastering the art of prayer is not necessarily hour-long sessions of mystical contemplation. To continue the analogy: an accomplished piano player can demonstrate just as much proficiency and ease in playing a minuet as in a full-scale concerto. So, too, the goal of learning the art of prayer should be a capacity to open our hearts to God at any time and place, regardless of the forms of our prayer.

What makes the analogy with learning a musical instrument so apt here (and the same could go for learning a language, sport, or nearly any other skill) is that children have an amazing capacity to absorb, adapt, and integrate knowledge. That's why we say that in family prayer, children often become the teachers.

Encountering Resistance

Lest we romanticize childhood too much, let's turn to a difficult issue that nearly every parent will have to confront at one point or another: what happens when a child doesn't want to pray? Given the premise of this book—that families should be praying together—the issue of a child's resistance to prayer is of paramount importance.

As a culture, we have become more willing to recognize the importance of a child's cooperation in behavioral change—child-rearing experts are more likely to promote incentives and encouragements than discipline and coercion. That tallies well with the experience of boomers and members of older generations who rebelled against religion and spirituality because it was forced on them in ways that made them feel like outsiders.

In addressing this issue, we think it is important to examine the different situations in which a child's reluctance to pray manifests itself. These involve (1) younger children who have not prayed before; (2) older children who have not prayed before; and (3) older children who decide to stop praying.

In our experience, children under the age of ten are unlikely to mount full-scale rebellion against prayer. Like human beings of any age, children tend to resist anything that is new and that breaks their sense of order and routine, from going off to nursery school to accepting responsibility for doing certain chores around the house. This type of resistance may appear strong at first, but it can be surmounted after only a brief transitional phase. If you as a parent begin to pray—at meals or at night, for example—you may find that your child is observing you carefully and may even ask if he can pray. And though there will be those who disagree with us, we don't think it is wrong to insist that your child say a brief prayer at bedtime. Since one of the typical bedtime prayers is to ask God's blessing on family members, a child's love will quickly take over and the initial parental insistence will be long forgotten.

The older children get, the more likely it is that their reaction to prayer will be more conscious and emotionally complicated. Let's face it: for millions of American kids, praying together as a family will hardly seem a cool thing to do. Our fifteen-year-old daughter Magdalen cringes when we say grace in a restaurant, and we understand her reaction. Though our voices are low, we make the sign of the cross and bow our heads. It is *our* decision—the decision to pray in public—that in Magdalen's eyes is the countercultural thing to do, as if we suffered from a particularly odd form of exhibitionism. Magdalen's instinctive embarrassment is today the *conventional* response, which is one reason we don't give her a hard time about it.

Despite the religiosity of the American people, there is precious little support in the public realm—and particularly in our popular culture—for something like family prayer. The climate may be changing, as the recent popularity of television programs about angels and ministers would seem to suggest, but many parents will find introducing prayer into family life to be an uphill battle.

The key to such situations is to avoid putting your children "on the spot," where they feel they have to *perform*. It is precisely at such moments that children will associate prayer with something imposed from above, rather than rising up from within. The first step might be for your child to merely be present while grace or other prayers are said. You might also say evening prayer after dinner and issue a standing invitation for anyone in the family who wishes to join you. If you are sincere about making prayer part of your life, that example will not be wasted. As Thich Nhat Hanh says, "If one person in a family is mindful, all the others will become more mindful."

The next stage might be to ask if you can pray out loud *for* your child. So long as your words celebrate and bless the child, avoiding any hint of condescension or emotional manipulation, it is hard to imagine the child objecting to this practice, once his initial self-consciousness passes. Yet another approach might be to ask the child to participate in a more formal liturgy, where his role would be merely to speak the responses. The glory of formal prayer is that it allows us to *grow into* the meaning of the words we say.

Does a child's personality have something to do with his willingness to pray? A great deal, in all likelihood. If one of your kids is extremely shy or has trouble articulating his feelings, then certain forms of prayer may prove intimidating at first. But there are so many different types of prayer that, with a little experimentation, you should be able to find something that works. We have made a concerted effort to include a wide variety of prayer-forms to help you find what will work in your particular situation.

There are times when a child who has been praying will want to stop. But except in situations where some extreme emotional trauma is present, this scenario usually occurs when the forms of prayer do not keep pace with the child's level of maturity. In other words, if the only model of prayer that a child experiences is that of bedtime prayer, that child's own developing mind and heart will sense a lack of spiritual stimulation and nourishment. For this reason we strongly suggest that you graduate from bedtime prayers to something more akin to an evening prayer service, or at least allow for the kinds of prayer that are more encompassing in nature. As we argued in the previous chapter, children's expanding consciousness will induce them not only to pray for the wider world but also to use prayer to understand their own personal and social development. Many of the prayers we have selected for this book may appear quite grown-up to you, but you may be surprised by how quickly your kids are ready for them. Adolescence is a rough time, but if you remain sensitive and adaptable, there is no reason why prayer can't keep pace with your child's life.

If your child ceases to pray, or refuses to begin, all is not lost. Your love remains. Make the commitment to pray for your children every day. How our prayers affect the universe is a mystery, but you can be sure of one thing—praying for your children will do them good, if only because it will do *you* good. Anyway, who knows how the divine economy works? In late adolescence Suzanne began a rebellion against religion that lasted for a number of years; she went through a great deal of personal trouble and anguish before returning to her childhood faith. When Suzanne did return, her grandmother told her that she had gone to daily Mass for several years to pray for her. Her grandmother had never breathed a word of this during the entire time she had been praying. Suzanne is convinced that her grandmother's prayers did play a role in the course of her life. A skeptic might laugh at this. But there are moments when even skeptics have doubts—when they suspect that there is more in heaven and earth than is dreamt of in their philosophy.

Giggles, Fidgets, and Prayers Gone Astray

Prayer has many connotations in people's minds, and one of them is of hushed cloisters and silent, candlelit temples. When prayer takes place in a home with children, however, "hush" is not a word that will spring to mind that often. For all their aptitude for prayer, kids are still kids and parents will have to deal with prayers being interrupted by flying toys, wrestling matches, wandering attention spans, and the question of what to do about childish prayers that don't seem to be spiritually correct. Bedtime prayers may be a perfect way to help tuck a child into peaceful sleep, but it is also when your kids are most tired—even if that is manifested in the manic activity of an overtired child!

One thing that we learned when our children were small was the difference between truly bad behavior and the high spirits that emerge out of the intimacy of family prayer. Some of the most raucously joyful moments we've ever had as a family have taken place just before, during, and after prayers. At such moments our hearts are light: we seem to be more witty and satirical than usual, and irreverent in the playful way that only reverent people can be. This shouldn't be surprising. In fact, it is for us the incontrovertible proof that, as we wrote in chapter 2, prayer is an intimate form of play. As parents, we tend to go easy on this sort of spirited behavior. We have also learned to recognize when our kids' restlessness is caused by prayers that are too long, too late in the evening, or too advanced for their comprehension.

At some point, however, high jinks must give way to some form of order. Kids have to settle down, TVs and CD players have to be turned off, and some effort made to create a spirit of quietness. If it is necessary to discipline the children in order to achieve this, then so be it. Just be careful that your own tiredness does not lead you to be so harsh with them that they associate your anger with the experience of prayer—something, alas, we have not always managed to avoid in our house. (During evening prayer, our children will occasionally parody Greg's gruff voice—"GLORY BE to the . . ."—thus holding up a funny, but somewhat discomforting, mirror to Dad's behavior.)

A trickier issue arises when your children pray in an

inappropriate manner—which usually means that they pray selfishly, asking for presents, candy, and other goodies. Of course, on the scale of sins that human beings are capable of, the wayward prayer of a tot has to rank at the very bottom. There are times when a smile of indulgence is the best response to a greedy prayer request. But there are also times when some gentle correction is justified. At such moments we try to steer the children toward prayers of gratitude for what they already have, as well as prayers for the good of others. And as children grow older, they are more able to understand that God may not grant our every wish.

Places, Postures, and Sacred Signs

C. S. Lewis once wrote: "The body ought to pray as well as the soul." Coming from a ferociously rational thinker like Lewis, this statement carries even greater weight. Words and thoughts are central to the experience of prayer, but without a "bodily" context they become dry and abstract. The environment in which we pray, the positions and postures of our bodies, and the signs and symbols we use are all vital to our experience of the spiritual. We would argue that every religious tradition has its own forms for embodying prayer. Even in certain Protestant traditions, which would never countenance incense, candles, statues, and icons, there are still a few key symbols—a large, leather-bound Bible, for example, to stress the centrality of the Word of God.

Since children live in and through their bodies more intensely than adults, they respond quickly to their environments. So while it remains true that prayers can be said anywhere and anytime, it is wise to give some attention to the environment.

If you are praying at night with small children, then the obvious place to pray is in their bedrooms. This will help to keep the elements of bedtime ritual—including reading aloud, brushing hair, and so on—in a single location. Our cultural memory is full of images of children kneeling by their bedside to pray, and that is certainly a hallowed tradition. When we kneel in prayer, we are assuming a position of humility and vulnerability. To kneel before someone is to place yourself at his or her mercy. In our real-life experience, however, we've discovered that our kids find kneeling more fatiguing than we at first imagined. Kneeling is always easier to sustain when you have something to lean on, such as a bed or chair. Some people use a small prayer bench known as a prie-dieu (literally, "pray God"), which consists of a padded kneeler attached to an upright section surmounted by a shelf on which a prayer book or hymnal can be placed.

But in our family we've chosen simply to sit for our prayers. This may be influenced by the fact that we kneel a fair amount in church on Sunday, so when we pray at home, sitting helps us avoid the distraction of aching bones and muscles. The only posture for prayer that we don't recommend is lying down—that's an invitation for your kids to drop off prematurely.

When your children are old enough, consider praying in a common area of the house. In some traditions, such as Judaism, there is even a specific *part* of a room that becomes the place of prayer. Edward Hays, in *Prayers for the Domestic Church*, suggests that every family should select its "shrine-place." "This can be the table, or a corner of a room or simply a spot beneath a religious icon or image," he writes. Just as we enter a church, synagogue, or mosque in order to find a sacred space conducive to prayer, so a shrine-place in the home can help us to step aside from our "profane" lives for a brief time.

Prayer can also be aided by positions other than kneeling, sitting, or standing. In recent years the ancient *orante* position—often seen in the catacomb paintings of early Christian Rome—has become popular. In this posture the lower arms are held out at about 45 degrees (with elbows against the ribs to avoid fatigue) and the palms up. Another custom is to hold hands with one another during prayer, such as when saying grace or the Lord's Prayer. We don't recommend holding hands for long periods of time because it's hard not to become self-conscious about sweaty palms or trembling arms. One of the most lovely—and most neglected—of sacred gestures is the bow, which can be done at the beginning and end of prayer, or at other times. Many Christians make the sign of the cross at certain points in their prayers and rituals. The "kiss of peace" (which can be an actual kiss, or a hug or handshake) offers us a chance to express our reverence for one another. As you explore the spiritual traditions that are most nourishing for you, you will discover more about these and other gestures.

Spontaneous versus Written Prayers

There is a famous passage in the book of Ecclesiastes that begins, "For everything there is a season, and a time for every matter under heaven: a time to be born and a time to die, a time to plant, and a time to pluck up what is planted." So it is with prayer. There is a time to use established words and forms, and there is a time to let the soul give vent to its needs and hopes in the language that comes straight from our hearts to our lips.

A book like this, with its large collection of written prayers, may seem to be weighted in the direction of formal prayer. But spontaneous prayer provides a necessary balance to written prayers: it reminds us that our words need to be intimately bound up with our feelings and intentions, and that any rift between these two things will lead to spiritual inertia and emptiness. We all know instinctively what the dangers of rote language are. How many people (particularly among the baby boomers) look back with anger and perhaps a touch of cynicism to childhood experiences of rote prayer that were merely perfunctory—praying was something that had to be done to "follow the rules" but that had no real meaning. How many people drifted away from religious life altogether because of such experiences?

Children are quick to spot gaps between feeling and expression. Because they have forgiving spirits, children will be tolerant of adults who are too tired and distracted to pray properly. But if they sense a lack of inner commitment on the part of the grown-ups who teach them, children will feel betrayed and in the long run they will shut down their spiritual sensibilities and just go through the motions required of them. The judgment of a child can be terrible indeed.

Of course, it is one thing to propose spontaneous prayer as a liberation from the tyranny of rote language, and another thing to achieve comfort and fluency when ad-libbing prayers. Many of those who begin to pray extemporaneously find that it is far more difficult than they expected. When this happens, their disillusionment leads them to abandon all types of prayer.

Children, however, are mercifully free from the kinds of self-consciousness and embarrassment that prevent adults from praying. The impromptu prayers of a child can pour out with an ease and earnestness that can fill jaded adults with awe. Kids have far fewer barriers, categories, and hierarchies than grown-ups; they haven't learned that some things are too trivial or too personal to pray for. They will beseech the Lord to look after a pet turtle and a dying grandparent in the same breath because their love is wonderfully democratic.

But children grow and change rapidly, and they too begin to find that their extemporaneous prayers become more and more repetitive, eventually becoming just another sort of formal prayer.

So how do you avoid "spontaneous prayer fatigue"? The novelist and spiritual writer Walter Wangerin Jr. suggests that spontaneous prayers work best when there is a specific occasion to give impetus to these prayers. An example would be hearing news that a loved one is seriously ill. The prayers that arise at that moment have the freshness of newly awakened compassion.

To the extent that you can encourage your children to share what troubles them—for instance, the difficulties they encountered at school that day—their impromptu prayers will connect with their deepest needs and longings. Of course, parents have to tread lightly here because children should not be coerced into talking about matters they feel are too private to reveal.

Another technique worth trying is to read a passage

from Scripture, then pause and ask the children to find a way to link that scripture to their own lives. After exploring the subject for a time, invite your children to pray about the scripture and its relevance to their lives.

Finally, don't worry too much about repetition in your kids' prayers. After all, litanies like "God bless Mommy and Daddy, Grandma and Grandpa . . ." are always said with love that can never be exhausted.

By Heart: Memorizing Prayers

Now that we've just put in a plug for making spontaneous prayer a part of your family devotions, we want to move back in the other direction and promote the habit of memorizing prayers. For many years now, memorization has been rather unpopular in America—at least in our educational system. Fewer and fewer children have to memorize anything longer than a ten-line passage from Shakespeare. And yet it can be argued that the act of memorizing classic literature, scriptures, and prayers may be one of the most liberating and enriching habits a human being can acquire. To memorize passages of profound wisdom and imaginative splendor is to possess great treasure indeed. To use an older term, memorization is learning something *by heart*. Notice that it isn't called learning *by head*—since this kind of knowledge helps to shape our emotions and judgment. It is much more than mere information.

And lo and behold, here is yet another faculty that children have in abundance. The flexible mind of a child can memorize vast amounts of material—amounts that adults would have to strain in order to remember. When it comes to prayer, memorization becomes a tremendous asset. As important as spontaneous prayer is, there are times when we don't have the mental or spiritual energy for making up our own words. And there are times when words that are far greater and wiser than ours will stand us in good stead. What could be more comforting when one is assailed by fear, or danger, or the tragic reality of illness and death, than to have the Twenty-third Psalm on one's lips?

Our own children know about thirty prayers by heart, including the Lord's Prayer and the Twenty-third Psalm. Often our evening prayer consists of a medley of prayers we've memorized, topped off at the end by the spontaneous requests and thanks that occur to us at that moment. We can do this anywhere, anytime, without needing books or props.

We've even taught our children several prayers in Latin. That may strike you as bizarre, pretentious, or just plain misguided. How can living prayer exist in a dead language? And yet when we say the Lord's Prayer in Latin, we see it through a different lens. It's also an opportunity to think about the Latin roots of words we use every day.

We're not advocating the revival of Latin, but we do believe that committing prayers to memory is something that will nourish your family's spirituality. The length and complexity of the prayers is not the issue. The key is to let them take up residence in your heart.

Fighting Boredom: Repetition and Variety

Whatever we do on a daily basis can, and does, become stale and routine. That's the human condition: we cannot sustain the kind of heightened awareness and emotional vitality that we ought to. The Zen masters teach that we need to practice certain habits of mind and body to achieve a state of mindfulness so that we do not sleepwalk through our lives. The spiritual life is always about strengthening our *conscious* love, gratitude, and sensitivity for others.

Many people fear that if they begin praying—on their own or with their children—they will not be able to avoid boredom. And yet a husband or wife would not dream of *not* saying "I love you" to a spouse every day just because tiredness or distraction cut down on the emotional intensity behind that phrase. Our hearts may not always be in sync with what is on our lips, but we *must* speak what is good and true and beautiful, if only to remind ourselves of the need to live up to those things as often as we can.

So here's the unvarnished truth: praying with your children *will* occasionally be perfunctory. You may also experience what spiritual writers call "dryness," the feeling that God is absent. At moments like these, the worst thing to do is to stop praying. As we stressed in chapter 2, prayer is an art and therefore depends on discipline. The great thing about discipline is that it enables us to span the gaps—to trek through dry spells to the oases that we will eventually discover. It is important that we exercise patience in our spiritual journeys, that we trust that over time we will experience real progress: a lessening of boredom and a greater serenity during periods of dryness. What a gift to children if you are able to help them learn this lesson early in their lives!

That said, we do practice a number of antiboredom tactics in our household. We use three different graces, for example. Our evening prayers also take different forms. The more formal evening prayer we say now with our three older kids has built-in variety: the prayer book has different psalms, scripture readings, and prayers each day. But we also practice that prayer medley mentioned above, as well as the occasional evening when *all* our prayers are spontaneous. Now and then we throw in a little Latin to spice things up. Discover your own seasoning and add to taste.

Prayer and Reading Aloud: From Scripture to Adventure Stories

Praying and reading aloud have gone together so naturally, have been so profoundly enriching for us and our children, that we can no longer imagine the two things separately. They are like the Fourth of July and fireworks, Gilbert and Sullivan, hot pastrami and rye. While these two activities are distinct, they share many wonderful resonances. Literature and prayer both use heightened forms of language to lift us out of our mundane existence and put us into a more contemplative frame of mind. Both require us to listen, and to speak, with care. They also call on us to use our imaginations actively, in a way that is simultaneously demanding and pleasurable.

Most of us have heard about the studies that show the link between reading aloud and a child's performance in school. But we think the analysis should be taken a step further. In an era that is dominated by passive media like television, and interactive media that are still better for practical information than they are for imagination, we believe that prayer and reading aloud provide a needed balance for your child's development—the spiritual and mental "food groups" that make a proper diet for the soul.

In her book *Homeward Voyage,* Emilie Griffin captures the essence of how prayer and reading aloud can reinforce each other. Writing of the role her grandmother and aunt played in her New Orleans childhood, Griffin recalls:

> They were charmers, spellbinders, storytellers. I loved to hear them talk, and their talk was always intermingled with a kind of prayer. They were the ones who taught me to pray, intertwining prayer and storytelling at bedtime, in a way so enjoyable that I hardly ever wanted it to end. . . . I remember how much both [of them] loved nursery rhymes and loved to read them with me. [My aunt] taught me how verses galumphed; she made it exciting to read. . . . They taught me prayer by example. Each morning they devoted time to Bible reading; at any time in their conversation, it seemed, a Bible saying could slip naturally in.

Griffin reminds us that faith and imagination are two human faculties that children love to exercise. Through metaphor, symbol, and rhythm they allow us to penetrate the surfaces of things and grasp meaning.

In our house we always pray first and then read aloud. That guarantees that if anyone gets sleepy, we can call it a night and prayer won't lose out. Since prayer can seem a little like work at times, this habit also allows the reading aloud to feel like the special treat. As our children have grown and schedules have gotten more hectic, it isn't possible to read long passages from novels like J.R.R. Tolkien's *The Lord of the*

Rings on school nights. So from time to time we'll read a single poem after our devotions. First we pray, then we galumph.

Interfaith Families: Finding Unity amid Differences

One of the most challenging situations facing anyone who wants to begin—or deepen—family prayer is when parents come from different faith traditions. In recent decades there has been a serious effort in our culture to celebrate the common elements in different religious traditions—an effort that has brought about greater understanding and important messages about tolerance. The truth remains that religious differences are real and should not always be passed over lightly. Some people choose to construct their own set of beliefs, but others prefer the concrete experiences of specific religious communions, experiences that are rooted in history, scripture, and culture. (We should add that "interfaith" is a term that doesn't encompass every possible scenario. One parent may believe in God while the other is agnostic or atheist. We hope our thoughts apply to such circumstances, too, at least to some extent.)

How can parents with divergent perspectives create an environment in which family prayer can take place?

The answers to this question are various and few of them are easy. Some couples make an agreement that their children will be raised in either the father's or the mother's religion. But there are times when agreements like this founder when one of the parents experiences a change of heart—and the inevitable tensions follow. Some parents attempt to expose their children to both traditions, even to the extent of going to two different weekly worship services. Others find that they simply have to eliminate any practice of prayer or devotion in the home in order to avoid creating a minefield.

It is the choice to live out some type of "both-and" approach that will prove to be the most challenging on a day-to-day basis. To try to understand the challenge better, we asked our friend Leah Buturain to share her experience with us. Leah is a Catholic and her husband Ed is Jewish. Leah spoke very frankly about the tensions and tribulations of an interfaith household, but she stressed that even in the muddle of daily life "prayer is all the more essential as a way to seek strength and unity beyond and in the midst of differences."

Like many parents in interfaith marriages, Leah works very hard to expose her children to the riches of both traditions. She takes the kids to Mass on Sunday, but they also frequently celebrate Shabbat and the seder. Also, as in many Jewish-Christian families, there is a special emphasis on the shared Jewish heritage. The most frequent prayers in the Buturain home are said in Hebrew: the Shema ("Hear, O Israel, the Lord our God, the Lord is One") and a grace ("Blessed art thou, O Lord our God, ruler of the universe, who bringest forth this bread from the earth").

Rather than dissecting the two traditions into doctrines, Leah tries to convey to her children the cultural richness that wells up from both Judaism and Christianity. As she wrote to us,

All the arts enrich our family's prayer life: when celebrating Shabbat or a Jewish holiday, I put on

CDs of klezmer music . . . my husband and I play the violin and piano and sing *"Havah Nigella"* while the children dance. During Advent, I play more Gregorian chants and Palestrina, the Brahms Requiem, and other classical selections, and at Christmas we play a variety of classical, R & B, and folk music. Ed plays Yiddish and Hebrew folk songs, such as *"Rozhinkes mit Mandelen"* ("Raisins and Almonds") and other beautiful songs. . . .

Still, for all the beauty of these moments, the Buturains acknowledge that conflicts continue to arise, symbolized in a bittersweet way by their son Samuel, who says to people, "I am Jewish and I am Christian," illustrating this by drawing a vertical line down the center of his body.

Ed wrote to us: "I believe that the prayers said by interfaith couples should be ones that weld together both faiths but offend neither. I love my four-year-old daughter's simple prayer: 'Thank you God for our food, thank you for everything.' " This may sound like nothing more than a "lowest common denominator" approach, but there is much to recommend in Ed's approach. Prayer and spirituality are such fertile things that even stripped down to the bare essentials, they can grow in your children's hearts.

We are grateful to Ed and Leah for being so honest about the ongoing struggles they face. Leah has taken comfort in the image of the pilgrim that she found in Dante's great poem, *The Divine Comedy.*

I am keenly aware of where I wish we would be, able to kneel down together and pray as a unified family. Yet, as Dante wrote, part of loving is learning to prefer the given. Instead of comparing ourselves to other families, I read aloud Psalm 139 and contemplate the unique identities we have been given. My hope is that all of our family prayers and rituals will participate in a procession much larger than ourselves, with a community of believers who have preceded us and who will follow us as well. . . .

May we all have the grace to find our place in that procession.

Moving Outward: From the Family to the Larger Community

As a child's horizons expand, so will his or her prayers, moving outward from the circle of the family to the larger world. At some point in this process you may find that you or your children develop a desire to act on this expanding awareness. One impulse will be to move from merely praying for the less fortunate to actively serving them. The other impulse will be to participate in a larger community of prayer.

We can think of few more important lessons to teach a child than the need to link our words to deeds—to practice what we preach. Prayer is a powerful means through which we develop the motivation to "walk the walk" as well as "talk the talk." One of the easiest ways to help your children make this connection is to set aside some money each week, even if it is little more than pocket change, for the poor, or for a particular cause. In many Christian churches, the season of Lent offers families the opportunity to practice self-denial by setting aside money for the poor. Teenagers are old enough to do volunteer work for soup kitchens and other relief organizations. Prayer may strengthen our desire to serve, but service will inflame and renew our prayers. The final section of prayers in this book is titled "Make Us Mindful of the Needs of Others" and is specially geared to prayers for justice and peace.

The desire to pray with a larger community of believers may prove to be a little more controversial or complicated than public service. After all, many of the boomers who left behind church or synagogue have fairly strong feelings about such matters—including a withering critique of the sins of the "institutional church." There are families who opt to do their own spiritual thing, independent of any institution.

And yet we have heard an increasing number of stories about boomers who have had second thoughts about leaving the institutional church, and also about Gen Xers who leave their parents at home on the Sabbath and seek out a variety of worshipping communities. This brings to mind something else that Leah Buturain shared with us. She believes that even if parents have bad memories of formal worship in their own childhoods, "giving the children an opportunity to experience the rituals and services in churches and synagogues, perhaps with friends or other family members, can give us the chance to see these things with fresh eyes." "As much as possible," Leah continues, "we try not to project our adult issues onto our children. I admire parents who, as Coleridge wrote, 'willingly suspend their disbelief' regarding rituals and religious observances to give their children the opportunity to feel for themselves, without any tincture of the parents' prejudice."

So if one or more family members feel the need to become involved in the larger community, our hope is that they will be encouraged in that quest. For those who may be apprehensive about full membership in a church or synagogue, there are many "para-church" organizations, from youth groups to Bible study groups to yoga classes, that provide something a little less in-stitutional and yet still embrace a larger concept of spiritual community.

How to Use This Book

We have tried to design this book so that it will be as useful as possible. If you can, read it straight through to discover the full range of prayers that we have in-cluded, as well as our thoughts and experiences with them. Then you can return to the book for daily or oc-casional prayers, as best suits your family's habits.

Of course, this book is really only an introduction—a gateway. We hope you will pass through it and enter the larger world of prayer and spirituality. There is a bibliography at the end of the book to give you some ideas about the multitude of available resources that can enrich your family's prayer life.

The prayers in each section always begin with selec-tions that are geared to younger children and become progressively more mature. Many of the prayers may strike you as being too demanding for a young child. Some of them undoubtedly are. But we believe that there is a greater danger of condescending to our chil-dren. Prayers that are overly cute, sentimental, or sim-plistic don't have the resonance and mystery to draw a child deeper into the life of the spirit.

How did we go about selecting the prayers? Our criteria were straightforward. We looked for prayers from every corner of the globe and every religious tra-dition. We also wanted examples of as many different types and occasions of prayer as possible. Finally, we wanted prayers that were substantial enough to be said again and again without becoming thin or trite. Since many hymn lyrics and poems have a powerful devotional dimension, we have included these as prayers as well.

Nearly all our quotations from the Bible come from two classic translations: the King James Bible and the recent, widely acclaimed New Revised Standard Version. The poetry of the King James Bible has never been matched, and is something that every child should hear, even if isn't the translation that satisfies you for everyday use.

With the beauty and wisdom of these prayers to inspire you, perhaps you will be motivated to try writing some of your own.

And now, instead of wishing you luck, we'll send you off into the adventure of prayer with a somewhat more spiritual and decidedly old-fashioned word.

Godspeed.

Part Two

WITHIN THE CIRCLE—THE PRAYERS

Chapter 5

THE RHYTHMS OF TIME

Raising children today gives a whole new meaning to the idea of time management. Between getting them up and off to school, juggling the afternoon rituals of homework, sports, and lessons, and engaging in battles over naps and bedtimes, parents' eyes rarely stray from their clocks and watches. Perhaps it is a blessing that our children are less aware of the passage of time than we are; otherwise they would grow up too quickly and feel the burden of adult cares. This is undoubtedly the reason for the enduring popularity of *Peter Pan*, both for kids and for adults. Oh for Never-Never Land!

And yet, despite their relative freedom from the burden of time, children need to have their lives organized according to certain basic routines or else their health and well-being will suffer. Young children especially need to have the comfort and reassurance of certain routines—such as eating, bathing, and going to sleep in the evening—or they become disoriented and irritable.

It's also easier for children to waste time nowadays than ever before, what with the constant presence of innumerable media, from radio and TV to music CDs, video games, and the Net. Entertainment is one thing, but a number of cultural critics and child psychiatrists have become alarmed at the myriad ways in which children can become couch potatoes. And despite the highly touted "interactivity" of computers, the evidence suggests that Web surfing is little different than channel surfing with the TV's remote control.

The great religious traditions all have much to teach us about how we use and manage time, and a good deal of this applies equally to children. Many of these traditions speak of the tendency of human beings to take life for granted, to sleepwalk through their lives rather than exist in a state of wakeful alertness to the beauty and wonder of the world.

Prayer can play a central role in helping parents and children alike to shape our attitudes to time and to the challenges and responsibilities we face every day. One definition of prayer might be that it is an attempt to use time to reach out to the timeless. Taking time out to pray slows us down and invites us to put our lives into perspective. (How rarely we think about that phrase—taking time *out*!) Because prayer is an intimate sharing of our hearts with God, it gives us the opportunity to gather as a family and place our concerns before one another and before the Lord.

For well over a thousand years, monastic orders from many traditions have developed a regular structure of prayers over the course of the day, creating a rhythm that has brought a deep peace not only to the monks and nuns but to all those who visit monasteries on retreat. Of course, it would be absurd to expect modern family life to resemble a monastery. But after all, millions have sampled the joys of the monastic life by playing CDs of Gregorian chant or eating the simple but hearty meals described in best-selling monastic cookbooks. Kathleen Norris's books, including *The Cloister Walk,* have taught us that even the busiest of people can incorporate the spirit of monasticism into their lives.

In the sections that follow, we present prayers that relate to certain times of the day as well as to the feasts and seasons that mark the Jewish and Christian calendars. These structures help to shape our souls, and children take to them with the ease and naturalness they bring to so many things. Our selections constitute only a tiny fraction of the prayers and rituals that we've inherited from the great spiritual traditions. In the bibliography you will find additional resources relating to the rhythms of time and all the other types of prayer discussed in these pages.

MORNING PRAYERS

In the myths and legends of most human cultures, the dawning of a new day has symbolized the creation and renewal of the world. Out of the symbolic death of the cold, dark night comes the resurrection brought by the sun, which gives light and life to all creatures. Every morning is thus a re-creation of the world, a new beginning. Over the millennia of human history, morning has been considered an appropriate time to give thanks for our existence and to acknowledge that as creatures we depend for life and health upon the Creator.

Mornings also seem to be the special province of young children. As long as they don't stay up too late, children have the ability to wake up with an ease and freshness that is truly impressive. Unfortunately (but understandably), most grown-ups find it a little hard to appreciate this fact at six or seven in the morning, when young feet begin scampering down stairs or the sides of the crib begin to rattle and small, insistent voices cry out for liberation.

Perhaps here, as in so many other aspects of our lives, children can remind us of something that we adults—with all our burdens, responsibilities, and anxieties—have lost sight of: that mornings should be greeted with wonder and gratitude.

If each morning is a new beginning, then it is also an opportunity to set the tone for the day, to put things into a certain perspective. Even the briefest of prayers in the morning can help lift adults out of the concerns and worries that all too quickly begin to preoccupy our thoughts and emotions. And for all their innocence, children too can become weighed down by the challenges of the coming day—a big test, a crucial sports event, or just the difficulty of finding friends and navigating the waters of their social life.

What kinds of prayer are appropriate for you and your children in the mornings? A lot depends on who gets up when. As members of the household straggle down at different times and in different conditions, the notion of the entire family joining together in prayer may be a little idealistic. Nevertheless, there may be a moment—between gulping down a bowl of cereal and running for the bus—when a common prayer might be offered.

In our family, where both Mom and Dad are emphatically "night people," it isn't practical to have family prayers in the morning: our older children take care of our four-year-old, so we catch a few extra winks. Instead we have encouraged our children to develop their own short, private devotions. In some religious traditions a physical gesture, such as the sign of the cross, is the first and simplest act of prayer. Or, to take another example, the first blessing in the book of Jewish prayers is the *"Al Netilat Yadayim,"* the blessing for the washing of hands.

When it comes to using words, a single verse of scripture or a classic prayer set to a simple rhyme scheme can also be sufficient. One of our favorite morning prayers is "This is the day the Lord has made; we will rejoice and be glad in it" (Psalm 118:24).

Praise and thanksgiving are natural sorts of prayers to offer in the morning, but so are requests for guidance and wisdom in facing the particular challenges that lie ahead. You may find that your child is able to express concerns in prayer that he or she is not as ready to share in normal conversation.

Even when morning prayers begin to fade from the mind, they can still serve, at a deep psychic and emotional level, to insulate your child from fears and temptations, and to inspire hope and courage.

Dear Father,
hear and bless
Your beasts
and singing birds;

and guard
with tenderness
small things
that have no words.
ANONYMOUS

...

Guardian angel, protect me today,
Watch over me while I work and play.
Let me be kind and loving and good,
Help me to do the things I should.
ANONYMOUS

...

Now, before I run to play,
Let me not forget to pray
To God Who kept me through the night
And waked me with the morning light.

Help me, Lord, to love Thee more
Than I ever loved before.
In my work and in my play,
Be Thou with me through the day. Amen.
ANONYMOUS

...

For this new morning and its light,
For rest and shelter of the night,
For health and food, for love and friends,
For every gift His goodness sends
We thank you, gracious Lord. Amen.
ANONYMOUS

...

Father we thank Thee for the night,
And for the pleasant morning light;

For rest and food and loving care,
All that makes the day so fair.

Help us to do the things we should,
To be to others kind and good,
In all we do, in work or play,
To grow more loving every day.
ABBIE C. MORROW

...

Dear Lord, I offer you this day
All I shall think, or do, or say.
ANONYMOUS

...

You, whose day it is, make it beautiful.
Get out your rainbow colors, so it will be beautiful.
NOOTKA SONG

...

Arise, you little glancing wings
and sing your infant joy!
Arise and drink your bliss!
For everything that lives is holy.
WILLIAM BLAKE

...

Day by day, dear Lord of you
Three things I pray:
To see you more clearly,
To love you more dearly,
To follow you more nearly,
Day by day.
ST. RICHARD OF CHICHESTER

...

Teach me, my God and King,
In all things thee to see,
That what I do in anything,
To do it as for thee.
GEORGE HERBERT

...

This is the day that the Lord has made; let us rejoice
and be glad in it.
PSALM 118:24

...

When morning gilds the skies
my heart awakening cries:
may Jesus Christ be praised!
FROM AN EIGHTEENTH-CENTURY GERMAN HYMN

...

I am thankful before You, Living and Sustaining
Ruler, Who returned my soul to me with mercy. Your
faithfulness is great.
JEWISH PRAYER KNOWN AS THE *"MODEH ANI"*

...

Today, O Lord, I say YES!
to you,
to life,
to all that is true, and good, and beautiful. Amen.
RICHARD J. FOSTER

...

Blessed art Thou, Lord our God, King of the universe,
    who has given the rooster intelligence to distinguish
    between day and night. . . .
Blessed art Thou, Lord our God, King of the universe,
    who sets forth the earth upon the waters.

Blessed art Thou, Lord our God, King of the universe, who directs the steps of man.

Blessed art Thou, Lord our God, King of the universe, who removes sleep from my eyes and slumber from my eyelids. . . .

Blessed art Thou, Lord, who bestows great kindnesses on His people Israel.

FROM "THE BLESSINGS ON ARISING," TALMUD (BERAKHOT)

...

Lord of all hopefulness, Lord of all joy,
Whose trust, ever childlike, no cares could destroy.
Be there at our waking, and give us, we pray,
Your bliss in our hearts, Lord, at the break of the day.
TRADITIONAL IRISH HYMN

...

Blessed art Thou, Lord our God, King of the universe, who sanctified us with His commandments and commanded us concerning the washing of hands.
"*AL NETILAT YEDAYIM,*" JEWISH MORNING PRAYER

...

Let the words of my mouth, and the meditation of my heart, be acceptable in Thy sight, O Lord, my strength, and my redeemer.
PSALM 19:14

...

O Lord, Our Heavenly Father, Almighty and Everlasting God, who has safely brought us to the beginning of this day; defend us in the same with Thy mighty power; and grant that this day we fall into no sin, neither run into any kind of danger; but that all our doings may be ordered by Thy governance, to do always what is righteous in Thy sight; through Jesus Christ our Lord. Amen.

BOOK OF COMMON PRAYER

...

Shew me thy ways, O Lord;
teach me thy paths.
Lead me in thy truth, and teach me:
For thou art the God of my salvation;
On thee do I wait all the day.

PSALM 25:4–5

...

O Lord our God, grant us grace to desire you with our whole heart, that, so desiring, we may find you; and so finding you, we may love you; and so loving you, may rejoice in you for ever; through Jesus Christ our Lord. Amen.

ST. ANSELM

...

Earth our mother, breathe forth life
all night sleeping
now awakening
in the east
now see the dawn.

Earth our mother, breathe and waken
leaves are stirring
all things moving
new day coming
life renewing.

PAWNEE PRAYER

...

...

O Lord, grant me to greet the coming day in peace. Help me in all things to rely upon thy holy will. In every hour of the day reveal thy will to me. Bless my dealings with all who surround me. Teach me to treat all that comes to me throughout the day with peace of soul, and with firm conviction that thy will governs all. In all my deeds and words guide my thoughts and feelings. In unforeseen events let me not forget that all are sent by thee. Teach me to act firmly and wisely, without embittering and embarrassing others. Give me strength to bear the fatigue of the coming day with all that it shall bring. Direct my will, teach me to pray, pray thou thyself in me. Amen.

EASTERN ORTHODOX PRAYER

...

May my mouth praise the love of God this morning.
O God, may I do your will this day.
May my ears hear the words of God and obey them.
O God, may I do your will this day.
May my feet follow the footsteps of God this day.
O God, may I do your will this day.

PRAYER FROM JAPAN

...

I bind unto myself today
The power of God to hold and lead,
His eye to watch, his might to stay,
His ear to hearken to my need;
The wisdom of my God to teach,
His hand to guide, his shield to ward;
The word of God to give me speech,
His heavenly host to be my guard.

FROM THE PRAYER KNOWN AS THE BREASTPLATE OF
ST. PATRICK

God, who hast folded back the mantle of the night
to clothe us in the golden glory of the day,
chase from our hearts all gloomy thoughts
and make us glad with the brightness of hope.

ANCIENT COLLECT

...

Lord Jesus Christ, you are the sun that always rises but
never sets. You are the source of all life, creating and
sustaining every living thing. You are the source of all
food, material and spiritual, nourishing us in both
body and soul. You are the light that dispels the clouds
of error and doubt, and goes before me every hour of
the day, guiding my thoughts and my actions. May I
walk in your light, be nourished by your food, be sustained by your mercy, and be warmed by your love.

DESIDERIUS ERASMUS

A Family Morning Prayer Service

*The following morning prayer service is adapted from a
Catholic prayer book, but it contains no Catholic-specific
prayers and thus is thoroughly ecumenical. In our house,
one of the parents serves as the "leader" of prayer, but we
ask our children to do most of the readings, including the
psalm. The antiphons are short sentences said before and
after the first two readings. Feel free to adapt this service
to your own family's needs. There are larger prayer books
that contain different readings and prayers for every
day of the year. See the bibliography for more resources.*

Leader: God, come to my assistance.
Response: Lord, make haste to help me.

All: Glory to the Father, and to the Son,
           and to the Holy Spirit:
           as it was in the beginning, is now,
           and will be for ever.
           Amen. Alleluia.

HYMN *(including a hymn is optional; it may be said or sung)*

PSALMODY

ANTIPHON 1
As morning breaks I look to you,
O God, to be my strength this day,
alleluia.

PSALM 63:1–8
O God, you are my God, for you I long;
for you my soul is thirsting.
My body pines for you
like a dry, weary land without water.
So I gaze on you in the sanctuary
to see your strength and your glory.

For your love is better than life;
my lips will speak your praise.
So I will bless you all my life,
in your name I will lift up my hands.
My soul shall be filled as with a banquet,
my mouth shall praise you with joy.

On my bed I remember you.
On you I muse through the night,
for you have been my help;

in the shadow of your wings I rejoice.
My soul clings to you;
your right hand holds me fast.

> Glory to the Father, and to the Son,
> and to the Holy Spirit;
> as it was in the beginning, is now,
> and will be for ever.
> Amen.

PSALM PRAYER
Father, creator of unfailing light, give that same light to those who call to you. May our lips praise you, our lives proclaim your goodness, our work give you honor, and our voices celebrate you for ever.

ANTIPHON 1
As morning breaks I look to you,
O God, to be my strength this day,
alleluia.

ANTIPHON 2
From the midst of the flames
the three young men cried out with one voice:
Blessed be God, alleluia.

DANIEL 3:57–88, 56 *(adapted)*
Bless the Lord, all you works of the Lord,
praise and exalt him above all forever.
Angels of the Lord, bless the Lord. . . .
You heavens, bless the Lord. . . .
All you waters above the heavens, bless the Lord. . . .
All you hosts of the Lord, bless the Lord. . . .
Sun and moon, bless the Lord. . . .
Stars of heaven, bless the Lord. . . .

Every shower and dew, bless the Lord,
praise and exalt him above all forever.
All you winds, bless the Lord. . . .
Fire and heat, bless the Lord. . . .
Cold and chill, bless the Lord. . . .
Dew and rain, bless the Lord. . . .
Frost and chill, bless the Lord. . . .
Ice and snow, bless the Lord. . . .
Nights and days, bless the Lord. . . .
Light and darkness, bless the Lord. . . .
Lightnings and clouds, bless the Lord. . . .

Let the earth bless the Lord,
praise and exalt him above all forever.
Mountains and hills, bless the Lord. . . .
Everything growing from the earth, bless the Lord. . . .
You springs, bless the Lord. . . .
Seas and rivers, bless the Lord. . . .
You dolphins and all water creatures, bless the
    Lord. . . .
All you birds of the air, bless the Lord. . . .
All you beasts, wild and tame, bless the Lord. . . .
You sons of men, bless the Lord. . . .

O Israel, bless the Lord,
praise and exalt him above all forever.
Priests of the Lord, bless the Lord. . . .
Servants of the Lord, bless the Lord. . . .
Spirits and souls of the just, bless the Lord. . . .
Holy men of humble heart, bless the Lord. . . .
Hananiah, Azariah, Mishael, bless the Lord,
praise and exalt him above all forever. . . .

Let us bless the Father, and the Son, and the Holy
    Spirit.

Let us praise and exalt him above all forever.
Blessed are you, Lord, in the firmament of heaven,
praiseworthy and glorious and exalted above all
forever.

ANTIPHON 2

From the midst of the flames
the three young men cried out with one voice:
Blessed be God, alleluia.

READING

REVELATION 7:10, 12

Salvation comes from our God, who is seated on the
throne, and from the Lamb! Amen. Blessing and
glory, wisdom and thanksgiving, honor, power, and
might be to our God forever and ever. Amen.

SILENCE

RESPONSE TO THE WORD OF GOD

Leader: Christ, Son of the living God, have mercy
on us.
Response: Christ, Son of the living God, have mercy
on us.

Leader: You are seated at the right hand of the
Father.
Response: Have mercy on us.

Leader: Glory to the Father, and to the Son, and to
the Holy Spirit.
Response: Christ, Son of the living God, have mercy
on us.

CANTICLE OF ZECHARIAH (LUKE 1:68–79)
Blessed be the Lord, the God of Israel;
he has come to his people and set them free.

He has raised up for us a mighty savior,
born of the house of his servant David.

Through his holy prophets he promised of old
that he would save us from our enemies,
from the hands of all who hate us.

He promised to show mercy to our fathers
and to remember his holy covenant.

This was the oath he swore to our father Abraham:
to set us free from the hands of our enemies,
free to worship him without fear,
holy and righteous in his sight all the days of our life.

You, my child, shall be called the prophet of the
    Most High;
for you will go before the Lord to prepare his way,
to give his people knowledge of salvation
by the forgiveness of their sins.

In the tender compassion of our God
the dawn from on high shall break upon us,
to shine on those who dwell in darkness and the
shadow of death,
and to guide our feet into the way of peace.

> Glory to the Father, and to the Son,
> and to the Holy Spirit:
> as it was in the beginning, is now,
> and will be for ever.
> Amen.

INTERCESSIONS

Leader: Christ is the sun that never sets, the true light that shines on every person. Let us call out to him in praise:
Response: Lord, you are our light and our salvation.

Leader: Creator of the stars, we thank you for your gift, the first rays of the dawn, and we commemorate your resurrection.

Response: Lord, you are our light and our salvation.

Leader: May your Holy Spirit teach us to do your will today, and may your Wisdom guide us always.
Response: Lord, you are our light and our salvation.

Leader: Each [Sun]day give us the joy of gathering as your people, around the table of your word and your body.
Response: Lord, you are our light and our salvation.

Leader: From our hearts we thank you for your countless blessings.
Response: Lord, you are our light and our salvation.

Together: Our Father, who art in heaven, hallowed be thy name; thy kingdom come, thy will be done, on earth as it is in heaven. Give us this day our daily bread, and forgive us our trespasses as we forgive those who trespass against us. And lead us not into temptation, but deliver us from evil. Amen.

CONCLUDING PRAYER

Leader: Father of love,
hear our prayers.
Help us to know your will
and to do it with courage and faith.

Grant this through our Lord Jesus Christ,
your Son,
who lives and reigns with you and the Holy
Spirit,
one God, for ever and ever.
Amen.

DISMISSAL

Leader: May the Lord bless us,
protect us from all evil,
and bring us to everlasting life.

Response: Amen

EVENING PRAYERS

Is there a more perfect time for prayer than bedtime? We doubt it. For generations of Americans,
kneeling by the bed to say our prayers before going
to sleep was one of the central rituals of childhood.
There is even evidence that recent generations, many
of whom were raised in secular or nominally religious environments that had abandoned evening
prayers, would like to restore the practice for their
own children.

What is it about evening that makes it such an appropriate time for prayer? Perhaps the most obvious answer is that the preoccupations and distractions of the day are over, and darkness brings with it a quieter, more introspective mood. But for a child there is more to it than that. Young children often find going to sleep a difficult and even scary experience. After all, it is the time when witches fly and "things go bump in the night." Bedtime prayers serve as a sort of bridge between the day and the unconsciousness of sleep— a moment to gather together thoughts of love and trust.

A parent's presence at bedtime prayers is essential, even if the parent doesn't pray with the child. A mother or father becomes a witness to the child's prayer, another ear besides God's. This point is worth emphasizing: the parent's presence at bedtime prayers is not just window dressing. A number of scholarly studies have demonstrated that a child's image of God is closely related to the character and personality of his parents. That's a daunting—perhaps a paralyzing— thought for most of us. Most parents know that they are fallible and far from Godlike (though we don't often admit it to our kids!). But in the long run there is something deeply encouraging about a child's linking of God and parents. To be given the task of communicating God's unconditional love to our children is an awesome responsibility, but it is also a privilege. We may be "broken vessels," to use biblical language, but despite the leaks, we can still pass along a taste of divine grace.

Ideally, parents should do more than simply witness their children praying: they ought to pray *with* and *for* their children. While it is crucial that parents allow children to develop their own spirituality and to pray in their own words, a parent's participation adds a whole new dimension. If we step outside the circle of prayer, we convey the message to our children that they are merely performing a duty. But when we enter that circle ourselves, we forge deep spiritual and emotional bonds with our children.

Needless to say, the rituals of bedtime are profoundly important to children. As soon as prayers are over, the child is tucked into bed, flush with the feelings of warmth and comfort generated by the intimate sharing that prayer brings about. It is at moments like this that we can see the *sacramental* dimension of faith, the necessary link between the body and the spirit. We all experience love through the senses, but children are the ultimate sensualists. The smell of our father's aftershave, the sound of our mother's voice crooning a lullaby, and above all the touch of caressing hands—these are the sacraments of love, the very foundations of our emotional well-being.

After evening prayers are over, we suggest one more action before kissing your kids goodnight. A wonderful practice that is now all but forgotten is the parental blessing (see page 153–154). Modern parents may be embarrassed at the idea of putting their hand on a child's head and pronouncing a blessing, as if they were some sort of priest or minister. But nothing can match the blessing of a parent for bringing a child a feeling of total security and love. We're confident that any embarrassment you may feel on blessing your children will quickly disappear as you look into their eyes.

We have blessed our children since they were infants. Over the years there have been evenings when we've put the kids to bed and collapsed onto the sofa, ready to watch a video or dive into a mystery novel, when we've heard the patter of little feet and seen a sleepy face at the door of the living room. "You forgot to bless me, Dadda," a child has said, somewhat indignantly, as if Greg were the world's worst-ever absent-minded professor. When Greg is out of town on business trips, our daughter Helena asks him to bless her over the phone.

Traditionally, evening prayer is the time when one makes an examination of conscience, going over one's actions during the day, confessing sins and failings, and asking for forgiveness and grace to improve. Far from being a merely negative activity or "downer," this examination of conscience can be an opportunity for a child to unburden himself or herself of guilt and hurt. As we've mentioned, a child can often find the sharing of painful emotions easier and more "objective" in the context of prayer than in a face-to-face confrontation with parents.

When children are older, the best time for saying evening prayer as a family is usually just before or just after dinner. By linking these prayers to the meal, we make it less likely that they will be missed. Of course, many families today don't even eat dinner together, so the idea of family prayers may strike some as hopelessly idealistic. But then we set up ideals so that we can at least strive to reach them.

Matthew, Mark, Luke and John,
Bless the bed that I lie on.
ANONYMOUS

...

God watches over us all the day,
At home, at school, and at our play,
And when the sun has left the skies,
He watches with a million eyes.
GABRIEL SETOUN

...

Lord, keep us safe this night.
Secure from all our fears.
May angels guard us while we sleep,
Till morning light appears.
SOURCE UNKNOWN

...

Father, unto thee I pray,
Thou hast guarded me all day;
Safe I am while in thy sight,
Safely let me sleep tonight.

Bless my friends, the whole world bless;
Help me to learn helpfulness;
Keep me ever in thy sight;
So to all I say good night.
HENRY JOHNSTONE

Some people have expressed reservations about the follow-
ing prayer, "Now I lay me down to sleep," particularly
the sentence "And if I die before I wake, I pray the Lord
my soul to take." It is true that this sentence might cause
some confusion and anxiety in the mind of a small child,
but we believe older children can handle it. After all,
human life is a fragile thing, and any spirituality that
does not take our mortality into account is little more
than escapism. In our family, our older children have

had to come to terms with the deaths of several school-
mates, and as parents we feel that this prayer is all the
more comforting because it takes all of reality into ac-
count and enfolds it in God's love.

Now I lay me down to sleep,
I pray the Lord my soul to keep.
Four corners to my bed,
Four angels there aspread:
Two to foot and two to head,
And four to carry me when I'm dead.
If any danger come to me,
Sweet Jesus Christ deliver me.
And if I die before I wake,
I pray the Lord my soul to take.
Angel sent by God to guide me,
Be my light and walk beside me;
Be my guardian and protect me;
On the paths of life direct me.
ANONYMOUS

...

Angel of God, my guardian dear,
to whom God's love commits me here;
Watch over me throughout the night,
keep me safe within your sight.
TRADITIONAL CHRISTIAN PRAYER

...

Protect us, Lord, as we stay awake; watch over us as we
sleep, that awake we may keep watch with Christ, and
asleep, rest in his peace.
TRADITIONAL CHRISTIAN PRAYER

...

Four angels gathered 'round my bed,
Ariel, angel of light, at my head,
Gabriel, messenger, at my feet,
watch over me now as I sleep.
Michael, defender, on my right,
keep me safe all through the night.
Raphael, healer, at my left stay,
bring me strength for a brand new day.
Four angels watching, bending near,
protect me now from harm and fear.
TRADITIONAL CHRISTIAN PRAYER

...

Evening Star, send for me.
NIGHT PRAYER OF THE OSAGE CHILDREN

...

From ghoulies and ghosties and long-leggity beasties,
and all things that go bump in the night, Good Lord,
deliver us.
ANCIENT SCOTTISH PRAYER

...

God be in my head, and in my understanding;
God be in my eyes, and in my looking;
God be in my mouth, and in my speaking;
God be in my heart, and in my thinking;
God be at my end, and in my departing.
SARUM PRIMER, FIFTEENTH CENTURY

...

Now the day is over,
Night is drawing nigh,
Shadows of the evening
Steal across the sky.

Jesus, give the weary
Calm and sweet repose;
With thy tenderest blessing
May our eyelids close.

Grant to little children
Visions bright of thee;
Guard the sailors tossing
On the deep blue sea.

Comfort every sufferer
Watching late in pain;
Those who plan some evil
From their sins restrain.

Through the long night watches,
May thine angels spread
Their white wings above me,
Watching round my bed.

When the morning wakens,
Then may I arise
Pure and fresh and sinless
In thy holy eyes.

SABINE BARING-GOULD

...

Jesus, Tender Shepherd, hear me;
Bless thy little lamb tonight;
Through the darkness be thou near me,
Keep me safe till morning light.

All this day thy hand has led me,
And I thank thee for thy care;
Thou hast warmed me, clothed and fed me;
Listen to my evening prayer!

Let my sins be all forgiven;
Bless the friends I love so well:
Take us all at last to heaven,
Happy there with thee to dwell.
MARY DUNCAN

...

Loving Father, put away
All the wrong I've done today;
Make me sorry, true, and good;
Make me love thee as I should;
Make me feel by day and night
I am ever in thy sight.

Heavenly Father, hear my prayer,
Take thy child into thy care;
Let thy angels pure and bright
Watch around me through the night. Amen.
SOURCE UNKNOWN

...

O God, my Guardian, stay always with me.
In the morning, in the evening,
by day, or by night, always be my helper.
PRAYER FROM POLAND

...

Good night! Good night!
Far flies the light;
But still God's love
Shall flame above,
Making all bright.
Good night! Good night!
VICTOR HUGO

O, holy Father, I thank thee for all the blessings of this
day. Forgive me that which I have done wrong. Bless me
and keep me through the night, for Jesus' sake. Amen.
SOURCE UNKNOWN

...

I will both lay me down in peace, and sleep: for thou,
Lord, only makest me dwell in safety.
PSALM 4:8

...

Lord, now you let your servant go in peace;
your word has been fulfilled:
my own eyes have seen the salvation
which you have prepared in the sight of every people:
a light to reveal you to the nations;
and the glory of your people Israel.
LUKE 2:29–32—A PRAYER KNOWN HISTORICALLY AS
THE NUNC DIMITTIS

...

The Lord is my shepherd: I shall not want.
He maketh me to lie down in green pastures:
he leadeth me beside the still waters.
He restoreth my soul:
he leadeth me in the paths of righteousness for his
    name's sake.
Yea, though I walk through the valley of the shadow
    of death,
I will fear no evil: for thou art with me:
thy rod and thy staff they comfort me.
Thou preparest a table before me in the presence of
    mine enemies:
thou anointest my head with oil:
my cup runneth over.

Surely goodness and mercy shall follow me all the
    days of my life:
and I shall dwell in the house of the Lord for ever.
PSALM 23

*Here is Psalm 23 from the New Revised Standard Ver-
sion of the Bible, in case you prefer modern English.*

The Lord is my shepherd, I shall not want.
He makes me lie down in green pastures;
he leads me beside still waters;
he restores my soul.
He leads me in right paths for his name's sake.
Even though I walk through the darkest valley,
I fear no evil; for you are with me;
your rod and your staff—they comfort me.
You prepare a table before me in the presence of my
    enemies;
you anoint my head with oil;
my cup overflows.
Surely goodness and mercy shall follow me all the
    days of my life,
and I shall dwell in the house of the Lord my whole
    life long.
PSALM 23

...

Visit this house,
we beg you, Lord,
and banish from it
the deadly power of the evil one.
May your holy angels dwell here
to keep us in peace,

and may your blessing be always upon us.
We ask this through Christ our Lord. Amen.
CATHOLIC HOUSEHOLD BLESSINGS AND PRAYERS

...

If at night when day is done
Kneeling by your bed,
You can only think of him
Though no words are said;
If in crowds you think of him
Who gives you light and air,
God will know in his love,
That you mean a prayer.
ANONYMOUS

...

Watch thou, dear Lord, with those who wake, or watch, or weep tonight, and give Thine angels charge over those who sleep. Tend Thy sick ones, O Lord Christ. Rest thy weary ones. Bless thy dying ones. Soothe thy suffering ones. Pity thine afflicted ones. Shield thy joyous ones. And all, for thy love's sake.
ST. AUGUSTINE

...

God, that madest earth and heaven,
    Darkness and light;
Who the day for toil has given
    For rest the night;
May thine angels guard and defend us,
    Slumber sweet thy mercy send us,
Holy dreams and hopes attend us,
    This livelong night.
REGINALD HEBER

Be thou my vision, Lord of my heart;
Naught be all else to me, save that thou art;
Thou my best thought, by day or night,
Waking or sleeping, thy presence my light.

EIGHTH-CENTURY IRISH HYMN, TRANSLATED BY MARY
BYRNE AND ELEANOR HALL

...

Lord Jesus, Son of God, from you all life and joy
    come forth this night;
the world and the gentle light of evening lamps
    reflect your glory.
Praise to you!

ORTHODOX HYMN (THIRD CENTURY), SUNG AT THE
LIGHTING OF CANDLES AT VESPERS

...

O Lord, grant that this night
we may sleep in peace.
And that in the morning
our awakening may also be in peace.
May our daytime
be cloaked in your peace.
Protect us and inspire us
to think and act only out of love.
Keep far from us all evil;
may our paths be free from all obstacles
from when we go out
until the time we return home.

BABYLONIAN TALMUD

...

Forgive me, Lord, for thy dear Son
The ill that I this day have done.

That with the world, myself, and thee,
I, ere I sleep, at peace may be.
BISHOP THOMAS KEN

A Family Evening Prayer Service

The following service has been adapted from the traditional Christian form of night prayer known as Compline, as found in the Book of Common Prayer. *It is appropriate for children aged ten and up. While this service may seem ambitious at first, it doesn't take long to say. It can be said every night, or perhaps once a week. (We pray Compline almost every night, using a monthly prayer book that we subscribe to. See the bibliography for resources.) The scripture selections and prayers can be changed to allow for variety.*

Leader: The almighty Lord grant us a peaceful night and a perfect end.
Response: Amen

Leader: Our help is in the name of the Lord.
Response: The maker of heaven and earth.

Leader: Let us confess our sins to God.

Together: Almighty God, our heavenly Father: We have sinned against you, through our own fault, in thought, and word, and deed, and in what we have left undone. For the sake of your Son our Lord Jesus Christ, forgive us all our offenses; and grant that we may serve you in newness of life, to the glory of your Name. Amen.

Leader: May the Almighty God grant us forgiveness
          of all our sins, and the grace and comfort of
          the Holy Spirit.
Response: Amen.

Leader: O God, make speed to save us.
Response: O Lord, make haste to help us.

Together: Glory to the Father, and to the Son, and to
          the Holy Spirit: as it was in the beginning, is
          now, and will be for ever. Amen.

PSALM

*One or more of the following psalms are sung or said.
Other psalms may be substituted.*

Psalm 4
Psalm 31
Psalm 91
Psalm 134

READING

*One of the following, or some other suitable passage of
Scripture, is read.*

Lord, you are in the midst of us, and we are called by
your Name. . . . Do not forsake us, O Lord our God.
(Jeremiah 14:9, 21)

Response: Thanks be to God.

Or this:

Come to me, all who labor and are heavy-laden, and I will give you rest. Take my yoke upon you, and learn from me; for I am gentle and lowly in heart, and you will find rest for your souls. For my yoke is easy, and my burden is light. (Matthew 11:28–30)

Response: Thanks be to God.

Or this:

May the God of peace, who brought again from the dead our Lord Jesus, the great shepherd of the sheep, by the blood of the eternal covenant, equip you with everything good that you may do his will, working in you that which is pleasing in his sight, through Jesus Christ; to whom be glory for ever and ever. (Hebrews 13:20–21)

Response: Thanks be to God.

Or this:

Be sober, be watchful. Your adversary the devil prowls around like a roaring lion, seeking someone to devour. Resist him, firm in your faith. (1 Peter 5:8–9)

Response: Thanks be to God.

A hymn may be sung here.

Leader: Into your hands, O Lord, I commend my spirit;
Response: For you have redeemed me, O Lord, O God of truth.

Leader: Keep us, O Lord, as the apple of your eye;
Response: Hide us under the shadow of your wings.

Leader: Lord, have mercy.
Response: Christ, have mercy.
Leader: Lord, have mercy.

Together: Our Father, who art in heaven, hallowed be thy Name; thy kingdom come, thy will be done, on earth as it is in heaven. Give us this day our daily bread, and forgive us our trespasses as we forgive those who trespass against us. And lead us not into temptation, but deliver us from evil. Amen.

Leader: Lord, hear our prayer.
Response: And let our cry come to you.
Leader: Let us pray.

The Leader then says one of the following prayers:

Be our light in the darkness, O Lord, and in your great mercy defend us from all perils and dangers of this night; for the love of your only Son, our Savior Jesus Christ.
Response: Amen.

Or this:

Be present, O merciful God, and protect us through the hours of this night, so that we who are wearied by the changes and chances of this life may rest in your eternal changelessness, through Jesus Christ our Lord.
Response: Amen.

Or this:

Look down, O Lord, from your heavenly throne, and illumine this night with your celestial brightness, that by night as by day your people may glorify your holy Name; through Jesus Christ our Lord.
Response: Amen.

Or this:

Visit this place, O Lord, and drive far from it all snares of the enemy; let your holy angels dwell with us to preserve us in peace; and let your blessing be upon us always; through Jesus Christ our Lord.
Response: Amen.

One of the following prayers may be added.

Keep watch, dear Lord, with those who work, or watch, or weep this night, and give your angels charge over those who sleep. Tend the sick, Lord Christ; give rest to the weary, bless the dying, soothe the suffering, pity the afflicted, shield the joyous; and all for your love's sake.
Response: Amen.

Or this:

O God, your unfailing providence sustains the world we live in and the life we live. Watch over those, both night and day, who work while others sleep, and grant that we may never forget that our common life depends upon each other's toil; through Jesus Christ our Lord.

Response: Amen.

Silence may be kept, and free intercessions and thanksgivings may be offered.

The service concludes with the Song of Simeon. The antiphon is sung or said by all:

Guide us waking, O Lord, and guard us sleeping; that awake we may watch with Christ, and asleep we may rest in peace.

Lord, you now have set your servant free to go in peace as you have promised;
For these eyes of mine have seen the Savior, whom you have prepared for all the world to see:
A Light to enlighten the nations, and the glory of your people Israel.
Glory to the Father, and to the Son, and to the Holy Spirit: as it was in the beginning, is now, and will be for ever. Amen.

Together:	Guide us waking, O Lord, and guard us sleeping; that awake we may watch with Christ, and asleep we may rest in peace.
Leader:	Let us bless the Lord.
Response:	Thanks be to God.
Leader concludes:	The almighty and merciful Lord, Father, Son, and Holy Spirit, bless us and keep us. Amen.

PARENTAL BLESSINGS

To bless your children, place one or both of your hands on their heads and speak the blessing. Some Christians then trace the sign of the cross on each child's forehead. In our house, we finish off with a hug and a kiss!

Lord Jesus Christ,
Protect, watch over, and bless this child [or substitute the child's name]
With a lively faith,
A fervent charity,
And a courageous hope of reaching your kingdom.
SOURCE UNKNOWN

...

Christ is shepherd over you,
Enfolding you on every side.
Christ will not forsake you, hand or foot,
Nor let evil come near you.
SOURCE UNKNOWN

...

May the peace of Jesus fill you,
The love of Jesus surround you,
And the presence of Jesus guard you,
Now as you sleep, and all your life.
ANGELA ASHWIN

The following are Jewish parental blessings, tradition-ally said on Shabbat (Sabbath). Shabbat commemorates the seventh day of Creation, on which God rested. It is ob-served on Friday, beginning at sundown.

For a girl:
May God make you like Sarah, Rebecca, Rachel, and Leah.

For a boy:
May God make you like Ephraim and Menasheh.

The above are followed by the priestly blessing:

May God bless you and keep you. May God turn toward you and be gracious to you. May God turn to you and grant you peace.

HOLY DAYS

Every December, columnists write editorials lamenting the commercialization of the holiday season that includes Christmas, Hanukkah, and Kwanzaa. It may be that these columns are the only items printed on the op-ed page during the course of the year that absolutely no one disagrees with. We read these columns, shake our heads, sigh, and think also of similar problems with Valentine's Day, St. Patrick's Day, and Halloween.

Who enjoys rushing out a dozen times to brave the teeming shopping malls, find the latest fad toys, and choose gifts that are perfectly appropriate for their recipients, and then rushing back home in order to cook, decorate, entertain, and clean?

Living as we do in a materialistic culture obsessed with consumption, our pursuit of holiday happiness seems to leave everyone dissatisfied. Even church services and performances of *The Nutcracker* can fail to lift the flagging emotions of parents and kids. For most of us, the hope is that we can somehow catch glimpses of the holiday spirit in the midst of all the holiday stress.

Though we may bemoan the incessant marketing of the holidays, at times there doesn't really seem to be much we can do about it. You can encourage the kids to hand-make a few special gifts for friends and family members. You can pledge to spend less and make the money go further. But to a great extent we're trapped in the system.

When do those fleeting moments of holiday joy seem to burst suddenly into our hearts? Isn't it in the quieter moments, when the family draws together and shares laughter, conversation, and the simple pleasures of good food and drink, that we experience that elusive happiness?

Prayer offers a similar oasis of quietness and intimacy. Prayer enables us to stop our relentless activity and enter a period of time that is sacred, time that is devoted to—set aside—for a high and holy celebration.

What we've lost in this secular, technocratic society of ours is a sense of *festivity*. The word is derived from the Latin for "feast," and of course another variation is "festival." A feast day, in our spiritual tradition, is not simply a day for gorging on food (although good food, and plenty of it, is an indispensable part!). Rather, on a feast day we set aside work and school in order to participate in a sacred ritual. These rituals recount stories that give meaning to our lives—stories like that of an infant born in obscurity and poverty whose life and teaching about the good news of God's unconditional love would turn the world upside down.

One of the most common misconceptions of our time is that prayer is necessarily bound up with a heavy, even burdensome, solemnity. Where's the fun in that? we wonder. But our ancestors did not divide their experience into airtight compartments the way we do nowadays. They experienced life as a seamless garment, where the time spent in the high and stately moments of prayer and ritual flowed directly into the release of laughter and enjoyment of feasts, parades and processions, games and competitions.

As we said in the introductory chapters of this book, prayer and laughter are close cousins. When we lift up our hearts, we are lifted out of ourselves and our daily anxieties. Laughter, like prayer, wells up when we are able to step outside the grind and see things in a new perspective. That's a liberating feeling.

Prayer can help us restore the spirit of festivity to family life. Children have a natural love for pomp and ceremony: the images, words, songs, and pageants of the holiday season form a sort of "sacred game" that fascinates many kids. It's also amazing how much knowledge and history children can absorb, with relatively little pain or resistance, when they enter into the spirit of a festive occasion.

The prayers and rituals that are associated with most of our spiritually rooted holidays—from Advent wreaths and calendars to playing the dreidel at Hanukkah—are rich and rewarding.

If singing is "praying twice," as the old saying has it, then the holidays, with their hymns and carols, are a veritable feast of prayer. We can offer only a small selection of the prayers that are traditionally said during these holidays, but our bibliography contains books that describe the customs and services appropriate to the Jewish and Christian communities. We want to emphasize once again that this book respects the uniqueness of Jewish and Christian traditions: by gathering prayers from both traditions, we do not mean to imply that these holidays are somehow interchangeable. We trust that parents will choose the prayers they feel to be appropriate for their families.

It is worth noting that the holy days and seasons of most faiths also involve fasting and other disciplines as well as feasts. Here, too, our culture has a hard time seeing the value in almost any form of self-denial: to some people, it leads only to a grim, masochistic frame of mind, where Puritanism and other repressive forces lurk. Once again, however, we have to disagree. G. K. Chesterton wrote that this form of self-denial is not a deprivation but a way of giving thanks. As Chesterton put it: "We should thank God for beer and Burgundy by not drinking too much of them." Spiritual disciplines such as fasting can enable us—children and parents alike—to learn a healthy detachment from the consumerist mentality, to develop a deeper sense of gratitude for the gifts and privileges we enjoy, and even to turn our self-denial into an opportunity to share our abundance with those who are less fortunate.

To supplement your family's prayers during the holidays, there are also many wonderful stories that encapsulate the spiritual meaning of festivals like Christmas and Hanukkah—stories that deserve to be read out loud. For younger children, there are many delightful holiday tales, such as Henry van Dyke's *The Other Wise Man* or Isaac Bashevis Singer's *The Power of Light: Eight Stories for Hanukkah*. Older children might find themselves caught up in Dickens's *A Christmas Carol* or Dylan Thomas's *A Child's Christmas in Wales*. If you don't feel up to dramatic readings of works like these, there are memorable versions on tape.

In a book like ours, which is intended for a broad audience, it isn't possible to delve into the full range of holidays associated with particular religious traditions. In most major religions, the year is divided into special seasons with their appropriate feasts and observances. Catholics and Eastern Orthodox Christians also observe certain feasts and memorials on saints' days. Learning to live according to the rhythms of the "church year" can be a rewarding experience for many families, and can be explored more fully by learning more about a specific religious tradition. Of course, certain religious faiths, including some Protestant denominations, do not have a place in their theology for the idea of a church year.

A Note on Kwanzaa: One holiday that has become extremely popular in the past thirty years is known as Kwanzaa, an African American observance celebrated from December 26 to January 1. Based on the ancient "first fruits" agricultural festivals of Africa, Kwanzaa provides a wonderful opportunity for African Americans to develop a deeper appreciation of their heritage. Among the rituals associated with Kwanzaa are special meals, the pouring of libations, candle-lighting ceremonies, and times set aside for meditation. According to movement founder Maulana Karenga, "Kwanzaa is not a religious holiday, but a cultural one with an inherent spiritual quality." It is intended not as a substitute for Christmas, Hannukah, or other religious customs but as a time of cultural enrichment—not only for African Americans, but for anyone who cares deeply about their rich cultural legacy. One of the key

elements of Kwanzaa is reflection on the seven principles of "unity, self-determination, collective work and
responsibility, cooperative economics, purpose, creativity, and faith." Though there are no official Kwanzaa prayers per se, we have included two books on this
festival in our bibliography for readers who are interested in learning more about it.

Jewish Holy Days

PASSOVER: THE FESTIVAL OF FREEDOM

This festival occurs in spring and commemorates the
Jews' liberation from slavery in Egypt. The first and (for
some families) second nights of the eight-day holiday
are celebrated with a Passover seder—a feast, the cen-
terpiece of which is the round seder plate on which are
placed five symbolic foods (a shank bone, symbolizing
the strong arm of God; a roasted egg, symbolizing fer-
tility and continuity; the bitter herb, symbolizing slavery; parsley, symbolizing spring and rebirth; and the
charoset, a mixture of apples, nuts, cinnamon, and
wine, symbolizing the mortar with which the Jews
made bricks in Egypt). It is also traditional to dip vegetables in salt water—another reference to the bitterness
of slavery. During the meal the Haggadah (a recounting
of the events of the Exodus and the rituals of the seder)
is read aloud and the ten plagues God visited on the
Egyptians are recited. During the course of the meal
four symbolic cups of wine or grape juice are drunk.

Why is this evening
different from all other evenings?
Because we were once slaves

of the Pharaoh in Egypt;
but the Lord heard our voice:
he felt our sorrow
and understood our oppression;
with his powerful hand
and his outstretched arm
he led us out of Egypt.
Then we were at last set free.
Blessed is the Lord,
who promised salvation to Israel:
he has kept his promise
and kept the Covenant he established with Abraham.
JEWISH PRAYER FOR PASSOVER

...

When the temple
was still standing firm and secure
in our city Jerusalem
our fathers used the sacrifice of the paschal lamb
as a reminder that God
spared the homes of the Israelites
and passed over them,
to punish only the Egyptian oppressors.
And our fathers bowed down before the Lord.
PRAYER FOR PASSOVER, RECITED WHILE THOSE AT
TABLE ARE SHOWN THE LAMB'S SHANK BONE

HANUKKAH: THE FESTIVAL OF LIGHTS

This festival, which occurs in early December, commemorates the reclaiming of the Temple in Jerusalem
by a small band of warriors led by the Maccabees.
When the temple light was relit, it was discovered that
there was only enough oil for it to last one day. Mi-
raculously, the oil in the lamp lasted for eight days,

giving the Jews enough time to acquire sufficient oil to keep the light burning continuously. On the first night of Hanukkah in millions of Jewish homes and synagogues today, a candle is lit in the menorah, an eight-branched candelabra; another candle is added each successive night, until all the candles are burning on the eighth day. The lighting of the candles each night is accompanied by a blessing traditionally spoken by the mother of the house.

Rock of Ages, let our song
Praise Thy saving power;
Thou, amidst the raging foes,
Wast our sheltering tower.
Furious, they assailed us,
But Thine arm availed us,
And Thy word
Broke their sword
When our own strength failed us.

Kindling new the holy lamps,
Priest approved in suffering,
Purified the nation's shrine,
Brought to God their offering.
And His courts surrounding,
Hear, in joy abounding,
Happy throngs
Singing songs
With a mighty sounding.

Children of the martyr race,
Whether free or fettered,
Wake the echoes of the songs
Where ye may be scattered.

Yours the message cheering
That the time is nearing
Which will see
All men free,
Tyrants disappearing.
TRADITIONAL HANUKKAH HYMN

...

These candles
which now we light
are in remembrance of the miracle of our deliverance,
of the wondrous and glorious deeds
that you performed for our fathers of old
and still perform for us today
through your holy priests.
For the eight days of Hanukkah
these candles are holy,
and we cannot look at them
without giving praise and honor to you, O Lord,
for the wonders and miracles that you have performed
and for your glory.
PRAYER FOR HANUKKAH, FROM THE TALMUD

YOM KIPPUR: THE DAY OF ATONEMENT

This important day in the Jewish calendar is the cul-
mination of Rosh Hashanah (the ten days of repentance over the sins of the previous year), and marks the
beginning of the Jewish New Year. Collectively, Rosh
Hashanah and Yom Kippur are known as the High
Holy Days. On Yom Kippur, Jews fast and attend services all day, asking God for forgiveness for any wrongs
they have committed at home or in the community.
The end of Yom Kippur is signaled by the triumphant
blast of the shofar (the ram's horn).

You reach out your hand to sinners
when they return to the narrow way
and hold out your hand
to greet those who are penitent:
O Lord God, you have taught us
to confess all our sins;
accept our humble repentance.
May it be an acceptable sacrifice to you
according to the promise you have given us!
FROM THE TALMUD, A PRAYER RECITED AT THE END OF
YOM KIPPUR

...

The Lord is merciful and compassionate;
he is the true God!
He pours out his goodness on the descendants of
    the just.
He forgives wickedness
and pardons the sins of those who turn their hearts
    to him.
Forgive us, O Lord!
Bear with us!
Our sin and wickedness are great.
But you, O Lord, are forbearing
and supremely full of compassion
toward those who seek your forgiveness.
You are always ready
to grant mercy and pardon
and are therefore even more
to be worshipped and adored.
PRAYER FOR YOM KIPPUR, BASED ON EXODUS 34:6 FF.

Christian Holy Days

ADVENT/CHRISTMAS

There's no better time of year to reconnect "holiday magic" to its ultimate sources in spirituality than the festivals of Christmas and Hanukkah. Ironically, the season of Advent, which is the four-week season of preparation for Christmas and boasts many of Christianity's most charming and memorable customs, is also one of the most neglected seasons in the church year. Like Lent, Advent traditionally involves some form of self-denial, the better to welcome the feast of the birth of Christ. But Advent is also the time for lighting candles, blessing candy canes, opening special calendars, and a host of other customs from around the world.

Children can't wait for Christmas, yet much of their joy comes from the anticipation of presents and good things to eat. Advent prayers can link the sacred and profane forms of expectation, reminding us that all gifts should evoke gratitude and a spirit of sharing with others.

Christmas offers us a wonderful chance to celebrate childhood itself. For Christians, the essence of Christmas is the mystery of God's willingness to take on flesh, to share our human life. The Christ child is not born into power or wealth but comes into the world in the humblest of circumstances, confounding the assumptions of worldly rulers and scholars. Christmas prayers encourage us all to become a little more childlike.

Blessing of an Advent Wreath

The Advent wreath, used in many Christian commu-nions, is made of four candles, three red and one pink, set within a circle of evergreen branches. One candle is lit the first week; two are lit the second week; three, including the pink candle, the third; and four on Christmas Eve. Some families, including ours, like to light the Advent wreath at dinnertime every evening with our usual grace before meals.

Leader: Our help is in the name of the Lord.

All: Who made heaven and earth.

Leader: In the short days and long nights of Advent, we realize how we are always waiting for deliverance, always needing salvation by our God. Around this wreath, we shall remember God's promise. Listen to the words of the prophet Isaiah:

The people who walked in darkness
have seen a great light;
Upon those who dwelt in the land of gloom
a light has shone.
You have brought them abundant joy
and great rejoicing. (Isaiah 9:2)

This is the Word of the Lord.

All: Thanks be to God.

Silence, followed by the Lord's Prayer.

Leader: Let us now pray for God's blessing upon us and upon this wreath.

Lord our God,
we praise you for your Son, Jesus Christ.
He is Emmanuel, the hope of the peoples,
he is the wisdom that teaches and guides us,
he is the Savior of every nation.

Lord God,
let your blessing come upon us
as we light the candles of this wreath.
May the wreath and its light
be a sign of Christ's promise to bring us
    salvation.
May he come quickly and not delay.

We ask this through Christ our Lord.

All: Amen.

The first candle is lighted

Leader: Let us bless the Lord.

All: Thanks be to God.

*All sing a verse from an Advent hymn such as "Come,
O Come, Emmanuel"*
ADAPTED FROM *CATHOLIC HOUSEHOLD BLESSINGS AND
PRAYERS*

*One way to fight the modern commercialization of
Christmas is to learn more about the spiritual roots of
this holiday. Though most of us are vaguely aware
that the jolly figure of Santa Claus is descended from
"St. Nick," few know anything about the real bishop of*

Myra in Asia Minor, who lived in the fourth century. Indeed, little is known about this saint, but from early tales of his generosity sprang legends and customs that made his feast an important part of European Christianity for more than a thousand years. His feast, celebrated on December 6, spawned a host of traditions, including that of placing cookies in the shoes of children early in the morning of the feast day. The following prayer, which uses the candy cane as its central symbol, is drawn from the countless rituals and practices of our faith traditions that are begging to be rediscovered. From simple celebrations like this may come family traditions that create lasting memories.

St. Nicholas Day Blessing of Candy Canes (December 6)

Good St. Nicholas, we honor you
   on this your holy feast day.
We rejoice that you are the patron saint
   and the holy symbol of joy
   for many peoples of many lands.
Come, great-hearted saint,
   and be our patron and companion
   as we, once again, prepare our homes and hearts
   for the great feast of Christmas,
   the birth of the Eternal Blessing, Jesus Christ.

May these sweets, these candy canes,
   be a sign of Advent joy for us.
May these candy canes,
   shaped just like your Bishop's staff,
   be for us a sign of your benevolent care.

We rejoice that you are the holy bringer of gifts
   and that so many have been delighted
   through your great generosity.
Help us to be as generous of heart.

Wherever these candy canes are hung,
   on tree or wall or door,
   may they carry with them
   the bright blessing of God.
May all who shall taste them
   experience the joy of God
   upon their tongues and in their hearts.

We ask God, now, to bless
   these your brightly striped sweets
   in the name of the Father,
   and of the Son,
   and of the Holy Spirit. Amen.

EDWARD HAYS

As we've suggested, Advent is a season that abounds in colorful, imaginative rituals. Even if you don't have the time or energy this year to do something more elaborate, why not simply add one or more of the following prayers as a substitute grace before meals in the month leading up to Christmas? Another alternative would be to get an Advent calendar and say one or more of these prayers when each of the daily "windows" is opened. Children love the thrill of anticipation; Advent provides a wonderful opportunity to add a deeply spiritual dimension to the idea of holy waiting or expectation for God's grace.

What can I give Him,
Poor as I am?

If I were a shepherd,
I would give Him a lamb;
If I were a wise man,
I would do my part;
But what can I give Him?
Give Him my heart.
CHRISTINA ROSSETTI

...

A babe lies in the cradle,
A little babe so dear,
With noble light he shineth
As shines a mirror clear,
This little babe so dear.

The babe within the cradle
Is Jesus Christ our Lord;
To us all peace and amity
At this good time afford,
Thou Jesus Christ our Lord!

O Jesus, babe beloved!
O Jesus, babe divine!
How mighty is thy wondrous love!
Fill thou this heart of mine
With that great love of thine! Amen.
TRADITIONAL GERMAN CAROL

...

Jesus Christ, thou child so wise,
Bless mine hands and fill mine eyes,
And bring my soul to Paradise.
HILAIRE BELLOC

...

Make me pure, Lord: Thou art holy;
Make me meek, Lord: Thou wert lowly;

Now beginning, and alway:
Now begin, on Christmas Day.
GERARD MANLEY HOPKINS

...

God, who became as we are,
may we become as you are.
AFTER WILLIAM BLAKE

...

Glory be to God in the highest,
and on earth peace,
good will toward men.
LUKE 2:14

...

Holy Child of Bethlehem,
whose parents found no room in the inn;
we pray for all who are homeless.

Holy Child of Bethlehem,
born in a stable;
we pray for all who are living in poverty.

Holy Child of Bethlehem,
rejected stranger;
we pray for all who are lost, alone,
all who cry for loved ones.

Holy Child of Bethlehem,
whom Herod sought to kill;
we pray for all in danger,
all who are persecuted.

Holy Child of Bethlehem,
a refugee in Egypt;
we pray for all who are far from home.

Holy Child of Bethlehem,
in you the Eternal was pleased to dwell;
help us, we pray, to see the divine image
in people everywhere.
In your name we offer this prayer.

DAVID BLANCHFLOWER

...

We pray you, Lord, to purify our hearts
that they may be worthy to become your dwelling-
    place.
Let us never fail to find room for you,
but come and abide in us,
that we also may abide in you,
for at this time you were born into the world for us,
and live and reign, King of kings and Lord of lords,
now and forever.

WILLIAM TEMPLE

...

Jesus, small poor baby of Bethlehem,
be born again in our hearts today
be born again in our homes today
be born again in our congregations today
be born again in our neighborhoods today
be born again in our cities today
be born again in our nations today
be born again in our world today. Amen.

MARIAN WRIGHT EDELMAN

NEW YEAR

The idea of using the first day of the new year for special prayers and resolutions for personal growth is
common in many religious traditions. In a number of

Christian churches, January 1 is celebrated as the feast of the Holy Name of Jesus.

Thanks be to Thee, Lord Jesus,
For another year to serve Thee,
To love Thee,
And to praise Thee.
ANONYMOUS

...

Dear God thank You for the gift of a new year to
  serve You
help me to talk right
help me to walk right
help me to see right
help me to feel right
help me to do right
in Your sight.
MARIAN WRIGHT EDELMAN

...

God, bless our year
giving us
time for the task
peace for the pathway
wisdom for the work
friends for the fireside
love to the last.
THE MOTHERS' UNION ANTHOLOGY OF PUBLIC PRAYERS

...

O Lord, as the years change, may we find rest in your eternal changelessness. Help us meet this new year bravely, in the faith that, while life changes all around us, you are always the same, guiding us with your

wisdom and protecting us with your love; through our
Saviour Jesus Christ.

WILLIAM TEMPLE

LENT/EASTER

Lent is a season that often gets a bad rap, as if it were
about nothing more than denying ourselves certain
pleasures. "What are you giving up for Lent?" is the
question everyone wants to ask in our house. It's been
said that to balance the seemingly negative idea of giving something up, it is worth considering taking something on, such as some form of service or prayer.

Whether you do without something or take on
some good work, the point is that Lent is a time of reflection and reevaluation. In the forty days between
Ash Wednesday, which reminds us of our mortality,
and Easter, when Christians celebrate the resurrection
of Christ and his triumph over death, Lent offers us an
opportunity to draw closer to God, to clear away some
of the debris in our hearts that gets in the way of a
more intimate relationship with the Creator.

There are some who consider Lent too grim to provide much that is edifying for children, but we beg to
differ. Children have an innate need to understand sin,
death, and suffering; we do them a disservice if we make
it seem that spirituality is about nothing more than emotional uplift. Also, they respond to the idea that sacrifice is a form of gratitude, that the best way to count our
many blessings is to share them with others. That's why
many Christians choose Lent as a perfect time to collect
money, clothing, and other things for the poor. Children quickly enter into the spirit of such efforts.

Easter, of course, is the holiest day of the year for

Christians, the victory of life over death. There's so much more to Easter than chocolate bunnies and fake plastic grass (essential as they may be). We invite you to adopt some of the prayers below to help deepen the meaning of Lent and Easter for your entire family.

Joyfully, this Easter day,
I kneel, a little child, to pray;
Jesus, who hath conquered death,
Teach me, with my every breath,
To praise and worship Thee.
SHARON BANIGAN

...

Christ is risen. He is risen, indeed. Alleluia!
ANCIENT CHRISTIAN PRAYER

...

Jesus Christ is ris'n today, Alleluia!
Our triumphant holy day, Alleluia!
Who did once upon the cross, Alleluia!
Suffer to redeem our loss, Alleluia!
HYMN BY CHARLES WESLEY

...

Purge me with hyssop; and I shall be clean: wash me, and I shall be whiter than snow.
Make me to hear joy and gladness; that the bones which thou hast broken may rejoice.
Hide thy face from my sins, and blot out all mine iniquities.
Create in me a clean heart, O God; and renew a right spirit within me.
PSALM 51:7–10

Table Liturgy for the Feast of Easter Sunday

The family stands in prayerful silence around their table, upon which there are two unlighted candles. After a few moments, the father (or single parent) of the family begins.

Father: Blessed are You, Lord our God,
         who raised up Jesus from the tomb
         and has gathered all of us around this table.

Mother: As the light of God
         overcame the darkness of death,
         may these candles we now light
         be for us a sign of the flame of life
         that burns within our hearts.

Candles are lighted

         As these Easter candles
            call us to the feast of this our table,
            may the light of Christ,
            call us to Your eternal Easter feast.
         May these candles delight our eyes
            and add splendor to our meal.

Father: With great joy,
         we come to our Easter dinner
         as we continue our celebration
         of the ever-newness of the resurrection
         of our Lord and Savior, Jesus Christ.
        We rejoice in the resurrection of spring,
         as birds, flowers, and fields come alive
         after the long sleep of winter.

May we, in this Easter Sunday meal,
    share with them the great joy of life.
Let us pause and, in silence,
    lift up our hearts to God
    in gratitude for this holy Easter meal.

Pause for silent prayer

    (As our Risen Lord came as a guest
        and ate with His disciples,
        may we be grateful for the presence at our
            table
        of our guests, [names],
        who bring to our table the holy presence
            of God
        and add to our celebration of this great
            and joyful feast.
    May God bless them,
        for together with the food of this feast,
        they give us reason for joy.)*

Mother: May the taste of goodness in this food
        be a promise of the eternal Easter meal
        we shall all share together with our Risen
            Lord.
    May this Easter dinner be a sacrament
        of springtime, peace, and eternal happiness.
    Alleluia, Alleluia!
    May God's blessing rest upon this table
        and each of us. Amen.

All toast: Happy Easter! *or* A Blessed Easter!
EDWARD HAYS

* *Include section in parentheses if there are guests present.*

Chapter 6

SPLENDOR IN THE ORDINARY

*The fascination of children lies in this: that with each of them
all things are remade, and the universe is put again upon its
trial. As we walk the streets and see below us those delightful
bulbous heads, three times too big for the body . . . we ought
always primarily to remember that within every one of those
heads is a new universe, as new as it was on the seventh day of
creation. In each of those orbs there is a new system of stars,
new grass, new cities, a new sea.*

—G. K. CHESTERTON

Watching each of our children change from an infant
to a toddler, we have never failed to marvel at the delight they take in their newfound ability to name the
things around them. A two-year-old can march around
a room and reel off the names of a dozen items, from
toys and siblings to birds and trees glimpsed through
the window. And that process of naming can go on
and on. Even if Mom and Dad may get a little bored
with the constant repetition of these mighty nouns,
the child never does.

In the book of Genesis, God gives to Adam the task
of naming the beasts. By delegating this authority to
man, God confers a sense of dignity as well as an intimacy with the created order. To name something is to

know it—and, in a profound and mysterious sense, to love it.

A child's in-built sense of wonder is inseparable from the spirit of gratitude. To a young child the world is a huge gift, full of endless surprises. What adult can look on these little Adams and Eves and not feel a sweet but poignant sense of loss? Those of us who have been blessed with children know that they can help us to revive our own capacity for wonder and gratitude.

But the culture we inhabit today is not kind to innocence and wonder. As parents we worry about preserving our kids' freshness and simplicity of spirit in the face of a culture that is increasingly cynical, violent, and self-obsessed. Nowadays gratitude has been replaced by a sense of entitlement, and all too quickly children learn to take the world for granted.

Prayer can help nurture a grateful heart. After all, when a toddler pronounces the name of a person or an object, he or she is really uttering something rather like a prayer. There are people who think that prayer is always bound up with esoteric and strenuous matters, but the simplest and most common prayer is the blessing we offer for the everyday pleasures that are all around us, from meals to sunsets, from loved ones to flowers. To sense the sacred in the ordinary is to develop a spirit of reverence.

In the Jewish tradition, for example, the primary mode of prayer is that of the blessing. According to Rabbi Lionel Blue, Jewish prayers "ask little and are God-centered. God is like this or that (or both), they say, and the world which he fashioned is [like this or that], and this is the way a wise and good man should journey through it. . . . Such prayers are important in an age when spirituality is easily confused with sentimentalism, and feeling with faith."

If our children don't possess a spirit of gratitude for simple, ordinary things, how can we expect them to develop the more mature virtues of responsibility and service as those are applied to the wider realms of society? Unless we are grounded in a love for the concrete world around us—the individual flowers and people—then all our talk about the environment or "the social fabric" will be nothing more than sentimental abstractions.

The prayers in this section offer blessings for daily bread, for the people and things that surround us, and for safety as we travel.

GRACES AND TABLE PRAYERS

Apart from bedtime devotions, there is no more frequently uttered form of prayer than grace before a meal. There is something so palpable, so inherently sacramental, about sharing food together that many of us who have relinquished other prayers have doggedly held on to this one moment of thanksgiving.

How many millions of human beings who have known all too well what it is to go hungry have said grace down through the centuries? How many say grace today in the same frame of mind? Even those of us who live in the midst of plenty, who get our food from the grocery store shelf rather than by planting and reaping, are dimly aware that the meal in front of us is truly a gift.

Saying grace is both an act of gratitude and an acknowledgment of our dependence on forces that are greater than we are. Though we eat to be refreshed and renewed, our contemporary way of life—with its driving pace and its fast-food habits—militates against any feeling of renewal. On the contrary, we live in the age of the Maalox Moment.

It would be wrong to condemn this situation as simply a matter of cultural decadence. The fact is that we are working longer hours to keep pace with the cost of living. We are attending night courses, or dropping kids off at sporting events. Single parents are struggling to earn a living and at the same time to provide a nurturing environment for their children. The family meal is a rare thing nowadays, and we can't always control that. But when it is possible to sit down to a family meal, saying grace is a wonderful way to draw together for a moment and transcend our busyness and preoccupations.

If you say only one form of grace before every meal, and fear that it has become just a mumbled formality, why not add one or two other graces and vary them? For this book we have gathered many beautiful and moving graces that have been composed through the centuries.

One common practice is to say a spontaneous prayer at mealtimes. This prayer may go beyond offering thanks for the meal: it can include thanks for the presence of guests, and even pressing concerns that affect one or more members of the family.

Some families make prayers before dinner more extensive. When we asked the well-known pastor and writer Eugene Peterson about his family's prayer habits, he told us that before his children grew into adulthood and left home, "table prayers" were a wonderful custom in his house. Beginning before the food was cooked, the Petersons would gather at the table and pray. The prayers, spontaneous and heartfelt, would be offered first by the eldest and descend in age. "They would just start gathering the whole world into those prayers," Peterson recalls.

Just remember: if you pray before a meal, don't go on so long that the food is either burnt or stone cold.

While it may be logical or comfortable for a parent to say the grace, we believe that children ought to be given regular opportunities to pray in their own voices and in their own words.

Many families enjoy holding hands during grace—a gesture that outwardly demonstrates an inward unity. For those who are especially unself-conscious, there are a number of graces that have been set to familiar music and can be sung before the meal.

Another practice worth considering is saying a grace *after* the meal. This provides a wonderful sense of closure to the meal before everyone scatters to the four winds.

How about saying grace in public? We mentioned earlier that our daughter Magdalen finds this distasteful. Most of us have an instinctive shyness about praying in public places, whether it be McDonald's or a four-star restaurant. We don't want to seem ostentatious, as if we are flaunting our faith in front of others. It's a natural form of reticence, perhaps, but in an era that promotes self-expression as a high value, perhaps we should be unself-conscious enough to pray anywhere.

Finally, saying grace before a meal is the ideal time to think about those who are less fortunate. During penitential seasons like Advent and Lent, eating a little less can be linked to church or community-related collections that give food to the poor.

Grace before Meals

Thank you for the world so sweet;
Thank you for the food we eat;
Thank you for the birds that sing;
Thank you, God, for everything.
E. RUTTER LEATHAM

...

God, we thank you for this food,
For rest and home and all things good,
For wind and rain and sun above,
But most of all for those we love.
MARYLEONA FROST

...

God is great and God is good,
And we thank him for our food;
By his hand we must be fed,
Give us, Lord, our daily bread. Amen.
ANONYMOUS

...

Bless, O Lord, this food to our use, and us to your
service.
TRADITIONAL GRACE

...

For what we are about to receive may the Lord make
us truly thankful. Amen.
TRADITIONAL GRACE

...

Be present at our table, Lord,
Be here and everywhere adored.

Thy creatures bless, and grant that we
May feast in paradise with thee.
JOHN WESLEY (THIS MAY BE SUNG TO THE TUNE OF
"THE OLD HUNDREDTH.")

...

For food and all Thy gifts of love,
We give Thee thanks and praise.
Look down, O Father, from above,
And bless us all our days. Amen.
ANONYMOUS

...

God bless the master of this house.
God bless the mistress, too;
And all the little children
That around the table go.
OLD ENGLISH GRACE

...

Thou openest
Thy hand, O Lord,
The earth is filled
with good;
Teach us with grateful
hearts to take
From Thee
our daily food.
ANONYMOUS

...

Father, bless the food we take
And bless us all for Jesus' sake.
ANONYMOUS

...

For health and food,
For love and friends,
For everything
Thy goodness sends,
Father in heaven,
We thank thee.
RALPH WALDO EMERSON

...

We thank thee, Lord, for daily bread
As by thy hands our souls are fed.
Grant us to grow more like to thee,
Today and through eternity.
ANONYMOUS

...

All things
Come of Thee,
O Lord,
And of Thine own
Have we given Thee.
1 CHRONICLES 29:14

...

Come, Lord Jesus,
Bc our Guest,
And let Thy gifts
To us be blessed. Amen.
ANONYMOUS

...

Bless Thou the work
That we have done,
Be it great or small;
On this, our food,

On us, each one,
Let now Thy blessing fall.
ANONYMOUS

...

Leader:	The eyes of all wait upon you.
Response:	And you give them their meat in due season.
Leader:	You open your hand.
Response:	And fill all living things with plenty.
Leader (or all):	We thank you, O Lord, for these your gifts, and we beseech you to grant that, whether we eat or drink, or whatsoever we do, all may be done to your glory. Amen.

TRADITIONAL MONASTIC GRACE, DERIVED FROM
PSALM 145:15–16

...

Our hands we fold,
Our heads we bow;
For food and drink
We thank Thee now.
ANONYMOUS

...

Heavenly Father,
Bless this food,
To Thy glory
And our good.
ANONYMOUS

...

To God, who gives our daily bread,
A thankful song we'll raise,

And pray that he who sends our food
May fill our hearts with praise.
THOMAS TALLIS

...

The bread is pure and fresh,
the water is cool and clear.
Lord of all life, be with us,
Lord of all life, be near.
AFRICAN GRACE

...

Bless us, O Lord, and these your gifts which we are
about to receive from your goodness. Through Christ
our Lord. Amen.
CATHOLIC HOUSEHOLD BLESSINGS AND PRAYERS

...

Bless me, O Lord, and let my food strengthen me to
serve thee, for Jesus Christ's sake. Amen.
THE NEW ENGLAND PRIMER

...

For food and all Thy gifts of love,
   We give thee thanks and praise.
Look down, O Father, from above,
   And bless us all our days.
ANONYMOUS

...

What God gives, and what we take,
'Tis a gift for Christ his sake:
Be the meal of beans and peas,
God be thanked for those, and these:
Have we flesh, or have we fish,
All are fragments from his dish.
ROBERT HERRICK

Here needy he stands,
And I am he.
OSAGE PRAYER

...

O give thanks unto the Lord, for he is good; his mercy
endureth forever. He giveth food to all flesh; he giveth
to the beast his food, and to the young ravens which
cry. The Lord taketh pleasure in those that hope in his
mercy.
MARTIN LUTHER

...

Come, dear Lord Jesus, be our guest, and bless what
thou hast given us. For Jesus' sake. Amen.
GERMAN PRAYER

...

All things come of thee, O Lord, and of thine own
have we given thee.
1 CHRONICLES 29:14

...

And of Joseph he said, "Blessed by the Lord be his
land, with the choicest gifts of heaven above, and of
the deep that couches beneath, with the choicest fruits
of the sun, and the rich yield of the months, with the
finest produce of the ancient mountains, and the abundance of the everlasting hills, with the best gifts of the
earth and its fullness, and the favor of him that dwelt
in the bush. Let these come upon the head of Joseph,
and upon the crown of the head of him that is prince
among his brothers."
DEUTERONOMY 33:13–16

...

Let them thank the Lord for his steadfast love, for his wonderful works to humankind. For he satisfies the thirsty, and the hungry he fills with good things.
PSALM 107:8–9

...

O give thanks to the Lord, for he is good, for his steadfast love endures for ever. . . . It is he who remembered us in our low estate, for his steadfast love endures for ever. . . . he who gives food to all flesh, for his steadfast love endures for ever . . . O give thanks to the God of heaven, for his steadfast love endures for ever.
PSALM 136:1, 23, 25–26, 9

...

Blessed are You, Our God, Ruler of the universe. We thank You for the bread which comes from the seeds which grow in the earth that You created.
"HA-MOTZI," JEWISH PRAYER

...

Blessed art Thou, Lord our God, King of the universe, who in His goodness, grace, loving-kindness, and mercy nourishes the whole world. He gives food to all flesh, for His loving-kindness is everlasting. In His great goodness, we have never lacked for food; may we never lack for food, for the sake of His great Name. For He nourishes and sustains all, He does good to all, and prepares food for all His creatures that He created. Blessed art Thou, Lord, who provides food for all.
"BIRKAT HA-MAZON," JEWISH BLESSING FOR FOOD

...

May the Merciful One bless the host and hostess and all who are seated about the table . . . just as our

forefathers were blessed in every way with every manner of blessing.
TRADITIONAL JEWISH GUEST BLESSING

...

This ritual is one.
The food is one.
We who offer the food are one.
The fire of hunger is also one.
All action is one.
We who understand this are one.
ANCIENT HINDU BLESSING

...

Our Father, hear us, and our Grandfather.
I mention also all those that shine, the yellow day,
    the good wind,
the good timber, and the good earth.
All the animals, listen to me under the ground.
Animals above ground, and water animals, listen
    to me.
We shall eat your remnants of food. Let them
    be good.
Let there be long breath and life.
Let the people increase, the children of all ages,
the girls and the boys, and the men of all ages and
    the women,
the old men of all ages and the old women.
The food will give us strength whenever the sun runs.
Listen to us, Father, Grandfather.
We ask thought, heart, love, happiness.
We are going to eat.
ARAPAHO PRAYER BEFORE EATING

...

We are thankful for this meal,
The work of many people
And the sharing of other forms of life.
ZEN PRAYER

Grace after Meals

Be known to us in breaking bread,
    But do not then depart.
Savior, abide with us and spread
    Thy table in each heart.
TRADITIONAL GERMAN GRACE

...

Blessed by He of whose [food] we have eaten and
from whose goodness we live.
JEWISH GRACE AFTER MEALS

...

God is blessed in all his gifts
and holy in all his works,
who lives and reigns for ever and ever. Amen.
CATHOLIC HOUSEHOLD BLESSINGS AND PRAYERS

...

Lord, you have fed us from your gifts and favors,
fill us with your mercy,
for you live and reign for ever and ever. Amen.
CATHOLIC HOUSEHOLD BLESSINGS AND PRAYERS

...

May the abundance of this table never fail and never be
less, thanks to the blessings of God, who has fed us and
satisfied our needs. To him be glory forever. Amen.
ANCIENT PRAYER FROM THE ARMENIAN APOSTOLIC
CHURCH OF LEBANON

We thank you, our God,
for the food you have given us.
Make our sharing this bread together
lead to a renewal of our communion with you,
with one another, and with all creatures.
We ask this through Christ our Lord. Amen.

CATHOLIC HOUSEHOLD BLESSINGS AND PRAYERS

Seasonal Graces

AT CHRISTMAS

For this day of the dear Christ's birth, for its hours of
home gladness and world gladness, for the love within
these walls, which binds us together as a family, for our
food on this table, for our surroundings in a land of
freedom, we bring to Thee, our Father, our heartfelt
gratitude. Bless all these, Thy favors, to our good, in
Jesus' name. Amen.

H. B. MILWARD

AT EASTER

This day, O Christ, we celebrate Thy victory over
death. Bring to us new life of body through this nourishment and new life of soul by Thy presence with us
now, and help us to say with Thy servant of old,
"Thanks be to God which giveth the victory through
Jesus Christ our Lord." Amen.

SOURCE UNKNOWN

...

Thou hast given so much to me,
Give one thing more—a grateful heart;
Not thankful when it pleaseth me,
As if Thy blessings had spare days,

But such a heart whose pulse may be
Thy Praise.
GEORGE HERBERT

Graces for National Holidays

We haven't come across many graces composed spe-
cifically for national holidays, but there are prayers
scattered through this book that you might use as
grace before your evening meal on a holiday. For example, a prayer from the section on "work" on Labor
Day or something relating to diversity or social justice
on Martin Luther King Jr.'s Birthday. However, the
following prayers seemed appropriate for two of our
national holidays, and so we offer them here.

ON INDEPENDENCE DAY

Bless our beautiful land, O Lord,
with its wonderful variety of people,
of races, cultures and languages.
May we be a nation
of laughter and joy,
of justice and reconciliation,
of peace and unity,
of compassion, caring and sharing.
We pray this prayer for a true patriotism,
in the powerful name of Jesus our Lord.
ARCHBISHOP DESMOND TUTU

...

God, source of all freedom,
This day is bright with the memory
Of those who declared that life and liberty
Are your gift to every human being.

Help us to continue a good work begun long ago.
Make our vision clear and our will strong:
That only in human solidarity will we find liberty,
And justice only in the honor that belongs
To every life on earth.

Turn our hearts toward the family of nations:
To understand the ways of others,
To offer friendship,
And to find safety only in the common good of all.

We ask this through Christ our Lord. Amen.
CATHOLIC HOUSEHOLD BLESSINGS AND PRAYERS

ON THANKSGIVING DAY

Come ye thankful people, come,
Raise the song of harvest home:
All is safely gathered in,
Ere the winter storms begin;
God, our Maker, doth provide
For our wants to be supplied;
Come to God's own temple, come,
Raise the song of harvest home.

HYMN BY HENRY ALFORD

Table Liturgy for Thanksgiving

The family stands in prayerful silence around their table, upon which there are two unlighted candles. After a few moments, the mother (or single parent) of the family begins.

Mother: Come, let us welcome the feast of
          Thanksgiving with joy and with light.
          Light is the symbol of the divine.

The Lord is our light and our salvation.
May the light of gratitude burn brightly
   in our hearts
   and around this table,
   not only on the feast of Thanksgiving
   but at all meals.

Candles are lighted

Mother: In the silence of our hearts,
     let each of us give thanks
     for all the many gifts that are ours.

Pause for silent reflection

Let us also be mindful of those today
   who are without food and a home.

Pause for silent reflection

And let us remember those whom we love
   who are not now present at our table.

Pause for silent reflection

Father: Lord of Gifts,
     from Your holy heart
     has come a flood of gifts to us.
With uplifted hearts, we have gathered
     around this table
     to thank You with prayer
     and with the worship of feasting.
We are grateful
     not only for the gift of life itself,

but for all the gifts
of friendship, love, devotion and
forgiveness
that we have shared.
On this feast of giving thanks, Lord God,
we thank You for showing us how to
return thanks
by lives of service,
by deeds of hospitality,
by kindness to a stranger
and by concern for each other.
(We thank You for the presence of our guests
[names],
who, by their being present in our home,
have added to the brightness of our
celebration.)*
We are most grateful, this feast day,
for the way You, our hidden God,
have become visible to us
in one another,
in countless daily gifts
and in the marvels of creation.
Come, Lord of Gifts,
and bless our table and all the food of this
feast.

Let us thank the Lord,
today and all days, Amen.

All toast: Happy Thanksgiving!
EDWARD HAYS

* *Include section in parentheses if there are guests present.*

BLESSINGS

Many people assume that only a priest, rabbi, or minister can confer blessings on something or someone. There's no doubt that it is utterly appropriate for an ordained minister to perform such actions at baptisms, bar and bat mitzvahs, weddings, funerals, and many other ceremonies by which we celebrate key moments in our lives.

But it would be a mistake to think that blessings can only be given by "official" representatives of religious communities. As we've suggested above, parents can, and should, bless their children. To bless something is nothing more or less than to pronounce it good.

The question may naturally arise here: if something is self-evidently good, why should it need to be blessed? Our answer is simple: to say something, especially to say it out loud, helps to make it more real to us and to others. We should bless things for the same reason that we say "I love you" to our parents or spouse or children. When we keep something bottled up inside us, it becomes abstract and distant. John Henry Newman once said that "faith follows action." By that he meant that we must embody our beliefs in tangible forms before they can be fully present to our minds and hearts.

Blessing is the essence of Jewish prayer. According to Ariel Burger, who writes for the on-line magazine *Jewish Family and Life,* "The Hebrew word *bracha* is related to the word for pool of water, which in the desert meant life. For a people wandering in a spiritual desert, a pool of water can mean renewal and hope. Like water in the desert, a blessing is something miraculous, unfamiliar, unexpected." Burger explains that in Judaism there are two forms of blessing, one that grows out of our encounter with the natural world and one that is based on our relationships to other people. "The first allows us to connect with and appreciate what is around us; the second allows us to give many gifts to the people around us."

Now don't get us wrong: we aren't advocating that families engage in some hyperactive effort to toss blessings around at the drop of a hat. Many blessings seem to be called for only at special, appropriate times. For example, there is something fitting about blessing a house or apartment soon after one moves in. When those times arrive, we ought not to be shy about blessing the things that give meaning to our lives.

The following blessings can be said on occasions such as moving into a home, getting a new pet, or taking leave of a visiting friend or relative. But they can also be added once in a while to your daily prayer time.

For the Home

Peace be to this house
And to all who dwell in it.
Peace be to them that enter
And to them that depart.
ANONYMOUS

...

May the house wherein I dwell be blessed;
My good thoughts here possess me;
May my path of life be straight and true;
My dreams as here I lie be joyous;
All above, below, about me
May the house I love be hallowed.
OMAHA INDIAN PRAYER

May God, the Father of goodness,
who commanded us to help one another
as brothers and sisters,
bless this building with his presence
and look kindly on all who enter here. Amen.
CATHOLIC HOUSEHOLD BLESSINGS AND PRAYERS

...

O God, protect our going out and our coming in;
let us share the hospitality of this home
with all who visit us,
that those who enter here may know your love and
   peace.
Grant this through Christ our Lord. Amen.
CATHOLIC HOUSEHOLD BLESSINGS AND PRAYERS

...

Peace be with this house and with all who live here.
Blessed be the name of the Lord. Amen.
CATHOLIC HOUSEHOLD BLESSINGS AND PRAYERS

...

O God, you fill the hungry with good things.
Send your blessing on us, as we work in this kitchen,
and make us ever thankful of our daily bread.
Grant this through Christ our Lord. Amen.
CATHOLIC HOUSEHOLD BLESSINGS AND PRAYERS

For Friends, Neighbors, Relatives

God bless all those that I love,
God bless all those that love me:
God bless all those that love those that I love,
And all those that love those that love me.
ON AN OLD NEW ENGLAND SAMPLER

...

May the road rise up to meet you,
may the wind be always at your back,
may the sun shine upon your face,
the rains fall soft upon your fields
and, until we meet again,
may God hold you in the palm of His hand.

ANCIENT IRISH BLESSING

...

The Lord bless you and keep you,
The Lord make his face to shine upon you and be
    gracious to you;
The Lord lift up his countenance upon you and give
    you peace.

NUMBERS 6:24–6

...

O Thou, who art the God of all the families of the
earth, we beseech thee to bless all our friends and kindred, wherever they may be, especially [names], and
grant that we may ever be knit together in bonds of
mutual love.

ANONYMOUS

...

Be gracious to all that are near and dear to me, and keep
us all in your fear and love. Guide us, good Lord, and
govern us by the same Spirit, that we may be so united
to you here as not to be divided when you are pleased
to call us hence, but may together enter into your glory,
through Jesus Christ, our blessed Lord and Savior.

AFTER JOHN WESLEY

...

O God of Love, we pray thee give us love: love in our
thinking, love in our speaking, love in our doing, and
love in the hidden places of our souls; love of our

neighbors, near and far; love of our friends, old and new; love of those with whom we take our ease; love in joy, and love in sorrow; love in life, and love in death: that so at length we may be worthy to dwell with thee, who art Eternal Love.

ANONYMOUS

The following prayer, a favorite of the novelist Flannery O'Connor, is a plea to the Archangel Raphael that we be led to meet those who will become good friends.

O Raphael, lead us toward those we are waiting for, those who are waiting for us: Raphael, Angel of happy meeting, lead us by the hand toward those we are looking for. May all our movements be guided by your Light and transfigured with your joy.

Angel, guide of Tobias, lay the request we now address to you at the feet of Him on whose unveiled Face you are privileged to gaze. Lonely and tired, crushed by the separations and sorrows of life, we feel the need of calling you and of pleading for the protection of your wings, so that we may not be strangers in the province of joy, all ignorant of the concerns of our country. Remember the weak, you who are strong, you whose home lies beyond the region of thunder, in a land that is always peaceful, always serene and bright with the resplendent glory of God.

ERNEST HELLO

For Pets

Hear our prayer, O Lord, our God, who gives us all good things. Bless all animals and protect them from danger. We pray for the animals who are sick, lost, or starving. Animals are a wonderful part of this world, especially our pets. Please help us to love them as you love us. Amen.

HELENA WOLFE

...

Hear our humble prayer, O God, for our friends the animals. We entreat for them all thy mercy and pity, and for those who deal with them we ask a heart of compassion and gentle hands and kindly words. Make us ourselves to be true friends to animals and so to share the blessing of the merciful. For the sake of thy Son, the tenderhearted Jesus Christ, our Lord.

TRADITIONAL RUSSIAN PRAYER

...

O God, source of life and power, Who feedeth the birds of the heavens, increase our tenderness towards all the creatures of Thy hand. Help us to refrain from petty acts of cruelty, or thoughtless deeds of harm to any living animal. May we care for them at all times, especially during hard weather, and protect them from injury so that they learn to trust us as friends. Let our sympathy grow with knowledge, so that the whole creation may rejoice in Thy presence.

ANONYMOUS

For Safe Travel

Parting, as the Bard has famously reminded us, is sweet sorrow. Whenever we travel, whether together as a family, or with parents and kids going off in different directions, there is a certain emotional resonance that everyone feels. We may be pulling out of the driveway for a summer vacation across the country, or just waving good-bye to Mom or Dad or a visiting relative at the airport, but at these moments we are reminded not only of our loves but also of our vulnerabilities.

It seems only natural to mark these moments with prayer—for good health and safety, for swift reunions and continued blessings. Some Protestant Christians have a beautiful phrase for this sort of prayer: they pray for "travel mercies."

Children, particularly young children, can feel especially fragile at partings. To commend ourselves to God's mercy and love can help a child feel protected and comforted. When a long road trip is ahead, and the minivan is pulling into traffic, a good way to start off the journey is with a request for those travel mercies. Another appropriate time to say these prayers is when a parent is leaving on a business trip, as more and more of us are doing these days.

The light of God surrounds me;
The love of God enfolds me;
The power of God protects me;
The presence of God watches over me.
Wherever I am, God is.
JAMES DILLET FREEMAN, "PRAYER OF PROTECTION"

...

Alone with none but you, my God,
I journey on my way.
What need I fear, when you are near,
O King of night and day?
More safe am I within your hand
Than if a host did round me stand.
ST. COLUMBA OF IONA

...

Go before thy servant this day;
　if Thou thyself go not forth with me,
　　carry me not up hence.

201

Thou, who didst guide the Israelites by an Angel,
    the wise men by a star;
  who didst preserve Peter in the waves,
    and Paul in the shipwreck;
be present with me, O Lord, and dispose my way;
go with me, and lead me out, and lead me back.
LANCELOT ANDREWES

...

O Thou who art the confidence of the ends of the earth, and of them that are afar off upon the sea, we commend to thine Almighty protection all travelers by sea and land; overshadow them by thy mercy, and surround them with thy love. When they cry in distress, do thou mercifully send them help and deliverance. Go with them on their journey, and grant to those who are afar from their homes that they may revisit them, in thy good name, in peace.
ANONYMOUS

...

You, O God, are the Lord of the mountains and the valleys. As I travel over mountains and through valleys, I am beneath your feet. You surround me with every kind of creature. Peacocks, pheasants, and wild boars cross my path. Open my eyes to see their beauty, that I may perceive them as the work of your hands. In your power, in your thought, all things are abundant. Tonight I will sleep beneath your feet, O Lord of the mountains and valleys, ruler of the trees and vines. I will rest in your love, with you protecting me as a father protects his children, with you watching over me as a mother watches over her children. Then tomorrow the sun will rise and I will not know where I am; but I know that you will guide my footsteps.
SIOUX PRAYER

Chapter 7

RITES OF PASSAGE:
Challenges and Transitions in a Child's Life

In the introduction to his book *The Spiritual Life of Children*, the renowned child psychiatrist Robert Coles confesses that it took nearly three decades before he was able to write on this particular subject. His career took shape in the South during the first stirrings of the civil rights movement and much of that career has been concerned with the political and ethical experiences of children.

But in the late 1970s Anna Freud, the distinguished psychoanalyst, suggested to Coles that he go back over the hundreds of interviews he had conducted with children and look for something that he had overlooked. After Coles and his wife sifted through those interviews, it soon became clear to them that he had omitted investigating the inward, spiritual dimension of the child's life. Even in the earliest days of his fieldwork in the South, Coles notes, he was getting clear signals from children about the importance of spirituality and religion in their ability to come to terms with poverty, discrimination, and depression. Coles recounts several important moments in his research when children cited the importance of prayer to their emotional life. Here he recalls one such moment:

> A black youth I was interviewing with relentless insistence in 1962, the year he pioneered school desegregation in Atlanta, said, "You've been asking me about how it feels, how it feels to be a Negro in that school, but a lot of the time I just don't think about it, and the only time I really do is on Sunday, when I talk to God, and He reminds me of what He went through, and so I've got company for the week, thinking of Him."

Coles eventually went over his early research and conducted new interviews all over the world in preparation for writing *The Spiritual Life of Children*, a book that contains a wealth of startling and moving stories.

Coles has become convinced that prayer can become an essential part of a child's psychic well-being, a deeply rewarding process that involves soul-searching, questioning, and the ability to find consolation and peace. Coles sees children as "seekers, as young pilgrims well aware that life is a finite journey and as anxious to make sense of it as those of us who are farther along in the time allotted us."

As we watch our own kids grow and move through the phases of childhood, we've come to a deeper appreciation of Coles's thesis. The argument made by skeptics over the centuries—that prayer is an "opiate" that makes people more resigned to their fate—couldn't be further from the truth, at least in our experience. If prayer is a conversation, even with an unseen presence or spirit, then it calls for an active engagement, not mere passivity.

In our home the after-dinner evening routine consists of prayer and, when there is time (and parental energy), reading out loud to our children. Over the years we have often had occasion to notice the similarities between our children's reactions to great literature and to prayer; both seem to evoke an active questioning, an imaginative probing into the deepest issues: the difficulty of choosing between good and evil, the perplexing mysteries of death and suffering. As we mentioned in chapter 3, our son Charles, who seems to be the resident philosopher in our house, once asked this question after prayers: "Mom, did God make Pepsi?" Well, Mom deferred to Dad, who of course resorted to some verbal ruse to evade the question entirely!

When we see our children engaging in this quest for meaning, it gives us hope that they have not succumbed to the passivity of a media-saturated generation. It also means that we can frequently substitute videos for reading out loud and not worry that we're rotting our kids' brains.

The prayers in this chapter relate to the emotional challenges that nearly all children experience—from the birth of siblings to the strains of academic and athletic competition to sickness and death. Since becoming parents we have realized, with a shock, that childhood seems to entail one arduous emotional transition after another. If grown-ups had to endure such constant change and adjustment, we'd all be basket cases.

George Herbert's famous poem known as "Prayer (1)" consists of a series of metaphors—some of them rather extravagant and baroque—that attempt to capture the essence of prayer. Herbert pictures prayer as "reversed thunder" and "the bird of Paradise," and even as a war machine that flings our words at God like a battering ram against the gates of Heaven. But after all these florid phrases are played out, he ends the prayer with two simple words. Prayer, Herbert concludes, is "something understood."

For children as well as adults, prayer can become a conversation in which we ask questions and seek answers, a dialectic that gives meaning to our struggles, our griefs, and our joys. Millions of people have testified that prayer has brought them to a place in their lives where some form of understanding was achieved, even if that understanding couldn't easily be put into words.

Children, as Robert Coles discovered, have the capacity to join in this search. We owe it to them to provide the prayerful context in which they can become seekers. In doing so, they will teach us more than we could ever imagine.

BIRTH/SIBLINGS

What we call "the family" comes in a lot more sizes and shapes today than it did even a generation ago. And yet, for all the changes that have taken place in our domestic lives, the essential meaning of "family" hasn't changed. Getting along with one's siblings is still just as hard as it ever was. That's why the family was once called "the school of charity": learning to live with one another in a family calls on us to learn forbearance and forgiveness.

The birth of a child can be an emotional challenge for older children—even if those children are much older. Everyone wants and needs attention and the arrival of a brother or sister can seem to threaten that. We've included prayers that deal with this sometimes tumultuous time.

Then there's the civil war that kids fight on a daily basis, which probably takes its biggest toll on Mom and Dad. Don't worry: we're not naïve enough to tell you that prayer will stop your kids from bickering and grousing. But our experience tells us that prayer—particularly evening prayer—gives children a chance to forgive and forget. That's not a miraculous cure, and it is almost always done "after the fact," but it helps to cultivate the habit of forgiveness. And we're convinced that over the course of years that habit *does* make a huge difference.

The first two prayers in this section can be said in the first weeks and months after the arrival of a new child. The second prayer, written by our daughter Magdalen, can be said by a child at any time.

Dear God, thank you for my baby [brother/sister]. Help me to be a loving [sister/brother]. Help me to understand that my baby [brother/sister] needs me even if all [he/she] wants to do all day is nurse and cry. I know that a baby needs to be hugged and kissed. Now that I am big, I understand why babies need so much attention from Mommy and Daddy. Help me to remember that I was once little. Help me not to get mad. Thank you for giving me this beautiful baby.
SUZANNE M. WOLFE

Dear Lord, please help me to be patient with my brothers and sister, especially when they trash my room and bug me with questions all the time. Help me understand what they need and who they are, even though I am so different from them. Help me to love them as you love me—unconditionally and constantly like my Mom and Dad love me. Amen.

MAGDALEN WOLFE

...

Ho! Sun, Moon, Stars, all that move in the heavens,
I bid you hear me!
Into your midst has come a new life.
Consent, I implore you!
Make its path smooth, that it may reach
the brow of the first hill!

Ho! You Winds, Clouds, Rain, Mist, all you that
   move in the air,
I bid you hear me!
Into your midst has come a new life.
Consent, I implore you!
Make its path smooth, that it may reach
the brow of the second hill!

Ho! You Hills, Valleys, Rivers, Lakes, Trees, Grasses,
   all you of the earth.
I bid you hear me!
Into your midst has come a new life.
Consent, I implore you!
Make its path smooth, that it may reach
the brow of the third hill!

OMAHA INDIAN PRAYER

...

BIRTHDAY PRAYERS

A birthday is not unlike any other holiday we celebrate during the course of the year: the essence of the day always seems in danger of being lost in the hustle and bustle of gifts and decorations and meals. It goes without saying that your child is rather interested in the presents and parties, but it would be a shame to leave it at that. After all, a birthday is an opportunity for a parent to remind a child of the miracle of life itself and of how precious and unique that child is.

While your child might be embarrassed for you to pray in front of his or her friends, you can take advantage of some quiet family time—say, at a meal—when you can pray for your child and give the child a prayer to recite.

A birthday also provides an opportunity to create family traditions and rituals that have a deeper spiritual meaning. For example, in *Jewish Family and Life,* Yosef I. Abramowitz and Rabbi Susan Silverman explain that for their daughter Aliza's fourth birthday, they sent out party invitations that asked for nonperishable food rather than gifts. "Then after the party we took Aliza to the local food pantry," they write. "She was proud to hand over her birthday *tzedakah* [righteous gift]. . . . Birthdays are a time to be thankful for the blessings we have in our lives. What better way to teach this idea to a child than having a celebration of her life be a celebration of sharing?"

God made the sun
And God made the tree,
God made the mountains
And God made me.
ANONYMOUS

Thank you, Lord, for this special day. Thank you
for the cake and the candles and the presents. All of
these things tell me that I am special. But most of all,
thank you for the love of my Mommy and Daddy and
brother(s) and sister(s).
SUZANNE M. WOLFE

...

O loving God, today is my birthday.
For your care from the day I was born until today
and for your love, I thank you.
Help me to be strong and healthy,
and to show love for others, as Jesus did.
PRAYER FROM JAPAN

...

My Father, all last year you took care of me and now
you have given me a birthday. I thank you for all your
goodness and kindness to me. You have given me loving parents, a home, gifts, and clothes. Thank you,
God. Help me to be a better child in my new year, to
grow strong, to study well, to work happily.
PRAYER FROM INDIA

...

But now thus says the Lord, he who created you . . .
Do not fear, for I have redeemed you;
I have called you by name, you are mine.
ISAIAH 43:1

Birthday Blessing Prayer for a Child
Lord our God,
   Not only [name] but each of us
   Rejoices in this birthday
   Because birthdays are among the best
   Of all our family feasts.

Today we celebrate that [name]
  Has been Your gift to all of us,
  A gift that grows more valuable in our hearts
  With each passing day.

Bless her/him on this her/his [number] birthday
  With blessings of good health,
  Of laughter and happiness.
On this birthday, may her/his heart overflow
  With good things and beautiful dreams.
Lord, Holy Creator of Fun and Song,
  Come and join us now as we wish [name]
  A happy birthday as we sing:

All sing: Happy Birthday.
EDWARD HAYS

SCHOOL

Outside of the home, the dominant influence on a child's life is usually his or her experience at school. Both as a place of learning and as the central location for your child's "socialization," school is the place where children have to begin to make their way in the world, without immediate support from their parents. From the day we drop our kids off at preschool or kindergarten to the day they graduate from college, our kids enter a microcosm of society itself. Indeed, school might be likened to a stage, where a young person begins to test and shape his character. On this stage many triumphs and tragedies are enacted. Here a child encounters the realities of academic and athletic competition, peer pressure, all the anxieties and pleasures of social life, and the mysterious fact that boys and girls are intriguingly different from one another.

You don't have to be a proponent of prayer in the public schools to see that there are times when children might benefit from putting their joys and sadnesses into the context of prayer. We have found in our own home that children frequently come back from school with emotional stresses and strains that they need to work out, even if they're too shy to approach such issues directly.

As many of the great writers have demonstrated—think of Charlotte Brontë's *Jane Eyre* or Charles Dickens's *Nicholas Nickleby*, for example—children have a keen and finely tuned sense of justice. If a teacher or a fellow student has been harsh or indifferent, a child's heart can be sorely wounded. One of the glories of childhood, of course, is that children seem to be able to forgive and forget with breathtaking ease. But at the same time they need to get things out in the open. Prayer offers them the perfect opportunity to unburden themselves and move on with their lives.

At the same time, our kids are eager to share their achievements and joys with us—if we make time to listen. Prayer provides at least one moment in the day (although it shouldn't be the only one) in which our kids can give thanks in our presence for those special triumphs.

The prayers that are gathered below relate primarily to the academic and athletic challenges of attending school. But there may be times when a child's experiences at school—from physical and emotional injuries to learning disabilities—will lead you to seek out prayers from other sections of this book. While it would be wrong for us as parents to be overly inquisitive about our kids' experiences at school, there are moments when we can give children a prayerful context in which to work through difficulties and challenges.

Lord of wisdom, who gives us minds and hearts to know and love your creation, make us eager to learn, patient with our mistakes and failures, and quick to forgive schoolmates who have been unfair to us, so that we use our knowledge to build a better world. Amen.

GREGORY WOLFE

...

Holy Spirit, help us in this school to live together in love and peace, patient with each other's faults and mindful of each other's wants. May we be gentle in words and helpful in deeds, not seeking our own profit only, but rather the good of all. Fill our hearts and minds so completely with thy presence that they may compel us to love one another.

ANONYMOUS

...

From the cowardice that dare not face new truth
From the laziness that is contented with half truth
From the arrogance that thinks it knows all truth,
Good Lord, deliver me.

KENYAN PRAYER

...

Grant, O Lord, to all teachers and students, to know that which is worth knowing, to love that which is worth loving, to praise that which pleases you most, and to dislike whatever is evil in your eyes. Grant us with true judgment to distinguish things that differ, and above all to search out and to do what is well-pleasing to you; through Jesus Christ our Lord.

AFTER THOMAS À KEMPIS

...

O Lord, who is the fountain of all wisdom and learning, you have given me the years of my youth to learn the arts and skills necessary for an honest and holy life. Enlighten my mind, that I may acquire knowledge. Strengthen my memory, that I may retain what I have learned. Govern my heart, that I may always be eager and diligent in my studies. And let your Spirit of truth, judgment, and prudence guide my understanding, that I may perceive how everything I hear fits into your holy plan for the world.

JOHN CALVIN

COMING-OF-AGE PRAYERS

Our oldest child just became the first teenager in the family and suddenly we feel like we're learning how to be parents all over again. Like countless parents before us, we find ourselves turning to each other and saying, "Just when we thought we were getting good at this. . . ."

So we step out onto the dance floor and try to master the new and intricate movements that now seem required of us. Our daughter, the child-woman, is struggling for independence, testing the limits of her freedom, and coping with the hormones that are beginning to surge inside her. We're stepping on each other's toes and trying not to lose our tempers. How to keep that precarious balance between the expressions of our unconditional love and the need to set boundaries?

Adolescence is also the time when everything is called into question, *especially* the beliefs and habits of adults. One of the most disconcerting aspects of adolescence is the extent to which the child draws a veil over her inner life. What once was transparent has become opaque. The temptation for the parent is to try to reach inside and find out what's going on, but that can't be done without violating the child's privacy and developing conscience. Sometimes the most important way to demonstrate love for a teen is to show respect for that private inner life.

Adolescence is a difficult but necessary period of adjustment for all concerned. It can also be profoundly rewarding, as we learn to relate to our children at a more adult level.

Perhaps because prayer has been so deeply embedded in our family life, our daughter has not become particularly restless or resentful about praying with us. What we have noticed is that her prayers now reach out beyond her immediate experience of school and friends. Now she adds prayers for the poor, the sick, the handicapped, the oppressed, and a list of people outside the family circle. It comforts us to know that as she explores the larger world around her, she is also bringing a sense of compassion and hope with her.

We've included prayers that would be appropriate when children are preparing for and then experiencing religious services such as confirmation and bar/bat mitzvah. These prayers are included not only to help mark these religious ceremonies, but also because they signify a child's coming of age. Of course, the Christian rite of confirmation is not practiced in all denominations, and it is theologically different from the bar/bat mitzvah. But these ceremonies do share a common spirit: they are rites of passage, formal declarations in the presence of the larger community of a serious commitment to a moral and spiritual life.

Be thou a bright flame before me,
Be thou a guiding star above me,
Be thou a smooth path below me,
Be thou a kindly shepherd behind me,
Today—tonight—and for ever.
ST. COLUMBA OF IONA

...

Lord,
this moment is yours;
mine for you,
and yours for me.
ANGELA ASHWIN

...

Lord, how glad we are that we don't hold you but that you hold us.
PRAYER FROM HAITI

...

Master of eager youth,
Controlling, guiding,
Lifting our hearts to truth,
New powers providing;
Shepherd of innocence,
Thou art our Confidence,
To thee, our sure Defense,
We bring our praises.
TRADITIONAL SUSSEX HYMN

Lord, I want to go where You want me to go
Do what You want me to do
Be what You want me to be.
Save me!
BLACK SPIRITUAL

...

Holy God who madest me
And all things else to worship thee,
Keep me fit in mind and heart,
Body and soul, to take my part.
Fit to stand and fit to run,
Fit for sorrow, fit for fun,
Fit for work and fit for play,
Fit to face life day by day.
Holy God, who madest me,
Make me fit to worship thee.
BISHOP R. MANT

...

Unbreakable, O Lord,
Is the love
That binds me to You:
Like a diamond,
It breaks the hammer that strikes it.

My heart goes into You
As the polish goes into the gold.
As the lotus lives in its water,
I live in you.

Like the bird
That gazes all night
At the passing moon,
I have lost myself dwelling in You.
MIRABAI

I am yours, I was born for you;
what is your will for me?
Let me be rich or beggared,
exulting or lamenting,
comforted or lonely;
since I am yours, yours only,
what is your will for me?
ST. TERESA OF ÁVILA

...

Somebody's knocking at your door,
Somebody's knocking at your door,
O children, why don't you answer?
Somebody's knocking at your door.

Knocks like Jesus, somebody's knocking at your door,
Can't you hear Him? Somebody's knocking at your
    door,
Jesus calls you, somebody's knocking at your door.
BLACK SPIRITUAL

...

Wherever I go—only Thou!
Wherever I stand—only Thou!
Just Thou, again Thou!
Always Thou! Thou! Thou! Thou!
When things are good, Thou!
When things are bad—Thou!
Thou, Thou, Thou!
HASIDIC SONG

The following prayer is a Jewish blessing that a parent says for a child.

Into our hands, O God, You have placed Your Torah,

to be held high by parents and children, and taught by one generation to the next.

Whatever has befallen us, our people have remained steadfast in loyalty to the Torah. It was carried into exile in the arms of parents that their children might not be deprived of their birthright.

And now I pray that you, my child, will always be worthy of this inheritance. Take its teaching into your heart, and in turn pass it on to your children and those who come after you. May you be a faithful Jew, searching for wisdom and truth, working for justice and peace. Thus will you be among those who labor to bring nearer the day when the Lord shall be One and His name shall be One.

JEWISH BLESSING

WORK

Most parents, it seems safe to say, want their children to achieve success in life, however variously the word "success" might be defined. We urge children to do well in school, we send them to music lessons, and enroll them in martial arts classes and soccer teams. Then we attend their recitals, or follow their bus around for hundreds of miles to cheer them on to victory.

Is it possible that in the last decade or two parents have become a little obsessed with urging their children to *perform* in one way or another? When we watch a movie like *Parenthood*, we laugh at the absurdity of the Rick Moranis character, who drills his child day and night in order to turn her into an intellectual prodigy—a child who is all "head" but no "heart."

But then we encounter news reports that are disturbing, like the story about the girl who died while attempting to become the youngest person in America to fly across the country.

When we make demands of our children, are we seeking their good, or somehow trying to live vicariously through them? How do we draw the line between instilling good habits—a "work ethic," if you will—and letting them enjoy the wonderful leisure of childhood?

Obviously there are no simple answers to these questions. Every parent has to struggle to find the golden mean. But there is no denying that children must learn to work, whether that work is merely the simple math problems of a third grader or the daily household chores or the pocket-money jobs of adolescence.

Because the work we do reveals who we are and what we care about, it is important that children understand that their efforts have a deeper meaning. If we make work into mere drudgery or the effort to achieve stardom and success, then we impoverish our lives and those of our children. To pray about the various kinds of work we undertake is to place those efforts in a larger context. There is a Hebrew phrase that helps Jews to define their sense of mission on this earth: *tikkun olam,* or "repairing the world." Children need to see their work as part of a larger human effort to repair, clean, and build up the world. So do grown-ups.

The prayers below can be said before embarking on some form of work, whether that be school, a paper route, or a summer job. Labor Day would be another appropriate time to say prayers relating to work. Or they can just be added on occasion to your daily prayers when you want to focus for a moment on the meaning and value of work.

O Lord! you know how busy I must be this day:
if I forget you, please do not forget me.
AFTER SIR JACOB ASTLEY

...

The things, good Lord, that I pray for, give me the grace to labor for.
ST. THOMAS MORE

...

Be my guide, O Lord, I pray,
Lest I stumble on my way.
Be my strength, dear Lord, I ask,
That I may fulfill each task.

Teach me, my God and King,
In all things thee to see,
And what I do in anything
To do it as for thee.
GEORGE HERBERT

...

O Lord, help me to understand that you ain't going to let nothing come my way that You and me together can't handle.
AN AFRICAN BOY, QUOTED BY MARIAN WRIGHT EDELMAN IN *GUIDE MY FEET*

...

My God, you are always close to me. In obedience to you, I must now apply myself to outward things. Yet, as I do so, I pray that you will give me the grace of your presence. And to this end I ask that you will assist my work, receive its fruits as an offering to you, and all the while direct all my affections to you.

BROTHER LAWRENCE

...

Lord Jesus,
take my mind and think through me,
take my hands and bless through me,
take my mouth and speak through me,
take my spirit and pray in me;
above all, Lord Jesus,
take my heart and love through me,
so that it is you who live and work in me.

AFTER LANCELOT ANDREWES

...

Lord, in union with your love, unite my work with your great work, and perfect it. As a drop of water, poured into a river, is taken up into the activity of the river, so may my labor become part of your work. Thus may those among whom I live and work be drawn into your love.

ST. GERTRUDE THE GREAT

...

Lord, when you call us to live and work for you,
give us the wisdom to remember
that it is not the beginning
but the faithful continuing of the task
that is most important in your eyes,
until we have completed it to the best of our ability.

AFTER SIR FRANCIS DRAKE

...

God of work and rest and pleasure,
grant that what we do this week may be for us
an offering rather than a burden;
and for those we serve, may it be the help they need.
A NEW ZEALAND PRAYER BOOK

...

Give me, dear Lord, a pure heart and a wise mind, that I may carry out my work according to your will. Save me from all false desires, from pride, greed, envy, and anger, and let me accept joyfully every task you set before me. Let me seek to serve the poor, the sad, and those unable to work. Help me to discern honestly my own gifts that I may do the things of which I am capable, and happily and humbly leave the rest to others. Above all, remind me constantly that I have nothing except what you give me, and can do nothing except what you enable me to do.
JAKOB BÖHME

ILLNESS AND TIMES OF NEED

When Greg was a boy he suffered from asthma and recurrent bouts of bronchitis—illnesses that had afflicted his father, too. Living as he did on Long Island, with its high humidity and pollen counts, he was frequently confined to bed for days on end.

Back in the 1960s, before the advent of preventive treatments and over-the-counter inhalers, asthma medicine was taken from a nebulizer made of intricate glass tubing and rubber. You poured the liquid medicine—a straight shot of adrenaline, essentially—into the nebulizer, placed the end of the tube in your mouth, squeezed the bulb, and inhaled. Then your heart would race with adrenaline and the passages in your lungs would open up for a while. But even then the bronchitis made it hard to breathe; Greg's chest would fill with phlegm and the coughing never seemed to end.

Nights were the worst times. Even with long naps, the effort of coughing all day took its toll. Being tired and yet unable to sleep was not easy for an eight-year-old to deal with. After Greg's mother had lovingly cared for him during the day, his father would come home from work and sit by his bedside at night. The fact that Greg's father had also suffered from asthma created a bond that somehow made the suffering easier to bear.

But what Greg remembers from those nights was the scripture passages and prayers that his father intoned in a quiet but soothingly rhythmic voice. The Gospel of John was Greg's dad's favorite. "In the beginning was the Word, and the Word was with God, and the Word was God." "Let not your hearts be troubled; believe in God, believe also in me. In my Father's house are many rooms; if it were not so, would I have told you that I go to prepare a place for you?"

There's no doubt in Greg's mind that it was the tone of his father's voice, even more than the content, that was so profoundly comforting. But would that voice have been as comforting if it had not been beseeching God for a boy's healing?

It has been said that prayer is love in action. When our children are ill or suffering from some sadness or distress, should we not demonstrate our love by praying for, with, and *over* them?

Blessed are You, our God, Ruler of the universe,
Who helps me when I am sad and tired.
TRADITIONAL JEWISH PRAYER IN TIMES OF DISTRESS

...

The King of love my Shepherd is,
Whose goodness faileth never.
I nothing lack if I am his
And he is mine forever.
HENRY WILLIAMS BAKER

...

Dear God, be good to me:
Thy sea is so wide, and my boat is so small.
PRAYER OF THE BRETON FISHERMEN

...

Lord, help me!
MATTHEW 15:25

...

O God our Father, bless all who suffer and give them
courage, strength, and peace. Amen.
JOHN G. WILLIAMS

...

When I am afraid, I put my trust in you.
PSALM 56:3

...

Bless all the children in hospitals. Help them to grow
stronger every day and to be happy, cheerful, and patient. Be with all the ill people everywhere. Help them
to know that Thou art with them and art taking care
of them.
BERTHA C. KRALL

...

Lord, I'm scared and alone. Help me!
SUZANNE M. WOLFE

...

Why should I feel discouraged?
Why should the shadows fall?
Why should my heart feel lonely
and long for heaven and home?
When Jesus is my portion
A constant friend is he.
His eye is on the sparrow
And I know he watches me.

I sing because I'm happy,
I sing because I'm free.

His eye is on the sparrow
And I know he watches me.
BLACK SPIRITUAL

...

Oh Lord,
Oh, my Lord,
O, my good Lord,
Keep me from sinking down.

I tell you what I mean to do,
Keep me from sinking down,
I mean to go to heaven too;
Keep me from sinking down.
ANONYMOUS

...

I believe in the sun even when it is not shining.
I believe in love even when feeling it not.
I believe in God even when he is silent.
JEWISH PRAYER

Dearest Lord, may I see you today and every day in
the person of your sick, and, whilst nursing them,
minister unto you. Though you hide yourself behind
the unattractive disguise of the irritable, the exacting,
the unreasonable, may I recognize you. . . .

MOTHER TERESA

...

Father of mercy,
Lover of all children,
Who in their form didst send Thy Son;
Gladly we bless thee,
Humbly we pray thee,
For all the children of the earth.

In thy compassion,
Helper of the helpless,
Tend them in sickness, ease their pain,
Heal their diseases,
lighten their sorrows,
And from all evil keep them free.

SILESIAN HYMN

...

Precious Lord, take my hand.
Lead me on. Let me stand.
I am tired. I am weak. I am worn.
Through the storm,
Through the night,
Lead me on to the light.
Take my hand, precious Lord,
and lead me home.

BLACK SPIRITUAL

...

Hear my prayer, O Lord, and let my cry come unto
    thee.
Hide not thy face from me in the day when I am in
    trouble;
incline thine ear unto me:
in the day when I call answer me speedily. . . .
My days are like a shadow that declineth;
and I am withered like grass.
But thou, O Lord, shalt endure for ever;
and thy remembrance unto all generations.
PSALM 102:1–2, 11–12

...

The Lord sustains them on their sickbed; in their illness you heal all their infirmities.
PSALM 41:3

...

O Lord, take care of me this day, and bring
me safely to my journey's end, for Jesus' sake. Amen.
ANONYMOUS

...

O Lord our God
and God of our fathers!
Mercifully direct and guide our steps
to our destination,
and let us arrive there
in health, joy, and peace!
Keep us from snares and dangers,
and protect us from any enemies
that we might meet along the way.
Bless and protect our journey!
JEWISH PRAYER

Save us, O God,
for your mercy's sake.
Protect us from our enemies
and keep far from us
evil and conflict,
hunger and affliction.
Keep us from stumbling
and falling into danger.
Shelter us in the shadow of your wings,
for you are our protection and salvation;
goodness and mercy are yours.
Watch over our going out and coming in.
Spread over us your mantle of peace.
PART OF A BLESSING RECITED ON THE EVENING OF
SHABBAT AND OF FESTIVALS, AFTER THE SHEMA

...

Send down your angel
who in his mercy gives comfort and relief
to those who suffer.
Let the sick and infirm be healed.
Lighten and relieve their pain.
Let them have respite from their suffering
that they may see your light.
Let healing come swiftly with the dawn.
Blessed arc you, O Lord,
who uphold the sick on their bed of sorrow!
May their days once more be good
and their years happy!
Blessed are you
who uphold, save, and restore the sick.
JEWISH PRAYER

...

Heal us, O Lord, and we shall be healed,
Save us and we shall be saved,
For Thou art our glory.
Send complete healing for our every illness,
For Thou, Divine King, art the faithful, merciful
    Physician.
Blessed are Thou, Lord, who heals the sick of His
    people Israel.

"REFUAH," JEWISH BLESSING

...

Tend thy sick ones, O Lord Christ,
rest thy weary ones.
Bless thy dying ones.
Soothe thy suffering ones.
Pity thy afflicted ones.
And all for thy love's sake.

ST. AUGUSTINE OF HIPPO

...

Who is my mother? Who is my father? Only you,
    O God.
You watch me, guard me, on every path, through
    every darkness,
and before each obstacle that you might hide or take
    away, O God, my lord,
O lord of the mountains and valleys.

KEKCHI MAYA

...

I will lift up mine eyes unto the hills, from whence
    cometh my help.
My help cometh from the Lord, which made heaven
    and earth.
He will not suffer thy foot to be moved: he that
    keepeth thee will not slumber.

Behold, he that keepeth Israel shall neither slumber
 nor sleep.
The Lord is thy keeper: the Lord is thy shade upon
 thy right hand.
The sun shall not smite thee by day, nor the moon by
 night.
The Lord shall preserve thee from all evil: he shall
 preserve thy soul.
The Lord shall preserve thy going out and thy coming
 in from this time forth, and even for evermore.
PSALM 121

...

Wa-kon'da, here needy he stands,
and I am he.
OMAHA INDIAN PRAYER

...

My Lord God, I have no idea where I am going. I do
not see the road ahead of me. I cannot know for certain where it will end. Nor do I really know myself,
and the fact that I think that I am following Your will
does not mean that I am actually doing so. But I believe that the desire to please You does in fact please
You. And I hope that I have that desire in all that I am
doing. I hope that I will never do anything apart from
that desire. And I know that if I do this, You will lead
me by the right road though I may know nothing
about it. Therefore will I trust You always though I
may seem to be lost and in the shadow of death. I will
not fear, for You are ever with me, and You will never
leave me to face my perils alone.
THOMAS MERTON

...

We wait in the darkness!
Come, all ye who listen,
Help in our night journey:
Now no sun is shining;
Now no star is glowing;
Come show us the pathway:
the night is not friendly;
The moon has forgot us,
We wait in the darkness!
IROQUOIS PRAYER

...

I am here abroad,
I am here in need,
I am here in pain,
I am here in straits,
I am here alone.
O God, aid me.
CELTIC PRAYER

...

O God, who knowest us to be set in the midst of so
many and great dangers, that by reason of the frailty of
our nature we cannot always stand upright; grant to us
such strength and protection as may support us in all
dangers, and carry us through all temptations; through
Jesus Christ our Lord.
BOOK OF COMMON PRAYER

WHEN SOMEONE DIES

Suzanne will never forget one day when she took our
firstborn, Magdalen, out shopping. Magdalen was just
two at the time. It was spring, and as they walked

along the main street of the small town where we lived, Suzanne spotted someone selling balloons. *"Boons!"* Magdalen cried. Suzanne bought her one and tied it to her wrist so it wouldn't fly off. The rest of the afternoon Magdalen gravely watched it bob and twist in the air above her head. Her delight in it, as with most toddlers, was solemn and intense.

Then it was time to go home. When they got to the car Magdalen insisted on holding the string to the balloon in her hand. Without thinking Suzanne opened one of the windows because the afternoon had turned very warm and the air-conditioning in the car didn't work. A few minutes later, while Suzanne was driving down the highway, she heard a heart-wrenching wail. Looking in the rear-view mirror she saw that the balloon had slipped out of Magdalen's fingers and disappeared through the window. Magdalen was craning her neck to watch it soar away up into the sky. Her grief was enormous, and there was little Suzanne could do to console her.

That day Suzanne realized that even the smallest child can suffer the most intense pain of loss. Whether it is a favorite stuffed animal that finally comes apart, a beloved blanket that shreds in the washer, or a cherished pet that gets lost, the loss of it is felt as a type of death. A child's grief, like its joy, has a burning purity that seems to blot out everything else.

So it is when a friend or family member dies. If adults have a difficult time coming to terms with death, how can a child, bursting with youth and energy, understand the mystery of human mortality? To complicate matters further, our culture has such an aversion to death that many critics have written about death being the "final taboo" in contemporary society.

How you decide to console your child when someone

near to you dies will depend on your own beliefs and traditions. What we have discovered in our family is that the long, slow process of grieving seems to stall without the aid of prayer. Because those who die depart from us, there is a basic human instinct to send our prayers after them. In prayer we cherish the memories of those whom we have loved and we come to a deeper understanding of the preciousness of every human life.

T. S. Eliot, who composed many poems that were at the same time prayers, once wrote that "Love is most nearly itself when here and now cease to matter." In a similar vein, the psalmist prayed with confidence that "love is stronger than death." Neither children nor adults will ever completely fathom the mystery of death, but when we focus our love into prayer for those who have passed on, we come as close to understanding death as it is humanly possible to do.

Lord Jesus, receive [name's] spirit.
ADAPTED FROM ACTS 7:59

...

God be in my head, and in my understanding;
God be in my eyes, and in my looking;
God be in my mouth, and in my speaking;
God be in my heart, and in my thinking;
God be at my end, and at my departing.
SARUM PRIMER, FIFTEENTH CENTURY

...

All shall be well,
and all shall be well,
and all manner of things shall be well.
JULIAN OF NORWICH

Yea, though I walk through the valley of the shadow
    of death, I will fear no evil;
For thou art with me; thy rod and thy staff they com-
    fort me.

PSALM 23:4

...

I want to die easy when I die.
I want to die easy when I die.
Shout salvation as I fly,
I want to die easy when I die.

BLACK SPIRITUAL

...

Lord Jesus, I am not an eagle. All I have are the eyes
and the heart of one. In spite of my littleness, I dare to
gaze at the sun of love, and I long to fly towards it.

ST. THÉRÈSE OF LISIEUX

...

Eternal rest grant unto them O, Lord, and may per-
petual light shine upon them. May they rest in peace.
Amen.

ANCIENT CHRISTIAN PRAYER

...

Let nothing disturb thee,
Nothing affright thee;
All things are passing;
God never changeth;
Patient endurance
Attaineth to all things;
Who God possesseth
In nothing is wanting;
Alone God sufficeth.

ST. TERESA OF ÁVILA

Blessed are they that mourn: for they shall be
comforted.
MATTHEW 5:4

...

Into Thy hands, Lord, I commend my spirit:
Thou hast redeemed me, O Lord God of truth.
PSALM 31:5

...

Abide with me: fast falls the eventide;
The darkness deepens; Lord, with me abide;
When other helpers fail, and comforts flee,
Help of the helpless, O abide with me.
HENRY FRANCIS LYTE, "EVENTIDE"

...

Bring us, O Lord, at our last awakening
into the house and gate of heaven,
to enter into that gate and dwell in that house
where shall be no darkness nor dazzling,
but one equal light;
no noise nor silence, but one equal music;
no fears nor hopes, but one possession;
no ends nor beginnings, but one equal eternity
in the habitations of your glory and dominion,
world without end.
JOHN DONNE

...

Give rest, O Christ, to your servants, with your saints,
where sorrow and pain are no more, neither sighing,
but life everlasting.
RUSSIAN ORTHODOX KONTAKION OF THE DEPARTED

...

Thy might is eternal, O Lord,
Who revives the dead,
Powerful in saving,
Who makes the wind to blow and the rain to fall,
Who sustains the living with loving-kindness,
Who revives the dead with great mercy,
Who supports the falling, heals the sick, frees the
     captive,
And keeps faith with the dead;
Who is like Thee, Almighty, and who resembles Thee,
O King who can bring death and give life,
And can make salvation blossom forth.
And faithful art Thou to revive the dead.
Blessed art Thou, Lord, who makes the dead live.
"GEVUROT," JEWISH BLESSING

...

O God, your Son chose the path which led to pain before joy and the cross before glory. Plant his cross in
our hearts, so that in its power and love we may come
at last to joy and glory; through your Son, Jesus Christ
our Lord.

LUTHERAN BOOK OF WORSHIP

...

The Lord is my shepherd; I shall not want.
He maketh me to lie down in green pastures:
he leadeth me beside the still waters.
He restoreth my soul: he leadeth me in the
paths of righteousness for his name's sake.
Yea, though I walk through the valley of the
shadow of death, I will fear no evil: for thou
art with me; thy rod and thy staff they comfort me.
Thou preparest a table before me in the

presence of mine enemies: thou anointest
my head with oil; my cup runneth over.
Surely goodness and mercy shall follow me all
the days of my life: and I will dwell in the
house of the Lord for ever.
PSALM 23

...

Lead, kindly Light, amid the encircling gloom,
Lead thou me on;
The night is dark, and I am far from home,
Lead thou me on.
Keep thou my feet; I do not ask to see
The distant scene; one step enough for me.

I was not ever thus, nor prayed that thou
Shouldst lead me on;
I loved to choose and see my path; but now
Lead thou me on.
I loved the garish day, and in spite of fears,
Pride ruled my will: remember not past years.

So long thy power hath blest me, sure it still
Will lead me on.
O'er moor and fen, o'er crag and torrent, till
The night is gone,
And with the morn those Angel faces smile,
Which I have loved long since, and lost awhile.
JOHN HENRY NEWMAN, "LEAD, KINDLY LIGHT"

...

May the Father take you
In his fragrant clasp of love,
When you go across the flooding streams
And the black river of death.
CELTIC BLESSING

Grandfather, Great Father,
let matters go well with me,
for I am going into the forest.
BAMBUTI PYGMY PRAYER

...

From delusion lead me to Truth.
From darkness lead me to Light.
From death lead me to Immortality.
THE UPANISHADS

...

O Father, give my spirit power to climb
To the fountain of all light, and be purified.
Break through the mists of earth, the weight of clay,
Shine forth in splendor, you who are calm weather,
And quiet resting-place for faithful souls.
You carry us, and you go before;
You are the journey, and the journey's end.
BOETHIUS

A Family Liturgy after Someone Has Died

OPENING RESPONSES

Come among us, God.
You who cast the planets into space
and cradle the sparrow in her nest.
Come God and meet us here.

Come among us, God.
You who bless the poor and the broken
and stand by the sad and the strong.
Come God and meet us here.

Come among us, God.
You who dance in the silence
and shine in the darkness.
Come God and meet us here.

READINGS

Psalm 139:7–10
Revelation 21:3–4
John 14:1–3

SPACE TO REMEMBER

This time may be devoted to remembering those who
have died. Here it would be appropriate to tell stories,
sing songs, share common memories, bring into the
present the things that you want to recall, and to share
silence. Use a ritual action that is meaningful to those
present: e.g., light a candle, place a stone or flower on
a grave, float petals in water, place centrally something
that recalls those who have died.

All our laughter, all our sadness,
Safe now in God's hands.

All our anger, all our gladness,
Safe now in God's hands.

All our stories, all our memories,
Safe now in God's hands.

Those we remember, those we love,
Safe now in God's hands.

Sing a song or listen to some favorite music.

CLOSING RESPONSES

We ask for the love of God
and the messages of angels.

The laughter of Jesus
and the stories of the saints.

The power of the spirit
and the strong hands of friends.

To bless us on life's journey
and lead us safely home, Amen.
RUTH BURGESS

Chapter 8

Prayers from the Heart

In her book *Children and Prayer*, Betty Shannon Cloyd recounts the story of a three-year-old boy whose mother had just given birth to a baby daughter. When the mother came home from the hospital, the three-year-old insisted that he be allowed to spend some time alone with his newborn sister. The mother hesitated at first, since the request seemed a little odd. Eventually she relented, but she decided to stand outside the door where she could listen to what her child would say to the baby. The three-year-old went to the crib, leaned over, and whispered to his sister: "Tell me about God. I think I'm beginning to forget."

One of the paradoxes of growing from childhood into adult life is that there is so much we seem to "unlearn" in the process. The thoughts, emotions, and desires of children have a purity and a searing intensity that adults, with our mixed motives and second thoughts, rarely experience.

We've often wondered if that is the reason why so

many grown-ups tend to sentimentalize childhood—
as a kind of unconscious escape hatch from having to
meet the needs of these remarkably subtle and sensitive creatures. Sentimentality has been defined as the
attempt to enjoy an emotional high without having to
put in the hard work of understanding the whole truth
of a thing.

We've noticed another tendency in many adults: the
habit of talking down to children when it isn't necessary. So often children seem to be in the same position
as the Oxford-educated "natives" in some Hollywood
comedy: the Anglo explorer meets them in the jungle
or village, assumes that they are "childlike," and starts
gesturing wildly and speaking in baby talk.

As the parents of four children, we're well aware that
kids are not "God's little angels." But we have often
gazed in wonder at their ease and unself-consciousness
when it comes to prayer and the life of the spirit. That's
why the story recounted by Cloyd, though it may have
a sentimental side to it, rings true. The many barriers
that seem to stand between us adults and a fuller prayer
life don't hinder small children: they aren't embarrassed
or shy or ashamed to pour their love and gratitude and
needs to God.

Nothing is too small or insignificant for a child to
address in prayer: there is no line of demarcation between Important and Not Important. In this sense,
Christ's words about God knowing the number of
hairs on our heads, and about being aware when a
sparrow falls, make perfect sense to a child. Either
God cares about everything (including those lost mar-
bles and bruised knees) or he cares about nothing;
either he listens to everyone with equal love and at-
tentiveness or he doesn't listen at all. It never occurs to

a child that he may not be worthy to speak to God or that God could ever "give up" on anyone. Even the shyest child can find in God a discreet conversational partner.

Some of the world's great mystics have written that the highest goal of the spiritual life is to make ourselves transparent before God—not because he doesn't know what is inside us, but because we must be willing to tear down the barriers we erect around our hearts. The reason we tell God what he already knows, according to C. S. Lewis, is that we must "unveil" ourselves: "The change is in us. The passive changes to the active. Instead of merely being known, we show, we tell, we offer ourselves to view."

One of the most poignant aspects of childhood is the transparency of children's souls: children have not yet learned to hide behind veils. The corollary to this is that children feel *known* and *loved* by God; they have a breathtaking confidence that he holds them in his hands. Adults often think with fear of being known by God, and it is true that even children can have some trepidation about God's knowledge of their sins and failures. But unless children are brought up to think of the Lord as a vindictive judge, they will count on his mercy and forgiveness. Thus prayer can become for a child a daily time for checking in with the Almighty.

But like any talent, even a child's natural talent for prayer can atrophy if it is not used and developed. At the very least, in our role as guardians of these creatures, we ought to provide the context in which they can begin their conversation with God. They really don't need complicated instructions on how to begin, just encouragement and a little prompting. Once they start sharing their hearts with God, you may find your-self relearning things you're amazed you ever forgot.

GIVING THANKS

When a toddler names the things around her, she isn't just stating the facts; she's making an exclamation. Doggy! Moon! Flower! Mommy! More often than not, when she utters these names she will have a look on her face that seems to say: "You're noticing this, right? You're paying attention? Can you believe this?" And if you fail to take sufficient notice, you're likely to feel a small hand grabbing your chin and yanking your head around in the right direction, in order to demonstrate the proper amazement. Only after you have shown the appropriate amount of reverence will the little taskmaster leave you in peace.

A child's capacity for wonder takes the stuff of everyday life and transforms it into the miraculous. As G. K. Chesterton once put it, "When we are very young children we do not need fairy tales [to astonish us]: we need only tales. Mere life is interesting enough. A child of seven is excited by being told that Tommy opened a door and saw a dragon. But a child of three is excited by being told that Tommy opened a door."

Indeed, there's a kind of holy selfishness about small children: they have an absolutely unshakable conviction that the cosmos has been created for one purpose alone: their personal pleasure.

Are they wrong about this? By nature, children are theologians, not scientists, and they believe that the universe was made for them. If that is true, then it makes all the difference in the world as to how we ought to think and act. Children tell us, in no uncertain terms, that the cosmos is a gift that has been given to each and every one of us.

And the natural human reaction to a gift is to feel gratitude and to return thanks. Each exclamation out of the mouth of the toddler is simultaneously a shout of thanks. The simplest prayers for small children are almost always thank-you prayers: "Thank you for Mommy, Daddy, Grandma, Granddad," and so on.

Precisely because the prayer of thanksgiving comes so readily to the lips of a child, we may be tempted to think that it is the easiest and least demanding sort of prayer. But perhaps that isn't true. From adolescence onward it gets harder and harder for us to cultivate hearts that resonate with gratitude. Indeed, it is hard to believe that the effort to maintain a grateful heart is any less difficult, or less costly, than the effort needed to offer praise, seek forgiveness, or any of the other common modes of prayer. We get so caught up in our own concerns and schemes that we make the mistake of thinking that we are the source of all that is good in our lives. We forget how dependent we are on others, how much of what we have is pure gift.

The sin of ingratitude may not get that much publicity—it's not among the Seven Deadlies—but much grief comes in its wake. Shakespeare based what many consider to be his greatest tragedy, *King Lear*, on the theme of ingratitude. Without a grateful heart, it is all too easy to take things for granted or just trash them and throw them away. It is nearly impossible to consistently abuse something that you feel grateful for. Will children vandalize, steal, or commit violence upon persons and institutions for which they are thankful? Would they put their own bodies at risk through drugs, sexual promiscuity, and violence if they felt truly grateful for the gift of life?

There are millions of people around the world who have far less to be thankful for than they should. But for those of us who have a superabundance of blessings, our gratitude should spur us on to what, spiritually speaking, is the next step: sharing our abundance with others.

O give thanks to the Lord, for he is good.
PSALM 106:1

...

All good gifts around us
Are sent from heaven above;
Then thank the Lord,
O thank the Lord,
For all his love.
HYMN BY MATTHIAS CLAUDIUS

...

May God give us grateful hearts
And keep us mindful
Of the need of others.
ANONYMOUS

...

Lord, you have given me so much; I ask for one more thing—a grateful heart.
AFTER GEORGE HERBERT

...

Thank you God for the rain which grows the trees and makes the leaves green.

Thank You God for Your Spirit which grows the will
and makes the soul strong.
Thank You God for everything.
MARIAN WRIGHT EDELMAN

...

O give thanks to the Lord, for he is good;
his steadfast love endures forever!
I was pushed hard, so that I was falling,
but the Lord helped me.
You are my God, and I will give thanks to you;
you are my God, I will extol you.
PSALM 118:1, 13, 28

...

For all that has been—Thanks!
For all that shall be—Yes!
DAG HAMMARSKJÖLD

...

O God, I thank Thee for all the joy I have had in life.
EARL BRIHTNOTH

...

Make a joyful noise to the Lord, all the earth.
Worship the Lord with gladness;
come into his presence with singing.
PSALM 100:1–2

...

I thank You God for this most
    amazing
    day: for the leaping greenly spirit of
    trees
    and a blue true dream of sky; and
    for everything

which is natural which is infinite
which is yes
e. e. cummings

...

O Lord, the Creator
of all the world,
all living things
bless you!
JEWISH PRAYER

...

Lord, behold our family here assembled.
We thank you for this place in which we dwell,
for the love that unites us,
for the peace accorded to us this day,
for the hope with which we expect the morrow;
for the health, the work, the food and the bright skies
that make our lives delightful;
for our friends in all parts of the earth. Amen.
ROBERT LOUIS STEVENSON

...

O Father of goodness,
We thank you each one
For happiness, healthiness,
Friendship and fun,
For good things we think of
And good things we do,
And all that is beautiful,
Loving and true.
PRAYER FROM FRANCE

...

Now thank we all our God with hearts and hands and
voices,

...

Who wondrous things hath done, in whom this
world rejoices;
Who, from our mothers' arms, has blessed us on
our way,
With countless gifts of love, and still is ours today.

O may this gracious God through all our life be near us,
With ever joyful hearts and blessed peace to cheer us;
Preserve us in this grace, and guide us in distress,
And free us from all sin, till heaven we possess.
MARTIN RINKART

...

If my lips could sing as many songs
as there are waves in the sea:
if my tongue could sing as many hymns
as there are ocean billows:
if my mouth
filled the whole firmament with praise:
if my face
shone like the sun and moon together:
if my hands
were to hover in the sky like powerful eagles
and my feet
ran across mountains as swiftly as the deer;
all that would not be enough
to pay you fitting tribute,
O Lord my God.
HYMN PROBABLY COMPOSED IN THE TALMUDIC PERIOD,
THIRD TO FIFTH CENTURY C.E.

...

Glorious Lord, I give you greeting! . . .
Let the birds and honeybees praise you,
Let the shorn stems and the shoots praise you. . . .

...

Let the seven days and the stars praise you,
Let the air and the ether praise you,
Let the books and the letters praise you,
Let the fish in the swift streams praise you,
Let the thought and the action praise you,
Let the sand-grains and the earth-clods praise you,
Let all the good that's performed praise you.
And I shall praise you, Lord of glory:
Glorious Lord, I give you greeting!
GAELIC BENEDICTION

...

Great Giver of all good gifts, we offer you back
our talents, our time and all that we possess.
Transform them, along with our lives,
into means of your life-giving freedom for all.
WORSHIP IN AN INDIAN CONTEXT

...

Holy God, I'm happy that I can bow in prayer before
you. Thank you very much. Thank you for the clothes
that we wear, and everything you give us, and for forgiving us our sins. As you died on the cross for us, be
with us always.
PRAYER OF A NAVAJO GIRL

...

Lord, we brought in the harvest.
The rain watered the earth,
the sun drew cassava and corn out of the clay.
Your mercy showered blessing after blessing over our
    country.
Creeks grew into rivers; swamps became lakes.
Healthy fat cows graze on the green sea of the
    savanna.

The rain smoothed out the clay walls, the mosquitoes
    drowned in the high waters.
Lord, the yam is fat like meat, the cassava melts on
    the tongue,
oranges burst in their peels, dazzling and bright.
Lord, nature gives thanks,
Your creatures give thanks.
Your praise rises in us like the great river.
WEST AFRICAN PRAYER

...

Glory be to God for dappled things—
    For skies of couple-colour as a brinded cow;
        For rose-moles all in stipple upon trout that swim;
Fresh-firecoal chestnut-falls; finches' wings;
    Landscape plotted and pieced—fold, fallow, and
    plough;
        And áll trádes, their gear and tackle and trim.
All things counter, original, spare, strange;
    Whatever is fickle, freckled (who knows how?)
        With swift, slow; sweet, sour; adazzle, dim;
He fathers-forth whose beauty is past change:
                                    Praise him.
GERARD MANLEY HOPKINS, "PIED BEAUTY"

...

We return thanks to our mother,
the earth, which sustains us.
We return thanks to the rivers and streams,
which supply us with water.
We return thanks to all the herbs,
which furnish medicines for the cure to our diseases.
We return thanks to the corn, and to her sisters,
the beans and squashes, which give us life.
We return thanks to the bushes and trees,
which provide us with fruit.

...

We return thanks to the wind, which, moving in the air,
has banished diseases.
We return thanks to the moon and stars,
which have given to us their light when the sun
   was gone.
We return thanks to our grandfather He-no, that he
   has protected
his grandchildren from witches and reptiles, and has
   given us his rain.
We return thanks to the sun, that he has looked upon
   the earth,
with a beneficent eye.
Lastly, we return thanks to the Great Spirit, in whom
   is embodied all goodness,
and who directs all things for the good of his children.
IROQUOIS PRAYER

PRAISE

The form of prayer that has traditionally gone under
the name of praise is often mentioned in the same
breath as that of thanksgiving. Both types of prayer
grow out of our loving response to the gifts we have
been given and the mystery and wonder of the world
in which we live. But if thanksgiving leads us to focus
on the gifts we enjoy, then praise calls us to turn our
thoughts toward the Giver. For that reason most of
the theologians, poets, and mystics who have written
on prayer situate praise on a somewhat higher plane
than thanksgiving. Praise is more vertical: it leads us
away from our own concerns and reaches out toward
the divine nature itself.

But it is precisely this focus on God that makes

praise just a bit more complicated for some people. Praise really requires you to decide what you believe about the Deity. After all, in order to praise someone or something, you have to know a little about the qualities you are singling out for commendation. In our own family experience, we've noticed that we're a bit shy about offering spontaneous praise to God. And yet when we play a CD of Handel's *Messiah*, we're not averse to joining in lustily with his famous Hallelujah Chorus. Similarly, there are plenty of psalms that we enjoy praying, like this passionate and rollicking catalog of praise to God: "Praise him with trumpet sound; praise him with lute and harp! Praise him with tambourine and dance; praise him with strings and pipe! . . . Let everything that breathes praise the Lord!" (Psalm 150:3–4, 6)

One thing we have discovered about praise, in spite of our shyness, is that it can bring with it a mysterious sense of liberation—an opportunity to lose oneself in the joyous celebration of God's goodness and love. Here the wisdom of the spiritual masters is made manifest: when you lose yourself in lifting up your thoughts to God, you can rediscover your inmost heart, and thus be more truly yourself.

Children lead the way in teaching us about praise. No words are more thrilling to a parent than hearing a child say "You're the best Mom/Dad in the whole wide world!" Children are unstinting with their praise, even if the words they use are less than churchly. In a child's mouth, "Cool!" and "Wow!" often say the same thing as "Alleluia" and "Gloria in excelsis."

Recently Greg has taken up astronomy as a hobby, and he takes the kids out stargazing whenever possible. Ever since he was a child, Greg has found that the glory of the night sky evokes his own wordless form of praise. Being able to point out the constellations, the rings of Saturn, and the fuzzy greenish haze that is the whirling Andromeda galaxy has been a delight for everyone—a chance to place ourselves in a praise-full mood. The psalmists loved to use the grandeur of nature as a springboard for prayer as they evoked mountains and hills leaping like mountain goats in an ecstatic vision of the cosmos offering up praise to its Maker.

The self-help industry has become extremely popular in recent years because it asks us to turn inward and pay attention to our own ego and its needs. But a lot of people, including many psychologists, think that we've become far too self-conscious as a culture. Praise calls us out of ourselves and enables us to rejoice in childlike wonder. But in uttering praise you just might find yourself feeling more "well-adjusted" than at any other time in your life.

Let the peoples praise you, O God;
let all the peoples praise you.
PSALM 67:3

...

Praise God from whom all blessings flow;
Praise Him, all creatures here below;
Praise Him above, ye heavenly host;
Praise Father, Son and Holy Ghost.
BISHOP THOMAS KEN

...

I shall sing a praise to God;
Strike the chords upon the drum.

God who gives us all good things—
Strike the chords upon the drum.
PRAYER FROM CONGO

...

O give thanks unto the Lord, for he is gracious,
and his mercy endureth for ever.
PSALM 107:1

...

Rejoice evermore.
Pray without ceasing.
In every thing give thanks.
1 THESSALONIANS 5:16–18

...

Let us with a gladsome mind
Praise the Lord for he is kind;
For his mercies shall endure,
Ever faithful, ever sure.

All things living he doth feed,
His full hand supplies their need:
For his mercies shall endure,
Ever faithful, ever sure.
JOHN MILTON

...

Let all the world in every corner sing
My God and King!
The heavens are not too high,
His praise may thither fly:
The earth is not too low,
His praises there may grow.
Let all the world in every corner sing
My God and King!
GEORGE HERBERT

...

Praise be to him who alone is to be praised.
Praise him for his grace and favor.
Praise him for his power and goodness.
Praise him whose knowledge encompasses all things.

ABU HAMID AL-GHAZALI

...

Bless the Lord, sun and moon, sing praise to him and
 highly exalt him for ever.
Bless the Lord, stars of heaven.
Bless the Lord, all rain and dew.
Bless the Lord, all winds.
Bless the Lord, fire and heat.
Bless the Lord, winter cold and summer heat.
Bless the Lord, dews and snows.
Bless the Lord, nights and days.
Bless the Lord, light and darkness.
Bless the Lord, ice and cold.
Bless the Lord, frosts and snows.
Bless the Lord, lightnings and clouds.
Let the earth bless the Lord; let it sing praise to him
 and highly exalt him for ever.
Bless the Lord, mountains and hills.
Bless the Lord, all things that grow on the earth.
Bless the Lord, you springs.
Bless the Lord, seas and rivers.
Bless the Lord, you whales and all creatures that
 move in the waters.
Bless the Lord, all birds of the air.
Bless the Lord, all beasts and cattle, sing praise to
 him and highly exalt him for ever.

"SONG OF THE THREE YOUNG MEN" FROM THE
APOCRYPHA

...

...

God,
to whom all hearts are open,
to whom all wills speak
and from whom no secret is hidden,
I beg you,
so as to cleanse the intent of my heart
with the unutterable gift of your grace,
that I may perfectly love you
and worthily praise you.

THE CLOUD OF UNKNOWING

...

Praise to the Holiest in the height,
And in the depths be praise,
In all his works most wonderful,
Most sure in all his ways.

JOHN HENRY NEWMAN

...

You are holy, Lord, the only God,
and your deeds are wonderful.
You are love, you are wisdom.
You are humility, you are endurance.
You are rest, you are peace.
You are joy and gladness.
You are all our riches, and you suffice for us.
You are beauty, you are gentleness.
You are our protector,
You are our guardian and defender.
You are courage,
You are our haven and hope.
You are our faith, our great consolation.
You are our eternal life, great and wonderful Lord,
God almighty, merciful Savior.

ST. FRANCIS OF ASSISI

Praise ye the Lord. Praise ye the Lord from the
heavens: praise him in the heights.
Praise ye him, all his angels: praise ye him, all
his hosts.
Praise ye him, sun and moon: praise him, all ye stars
of light.
Praise him, ye heavens of heavens, and ye waters that
be above the heavens.
Let them praise the name of the Lord: for he
commanded and they were created.
He hath also stablished them for ever and ever: he
hath made a decree which shall not pass.
Praise the Lord from the earth, ye dragons, and all ye
deeps:
Fire, and hail; snow, and vapours; stormy wind
fulfilling his word:
Mountains, and all hills; fruitful trees, and all cedars;
Beasts, and all cattle; creeping things, and flying fowl:
Kings of the earth, and all people; princes, and all
judges of the earth;
Both young men, and maidens; old men, and children:
Let them praise the name of the Lord: for his name
alone is excellent; his glory is above the earth and
heaven.
He also exalteth the horn of his people, the praise of
all his saints; even the children of Israel, a people
near unto him.
Praise ye the Lord.
PSALM 148

...

We will sing thy praises, O God almighty.
We will now and evermore sing thy praises, even as
they were sung of old.

For thy laws are immutable, O God:
They are firm like the mountains.
THE VEDAS

...

All you big things, bless the Lord
Mount Kilimanjaro and Lake Victoria
The Rift Valley and the Serengeti Plain
Fat baobabs and shady mango trees
All eucalyptus and tamarind trees
Bless the Lord
Praise and extol Him for ever and ever
All you tiny things, bless the Lord
Busy black ants and hopping fleas
Wriggling tadpoles and mosquito larvae
Flying locusts and water drops
Pollen dust and tsetse flies
Millet seeds and dried dagaa
Bless the Lord
Praise and extol Him for ever and ever.
EAST AFRICAN CANTICLE

...

It is right, O God, that peoples sing thy praises, and
that they are glad and rejoice in thee. . . .

Thou God from the beginning, God in man since man
was. Thou Treasure supreme of this vast universe. Thou
the One to be known and the Knower, the final resting
place. Thou Infinite Presence in whom all things are.

Adoration unto thee who art before me and behind
me: adoration unto thee who art on all sides, God of
all. All-powerful God of immeasurable might. Thou
art the consummation of all: thou art all.
THE BHAGAVAD GITA

My soul doth magnify the Lord,
And my spirit hath rejoiced in God my Saviour. . . .
For he hath done great things for me, and holy is
    his name.
His mercy is upon them that fear him from
    generation to generation.
He hath showed the might of his arm; he hath
    scattered the proud in their conceit.
He hath put down the mighty from their thrones,
    and hath raised up the lowly.
He hath filled the hungry with good things, and the
    rich he hath sent empty away.
LUKE 1:46–47, 49–53, FROM THE PRAYER OF MARY
TRADITIONALLY KNOWN AS THE MAGNIFICAT

PETITION: ASKING GOD FOR THINGS

If thanksgiving is one of the most natural forms of
prayer to rise to our lips, so is petition. All of us are
needy creatures. Even if we are blessed with material
abundance, we have emotional, spiritual, and physical
requirements that need to be met every single day of
our lives. And so we turn to others and to God to ask
for things.

Of course, we don't always want what's best for us.
Our motives are frequently mixed and we may ask for
something we don't need or shouldn't have. But
throughout human history—no matter how secular
society has become, no matter how mighty a culture
has become—people have turned to God to ask that
their needs be met.

Children are the neediest of all, since they are dependent on grown-ups for almost everything. How

easy it is for parents to become exhausted and irritated by their children's incessant clamoring for things. Toys. Snacks. Candy. Clothes. Outings to parks, movies, malls. Staying up at night for just another hour. Friends to sleep over. The keys to the car. How much of our time is spent saying "No!" "Not yet!" "In your dreams!"

As parents we want our children to learn self-restraint, to place their needs in the larger context of the family and the world. But there are also things that we hope they *will* ask for. We want them, for example, to know when to ask for help—from family, friends, teachers, and God. We hope they will come to us when they are sad, afraid, or lonely, and find us to be willing listeners.

Here we touch on one of the central themes of the spiritual life: the need to purify our desires, to learn how to want what is best for us. The human heart is a restless thing, always ready to believe that if only it gets what it desires, happiness will be sure to follow. And yet most of us suspect that our heart, like an untended garden, will quickly become choked with weeds if we don't cultivate it. So we make New Year's resolutions or give things up for Lent, or just vow to set our sights higher.

This is not an easy task in a culture where we are constantly assaulted by messages that inflame our desires and tell us that happiness is found in maximizing our personal pleasures. Advertisers know that our habits of consumption are learned early in life; that's why every year they spend billions of dollars with a single purpose: selling things to children.

Prayer can help us to cultivate our own hearts as well as those of our children. When we place our needs, hopes, and wishes before God, we are already beginning to put things into perspective. The very act of prayer asks us to step out of our subjective preoccupations for a time and set them against the higher values of faith, hope, and love. A child who asks for these gifts, and for God's blessings on those he loves, near and far, will be less likely to fall into the self-absorption that is so common among young people today.

At the same time, prayer is not just about denying oneself; it also summons us to boldly offer up to God's mercy whatever is in our hearts. Children ought to know that nothing that troubles them is off-limits in prayer. The Bible is full of stories about men and women who challenge, question, and even bargain with God.

One of the great Hasidic rabbis was asked by his disciples to explain a phrase from the book of Psalms in which King David says, "And I am prayer." The rabbi turned to his disciples and said: "It is as if a poor man, who has not eaten in three days and whose clothes are in rags, should appear before the king. Is there any need for him to say what he wants? That is how David faced God—he was the prayer."

To become transparent before God, to tear down the walls of fear and hurt—that is what authentic prayer requires of us. Children, with their characteristic candor and unself-consciousness, have little problem opening their hearts and asking God for what they need.

The most challenging thing about petitionary prayer is not the asking but the more complicated process of waiting for an answer. A child does not come equipped with explanations about why God might not give him or her what was asked for. That's where we as parents have to summon our courage and venture out into the

realm of Ad Hoc Theology. Though we may feel uncomfortable offering answers that sound hollow in our
ears, it is important that we be willing to think out
loud about these matters. The simplest explanation
we, the authors, can think of is that God's responses to
our prayers are like the colors of a stoplight: sometimes God replies with green for yes, sometimes with
red for no, and often with yellow, which means that
we have to slow down and wait for the answer.

Another analogy that children understand instinctively is that of God as a parent, someone who loves us
unconditionally and wants us to grow and flourish. A
child can comprehend that God, like any parent, will
sometimes refuse to give us what we ask for if it isn't
what's best for us. On the other hand, God can sur-
prise us with presents we never expected to receive.

When a friend of ours, the singer-songwriter Jan
Krist, heard that we were writing this book, she wrote
to us about her experiences in teaching her children to
pray. One of her stories had to do with the problem of
God's answers to prayer. "Some of my children's
prayers were answered swiftly," Jan wrote, "but others
went unanswered for years. My daughter Amon
prayed every night for five years for God to give her a
'best friend.' We lived in the city and there were few
children her age in our neighborhood. She went to a
private school where most of the children came from
more affluent families than ours and she didn't feel
accepted there. Her prayers were not met until we
moved to a new neighborhood and put her in a new
school, where she found her best friend. She is twenty-
three now and is quick to remind me these days about
how slow God can be in his answers to our prayers."

Petitionary prayer, like any kind of prayer, does not

consist merely of the specific things we ask for; the process of asking is just as important (if not more so) than what we ask for. Before God we should all become like children—dependent and wayward at times, but willing and able to send up our requests, large and small, with the confidence that a loving heart is listening to us and responding in myriad ways.

God whose Name is Love, happy children we;
Listen to the hymn that we sing to thee.

Help us to be good, always kind and true,
In the games we play or the work we do.

Bless us every one singing here to thee,
God whose name is Love, loving may we be! Amen.
FLORENCE HOATSEN

...

Our Father who art in heaven,
Hallowed be thy name.
Thy kingdom come.
Thy will be done on earth, as it is in heaven.
Give us this day our daily bread.
And forgive us our trespasses, as we forgive those
    who trespass against us.
And lead us not into temptation, but deliver us
    from evil:
For thine is the kingdom, the power and the glory,
    for ever and ever. Amen.
MATTHEW 6:9–13

...

Ask and you shall receive.
JOHN 16:24

Be Thou my Guardian and my Guide
And hear me when I call;
Let not my slippery footsteps slide
And hold me lest I fall.

And if I tempted am to sin,
And outward things are strong,
Do Thou, O Lord, keep watch within
And save my soul from wrong.
ISAAC WILLIAMS

...

Stay with me, and then I shall begin to shine as Thou
shinest so as to be a light to others.
JOHN HENRY NEWMAN

...

Keep me as the apple of the eye,
hide me under the shadow of thy wings.
PSALM 17:8

...

O God, look on us and be always with us that we may
live happily.
PRAYER OF THE AMAZULU PEOPLE

...

Lord God Almighty, Shaper and Ruler of all creatures,
we pray for Thy great mercy to guide us to Thy will,
to make our minds steadfast, to strengthen us against
    temptation,
to put far from us all unrighteousness. Shield us
    against our foes,
seen and unseen, teach us so that we may inwardly
    love Thee
above all things with a clean mind and a clean body,

...

for Thou art our Maker and our Redeemer, our Trust
   and our Hope. Amen.

KING ALFRED THE GREAT

...

O God, forasmuch as our strength is in Thee,
mercifully grant that Thy Holy Spirit may in
all things direct and rule our hearts; through
Jesus Christ our Lord. Amen.

GELASIAN SACRAMENTARY

...

O Christ,
tirelessly you seek out those who are looking for you
and who think that you are far away;
teach us, at every moment,
to place our spirits in your hands.

BROTHER ROGER OF TAIZÉ

...

O gracious and holy Father,
give us wisdom to perceive you,
intelligence to understand you,
diligence to seek you,
patience to wait for you,
a heart to meditate upon you,
and a life to proclaim you,
through the power of the Spirit
of our Lord Jesus Christ.

ST. BENEDICT

...

Help us so to know you that we may truly love you,
and so to love you that we may fully serve you,
whom to serve is perfect freedom;
through Jesus Christ our Lord.

ST. AUGUSTINE OF HIPPO

Open unto me—light for my darkness.
Open unto me—courage for my fear.
Open unto me—hope for my despair.
Open unto me—peace for my turmoil.
Open unto me—joy for my sorrow.
Open unto me—strength for my weakness.
Open unto me—wisdom for my confusion.
Open unto me—forgiveness for my sins.
Open unto me—tenderness for my toughness.
Open unto me—love for my hates.
Open unto me—Thy Self for my self.
Lord, Lord, open unto me!
Amen.

HOWARD THURMAN

...

Lord, you are my lover,
My longing,
My flowing stream,
My sun,
And I am your reflection.

MECHTILD OF MAGDEBURG

...

O God, grant me light in my heart and light in
    my tomb,
light in my hearing and light in my seeing,
light in my flesh, light in my blood, and light in my
    bones.
Light before me, light behind me, light to right of me,
light to left of me, light above me, light beneath me.
O God, increase my light and give me the greatest
    light of all.
Of thy mercy grant me light, O thou most merciful.

ABU HAMID AL-GHAZALI

I pray not for wealth, I pray not for honours, I pray
not for pleasures, or even the joys of poetry. I only
pray that during all my life I may have love: that I may
have pure love to love Thee.

CHAITANYA

···

I asked for strength that I might achieve;
I was made weak that I might learn humbly to obey.

I asked for health that I might do greater things;
I was given infirmity that I might do better things.

I asked for riches that I might be happy;
I was given poverty that I might be wise.

I asked for power that I might have the praise
   of men;
I was given weakness that I might feel the need
   of God.

I asked for all things that I might enjoy life;
I was given life that I might enjoy all things.

I got nothing that I had asked for,
but everything that I had hoped for.
Almost despite myself my unspoken prayers were
   answered;
I am, among all men, most richly blessed.

PRAYER OF AN UNKNOWN CONFEDERATE SOLDIER

···

You made me to find you; give me strength to seek you.
My strength and my weakness are in your hands:
preserve my strength and help my weakness.
Where you have opened the door, let me enter in;
where it is shut, open to my knocking.

Let me ever increase in remembering you,
understanding you, loving you,
until you restore me to your perfect pattern.

ST. AUGUSTINE OF HIPPO

SEEKING FORGIVENESS

After various altercations with our kids, we've found, on retiring for the night, apology notes left on our beds. Some of them are priceless and are stored away in our special archive for such masterpieces. One of the best came in an elaborately decorated envelope that was covered with the "peace" sign, marked "Sorry Mail!" and addressed to us at "323 South Bedroom, Sleepytown, PA 1934-bed." The letter of apology inside was accompanied by a special "Coupon Pack" that entitled us to a number of free services, including taking the baby "all day," helping Dad paint the house, and cleaning the bathrooms. Another favorite—less literary, but no less imaginative—was addressed "Dear Mummy." It reads: "I love you. I'm sorry I acted the way I did. Please forgive me. Send my love to Dad. P.S. I just couldn't sleep so I drew." The illustrated poem on the left-hand page reads: "Your as sweet as candy, as hip as a mummy [picture of Egyptian mummy], as bright as the sun, as cool as the breeze." Finally, a somewhat more earthy (and ambivalent) note, written after a dispute about the wearing of a pair of jeans, says: "Dear Mum, I'm sorry very much. I just don't like jeans. My legs aren't fit for jeans my legs get soar and tired. I'm very sorry about all this. It even gives me a wedgie. Worse than yours."

We treasure these notes not so much for their sense

of humor (intended or unintended) as for what the humor signifies—that our children have an unshakable trust that we will forgive them. Though our family has its fair share of knock-down-drag-out fights, grumpy outbursts, and recurrent skirmishes, it's comforting to know that we have done something to lay down a bedrock of forgiveness that everyone unconsciously relies on.

It's hard to imagine something that is more desperately needed in our world today than the spirit of forgiveness. From the intractable civil wars in the world's hot spots to the violence on our streets and in our homes, the lack of forgiveness creates a vicious circle of conflict.

In the last thirty years or so, the rise of therapeutic psychology has popularized words like "tolerance," "self-acceptance," and "personal values" as keys to conflict resolution. The thought is that people need to learn to accept their differences and not to condemn others. While this perspective makes sense in terms of large issues like race, ethnicity, and gender, it is far less effective when it comes to individual moral actions. Educational techniques such as "values clarification" have taught children that everyone chooses his or her own set of values and that no one has a right to criticize the values of others. But if all values are relative, then there can be nothing wrong about the "values" of drug dealers or sexual abusers.

Though well-intentioned, the therapeutic effort to be nonjudgmental at all costs has caused us to drift away from the anchor of traditional moral concepts like personal responsibility. When we harm someone we need to ask for that person's forgiveness, not the acceptance of our "differences." Our offense not only

271

causes pain, it erects a barrier that stands between us and the person we have hurt. Forgiveness is the act of tearing down that barrier, of joining together what has been torn asunder.

Because children haven't learned how to disguise their emotions, it is often possible to see in their faces how deeply they long for the reunion that forgiveness brings. Still, it isn't easy for two people who feel aggrieved to find the humility to lay down their battle of wills and find reconciliation. That's why seeking forgiveness in prayer can be so essential to the peace and harmony of family life. There is an old religious saying that marriage involves three partners: the husband, the wife, and God. The meaning of the saying is simple: without the grace and love of God, a marriage can become little more than a battle of wills—a standoff without the hope of resolution. Given the high rate of divorce today, it's hard not to have some sympathy with the spirit of this old saying.

The truth of the saying is enacted every time a family prays together for forgiveness. When God is the unseen partner in prayer, surrendering our pride becomes much easier. In the section on evening prayer, we discuss the tradition known as the examination of conscience, in which we are to reflect on the day and confess any sins we have committed that day. In our family, this part of our nighttime prayer has provided many opportunities for apologies and reconciliations.

Theologians have often debated whether forgiving also means forgetting. Some scholars point out that forgiveness doesn't automatically blot out the memory, or the pain, of an offense. There's a great deal of truth to that, but it sounds to us like an adult truth. Children are less brittle and less interested in nurturing grudges: they really *do* tend to forget when they've been forgiven. May we all learn a little of that holy forgetfulness.

Sweet Jesus, ever watchful over me,
Let not my thoughts be evil,
Let not my words be wild,
Let not my acts be willful.
Watch the door of my lips
That I may tell no lie.
Grant me grace to guard my senses,
Strength to keep my temper,
Courage to deny myself. Amen.
W. ROCHE, S.J.

...

Forgive us our trespasses, as we forgive those who trespass against us.
FROM THE LORD'S PRAYER

...

O thou great Chief, light a candle within my heart that I may see what is therein and sweep the rubbish from thy dwelling place.
PRAYER OF AN AFRICAN GIRL

...

Lord, I am not worthy to receive You, but only say the word and I shall be healed.
FROM THE LITURGY OF THE EUCHARIST (CATHOLIC)

...

Jesus Christ, have mercy on me,
As Thou art king of majesty;
And forgive my sins all

That I have done, both great and small;
And bring me, if it be Thy will
To heaven to dwell aye with Thee still.
RICHARD ROLLE

...

O Almighty God, we humbly ask you to make us like trees planted by the waterside, that we may bear fruits of good living in due season. Forgive our past offenses, sanctify us now, and direct all that we should be in the future; for Christ's sake.
PRAYER FROM NIGERIA

...

O God, help us not to despise or oppose what we do not understand.
WILLIAM PENN

...

Lord, replace my blindness with Your vision
My deafness with Your healing voice
My insensitivity with Your understanding
My sinfulness with Your love.
MARIAN WRIGHT EDELMAN

...

In your mercy, O my God,
save me from the proud,
and help me not to be proud myself.
Deliver me from sin
and keep my tongue from doing wrong
by committing slander, speaking evil
and quarreling
with anyone at all.
PART OF A TEXT QUOTED IN THE TALMUD

...

Our Father,
forgive all our misdeeds
and wipe away our sin,
for you are great and compassionate;
your mercy knows no bounds.
JEWISH PRAYER

...

My heart lies before you, O my God.
Look deep within it.
See these memories of mine, for you are my hope.
ST. AUGUSTINE OF HIPPO

...

Holy Spirit,
giving life to all life,
moving all creatures,
root of all things,
washing them clean,
wiping out their mistakes,
healing their wounds,
you are our true life,
luminous, wonderful,
awakening the heart
from its ancient sleep.
HILDEGARD OF BINGEN

...

From all blindness of heart, from pride, vainglory,
    and hypocrisy;
from envy, hatred, and malice, and all uncharitableness,
Good Lord, deliver us.
BOOK OF COMMON PRAYER

...

...

Amazing grace! how sweet the sound,
That saved a wretch like me!
I once was lost, but now am found,
Was blind, but now I see. . . .

The Lord has promised good to me,
God's word my hope secures;
God will my shield and portion be
As long as life endures.

Through many dangers, toils and snares,
I have already come;
'Tis grace has brought me safe thus far,
And grace will lead me home.

JOHN NEWTON

...

Loving God, our source of life,
you know our weakness.
May we reach out with joy to grasp your hand
and walk more readily in your ways.

CATHOLIC HOUSEHOLD BLESSINGS AND PRAYERS

...

Love bade me welcome: yet my soul drew back,
    Guilty of dust and sin.
But quick-eyed Love, observing me grow slack
    From my first entrance in,
Drew nearer to me, sweetly questioning
    If I lacked any thing.

"A guest," I answered, "worthy to be here":
    Love said, "You shall be he."
"I the unkind, ungrateful? Ah, my dear,
    I cannot look on thee."
Love took my hand, and smiling did reply,
    "Who made the eyes but I?"

"Truth, Lord, but I have marred them; let my shame
  Go where it doth deserve."
"And know you not," says Love, "who bore the
    blame?"
  "My dear, then I will serve."
"You must sit down," says Love, "and taste my meat."
  So I did sit and eat.
GEORGE HERBERT, "LOVE (3)"

...

Cut through, O Lord,
my heart's greed,
and show me
your way out.
MAHADEVIYAKKA

...

O great God of Heaven,
Draw Thou my soul to Thyself
That I may make repentance
With a right and a strong heart,
With a heart broken and contrite,
That shall not change nor bend nor yield.

O great God of the angels,
Bring Thou me to the dwelling of peace;
O great God of the angels,
Preserve me from the evil of the fairies;
O great God of the angels,
Bathe me in the bathing of Thy pool.
CELTIC PRAYER

...

O Heavenly King, the Comforter, the Spirit of Truth
  who art everywhere and fillest all things,

Treasury of Blessings, and Giver of Life: Come and
   abide in us,
and cleanse us from every impurity, and save our souls,
   O Good One.

O most-holy Trinity: have mercy on us.
O Lord: cleanse us from our sins.
O Master: pardon our transgressions.

O Holy One: visit and heal our infirmities, for Thy
   name's sake.
ST. JOHN CHRYSOSTOM

...

I love you, Jesus, my love, above all things;
I repent with my whole heart for having offended you.
Never permit me to separate myself from you again.
Grant that I may love you always, then do with me
   what you will.
STATIONS OF THE CROSS (CATHOLIC)

...

Give me the strength that waits upon You in silence
and peace. Give me humility in which alone is rest, and
deliver me from pride which is the heaviest of burdens.
THOMAS MERTON

...

Blessèd sister, holy mother, spirit of the fountain,
   spirit of the garden,
Suffer us not to mock ourselves with falsehood
Teach us to care and not to care
Teach us to sit still
Even among these rocks,
Our peace in His will
And even among these rocks

Sister, mother,
And spirit of the river, spirit of the sea,
Suffer me not to be separated

And let my cry come unto Thee.
FROM "ASH WEDNESDAY," BY T. S. ELIOT

...

All that we ought to have thought, and have not
    thought,
All that we ought to have said, and have not said,
All that we ought to have done, and have not done;
All that we ought not to have thought, and yet have
    thought,
All that we ought not to have spoken, and yet have
    spoken,
All that we ought not to have done, and yet have done;
For thoughts, words, and works, pray we, O God, for
    forgiveness.
PERSIAN PRAYER

...

I come before thee as one of thy many children.
See, I am small and weak; I need thy strength and
    wisdom.
Grant me to walk in beauty and that my eyes may
    ever behold the crimson sunset.
May my hands treat with respect the things which
    thou hast created,
may my ears hear thy voice!
Make me wise, that I may understand the things
    which thou hast taught my people,
which thou hast hidden in every leaf and every rock.
I long for strength, not in order that I may overreach
    my brother but to fight my greatest enemy—myself.

Make me ever ready to come to thee with pure hands
and candid eyes,
so that my spirit, when life disappears like the setting
sun,
may stand unashamed before thee.
SIOUX PRAYER

...

Mother of gods, father of gods, Ancient God . . .
a common man has come.
He comes crying, he comes in sadness, he comes
with guilt.
Perhaps he has slipped, perhaps he has stumbled,
perhaps he has touched the bird of evil, the spider's web,
the tuft of thorns:
It wounds his heart, it troubles him.
Master, Lord,
Ever Present, Ever Near,
take it from him: hear the pain of this common man.
AZTEC PRAYER

...

God, give us grace to accept with serenity
the things that cannot be changed,
courage to change the things that should be changed,
and the wisdom to distinguish the one from the other.
REINHOLD NIEBUHR

SILENT PRAYER AND MEDITATION

At first glance, the notion of putting the words "silence" and "children" in the same sentence might strike
you as hysterically funny. And we'd concede that you
may have a point. Recently, we tried to encourage our

older kids (currently aged eleven, thirteen, and fifteen) to observe a period of silence *before* we said evening prayers as a way of quieting down their thoughts and preparing to enter into a spirit of prayerfulness. For at least five minutes we tried to stop the kids from breaking the silence with questions, giggles, and wiseacre comments. Then, when silence had descended for all of thirty seconds, one of the kids made a loud noise—which, out of courtesy, we will not describe for you, dear reader. (Suffice it to say that it was what Suzanne calls one of the "sins of emission.") Suddenly all of us were rolling on the floor, laughing uproariously.

So much for our first experiment in silent prayer.

Nonetheless, we have persisted, and we have achieved a modest amount of success (more on that in a moment). But why should we even bother with silent prayer? It might seem more likely that rivers will flow uphill before kids manage to be quiet for more than a few seconds at a time.

But silence and prayer are intimately linked, and any attempt to pray without a grounding in quietness will never amount to much. Our friend Leah Buturain shared with us something that she explains to her children. Leah reminds them that if we forget to be quiet and listen, that is tantamount to calling someone on the phone, talking away, then hanging up before the person has a chance to respond. We listen to those we love in silence.

Dale C. Allison Jr., in his book *The Silence of Angels*, writes that silence has been revered by every religion in the world: "Silence is praised in the Koran and the Talmud, the Bible and the Avesta, the Darshanas and the Analects. Religions are at one in teaching that, without quiet, the roots of piety will be shallow. The idea that

God speaks not with the wind or the earthquake or the fire, but with a still, small voice is a commonplace; it is general religious wisdom. . . . 'Be still, and know that I am God.' "

We need silence to quiet our restless thoughts and anxieties, the constant temptation to always worry about the future and not dwell peacefully in the present moment. In silence, not only is it possible to know our own hearts better, but we are also in a better position to hear God's still, small voice. Against the backdrop of silence, our words are more measured; they emerge from our lips with more meaning and dignity.

Children *are* capable of being silent. When they are absorbed in some new experience, whether they are encountering a wonder of nature or learning something that fascinates them, they can become extremely still, like a radar dish turned to receive a signal from a particular direction. At these moments, children can take in vast amounts of knowledge and experience.

But when do children encounter silence these days? Modern technology and media leave no room for quietness. Radio, television, computers, stereos, movie theaters, Muzak piped in over the shopping mall's P.A. system, boom boxes, portable media players with headphones—the wall of sound, news, and information surrounds us with a constant drone. Despite numerous scientific studies that show the deleterious effects of media overload on a child's ability to concentrate, learn, and retain knowledge, we remain attached to our media noisemakers. Everyone needs distraction from time to time, but today we are distracting ourselves to death.

There are many ways to try to introduce a little healing silence into your children's lives, including silent reading and outdoor walks. (Greg tries to get our kids to be silent when they're out stargazing, with at least occasional success.) Silent prayer is another option. Praying in silence allows us to cultivate a sense of intimacy with God; it can consist of words said in the mind or in wordless meditation and wonder.

Silent prayer can be a part of your family prayer time, or it can be something you and your kids practice on your own. We have managed to preface our family evening prayers with a minute or so of silence, and have found it to be an effective method for making the transition between our busy, distracted selves to our more meditative selves. Both Eastern and Western religious traditions celebrate silent meditation and offer techniques that older children, at least, can begin to practice. (See the bibliography for some resources in this area.)

We've also begun to experiment with icons and other classic works of art as a focal point for silent meditation. Children and adults alike often find that an image can provide the necessary gateway into a deeper state of consciousness. Depending on your personal beliefs and tastes, you might find that a painting of a biblical scene, a saint, or a heroic person, or even a photograph of natural beauty is conducive to silent meditation.

Another pathway to meditation is music: playing Gregorian chant or Native American flute songs or even a graceful slow movement from Handel or Mozart can lead a child into a quiet mood. If you can preface the music with a brief story that will help to focus their thoughts, so much the better.

Dale Allison notes that the proverb "Silence is golden" seems quaint, if not downright corny, to modern ears. Perhaps as our cacophonous media-saturated culture overdoses on noise and flickering images, that old saying will begin to sound better and better.

The prayers in this section require us to speak (if only in our minds). But they summon us to a deeper relationship with silence. St. Francis always began his prayers with the sentence "Let us place ourselves in God's presence." Many of these prayers can be said immediately before a period of silent prayer is observed.

There are other prayers that resonate well with silence. An example can be found in the first prayer here, often called the Jesus Prayer. Traditionally this prayer is said many times so that it may become a gateway to the contemplation of God's love. Another approach might be to say this prayer less frequently, repeating it only when our minds begin to wander too far from God.

Lord Jesus Christ, son of God, have mercy on me, a sinner.
ANCIENT CHRISTIAN PRAYER KNOWN AS THE JESUS PRAYER

...

O make my heart so still, so still,
When I am deep in prayer,
That I might hear the white mist-wreaths
Losing themselves in air!
"*UTSONOMIYA SAN,*" A PRAYER FROM JAPAN

...

Christ be with me, Christ be within me,
Christ behind me, Christ before me,
Christ beside me, Christ to win me,
Christ to comfort and restore me.

Christ beneath me, Christ above me,
Christ in quiet, Christ in danger,
Christ in hearts of all who love me,
Christ in mouth of friend or stranger.
FROM THE PRAYER KNOWN AS THE BREASTPLATE OF
ST. PATRICK

...

Like weary waves,
thought flows upon thought,
but the still depth beneath
is all thine own.
GEORGE MACDONALD

...

Teach me the power and the strength of silence,
that I may go into the world
as still as a mouse
in the depths of my heart.
AFTER MECHTILD OF MAGDEBURG

...

Drop thy still dews of quietness,
Till all our strivings cease;
Take from our souls the strain and stress,
And let our ordered lives confess
The beauty of thy peace.
JOHN GREENLEAF WHITTIER

...

Let me seek you in my desire,
Let me desire you in my seeking.
Let me find you by loving you,
Let me love you when I find you.
ST. ANSELM

Lord, teach me to seek you,
and reveal yourself to me as I look for you.
For I cannot seek you unless first you teach me,
nor find you unless first you reveal yourself to me.
ST. AMBROSE

...

My Father,
I abandon myself into your hands.
Do with me as you will.
Whatever you may do with me,
I thank you.
I am prepared for anything,
I accept everything,
provided your will is fulfilled in me
and in all creatures.
I ask for nothing more,
my God.
I place my soul in your hands,
I give it to you, my God,
with all the love of my heart,
because I love you.
And for me it is a necessity of love,
this gift of myself,
this placing of myself in your hands,
in boundless confidence,
because you are
my Father.
CHARLES DE FOUCAULD

...

Take, Lord, all my liberty,
my memory, my understanding,
and my whole will.

You have given me all that I have,
all that I am,
and I surrender all to Your Divine Will.
Give me only Your love and Your grace.
With this I am rich enough,
and I have no more to ask.
Amen.

ST. IGNATIUS OF LOYOLA

...

Govern everything by your wisdom, O Lord, so that my
soul may always be serving you
in the way you will
and not as I choose.
Let me die to myself so that I may serve you;
let me live to you who are life itself.
Amen.

ST. TERESA OF ÁVILA

...

In the Name of God, the merciful Lord of mercy.
Praise be to God, the Lord of all being,
the merciful Lord of mercy,
Master of the day of judgment.
You alone we serve: to you alone we come for aid.
Guide us in the straight path,
the path of those whom You have blessed,
not of those against whom there is displeasure,
nor of those who go astray.

THE KORAN, "OPENER PRAYER"

...

O love, O pure deep love, be here, be now
Be all; worlds dissolve into your stainless endless
    radiance,

Frail living leaves burn with you brighter than cold
   stars:
Make me your servant, your breath, your core.
JELALUDDIN RUMI

...

In the beginning was God,
Today is God,
Tomorrow will be God.
Who can make an image of God?
He has no body.
He is the word which comes out of your mouth.
That word! It is no more,
It is past, and still it lives!
So is God.
PYGMY PRAYER

...

We were enclosed,
O eternal Father,
within the garden of your breast.
You drew us out of your holy mind like a flower
petaled with our soul's three powers,
and into each power you put the whole plant,
so that they might bear fruit in your garden,
might come back to you with the fruit you gave them.
And you would come back to the soul,
to fill her with your blessedness.
There the soul dwells—
like the fish in the sea
and the sea in the fish.
ST. CATHERINE OF SIENA

...

O Thou who art at home deep in my heart
Enable me to join you deep in my heart.
THE TALMUD

...

Come then, Lord my God, teach my heart where and
how to look for you, where and how to find you.
AFTER ST. ANSELM

...

Thou my mother, and my father thou
Thou my friend, and my teacher thou
Thou my wisdom, and my riches thou
Thou art all to me, O God of all Gods.
RAMANUJA

"SHORT ATTENTION SPAN PRAYERS"

We owe this slightly facetious phrase to our friend William Griffin, a Christian writer who has the ability to send everyone around him into fits of laughter. Though Bill often writes about spiritual things, his feet are always firmly planted on terra firma; he's what you might call a spiritual realist. When Bill gave a brief talk on "short attention span prayers" (or SASPs, as he called them), he pointed out that Catholics used to call these brief prayers ejaculations. It's not a word we, he noted with a twinkle in his eye, tend to associate with prayer these days.

But Bill Griffin had a practical, down-to-earth point to make, and it's simply this: most of us lead busy lives and are either too distracted or too preoccupied to set aside much time for prayer. And though we like to think of our children as having lots of free time, the truth is that school, homework, sports, lessons, summer camp, and all the other activities kids participate in nowadays have made their lives more rushed and harried than we parents would like to admit. It's all too easy to be caught up in the daily grind and lose any sense of connection to the sacred.

Many religious traditions encourage their followers to say brief prayers—often a single sentence or just a phrase—at various times and for various occasions. Most of the daily emotions and experiences we have can become the occasion for prayer. A beautiful sunny day might evoke in us a passing feeling of gratitude. To give that feeling some depth or resonance, to celebrate it more vividly, we can offer up a brief prayer: "Thanks be to God!" Far from being merely sentimental, such prayers enable us to live in a heightened state of awareness, or what Zen masters call mindfulness.

From a child's perspective, there are many times when prayer would offer comfort, strength, and peace. When someone is afraid, as a child might be before taking a test, going to the doctor or dentist, or dealing with the emotional highs and lows of his or her social life, a prayer for protection and grace can settle a fast-beating heart. Fear, anger, insecurity—these and similar emotions sometimes lead us to get too caught up in the moment, unable to step back and see the bigger picture. When we're under stress, we often break the tension through some form of violence, even if that violence is only a harsh word. A short prayer, while it can't solve all our problems or make them go away, can help us to calm down and take stock of our situation.

When we asked our daughter Magdalen about the times when she prayed on her own, she offered some examples that helped us see how "short attention span prayers" become part of a child's experience. Realizing that she had lost a library book, Magdalen prayed for the peace of mind she needed to track it down. Once, when walking back home after a couple hours in a nearby park, Magdalen saw at the end of our street a bevy of fire engines near our house. Filled with panic, she prayed: "Lord, keep my family safe!" A silly, childish fear, we might be tempted to say, but how often do such thrills of panic fill our own hearts? The prayer of distress has always been one of the most frequently uttered types of prayer.

It might be objected that these one-line prayers could degenerate into something akin to superstition, as if they were charms or amulets to ward off evil spirits. This is a legitimate concern. Any good thing has its potential abuse and the ever-present danger with prayer is that it becomes merely rote, a muttered formula rather than a cry from the heart.

However, we think that such short prayers, if they are suggested to children in the right spirit, ought to be no different than *any* type of prayer: shouts of praise or calls for help. Some of the short prayers we list below are classics, but there is no reason why you and your children shouldn't use the words that rise spontaneously to your lips.

St. Paul admonished his fellow believers to "pray without ceasing." In a similar vein, the Talmud directs Jews to say one hundred blessings every day. These are just two of the lofty pronouncements one encounters when reading the spiritual classics; they're the kind of saying that can stop us in our tracks. Who, aside from contemplative monks on mountaintops or in hushed cloisters, can possibly be expected to pray all the time?

But, as Bill Griffin reminds us, even the most distracted and preoccupied person can find many moments in the day to fire off a prayer. We'd venture to say that these simple bursts of prayer, emerging as they do out of the chaos and distractions of our days, help us to cultivate the spirit of devotion of which the masters speak.

Thanks be to God.

Glory to God in the highest.

Alleluia!

Lord, stay with me.

Thy will be done.

Help me, Lord.

The Lord is my shepherd, there is nothing I shall want.

Blessed are you, Lord God, ruler of the universe.

Blessed is he/she who comes in the name of the Lord.

Lord, I am not worthy, but only say the word and I shall be healed.

Lamb of God, who takes away the sins of the world, grant me peace.

Lord, I believe. Help thou my unbelief.

Lord, make me a channel of your peace.

This is the day the Lord has made. Let us rejoice and be glad in it.

PRAYERS FOR PARENTS, GRANDPARENTS, AUNTS, UNCLES, AND ALL THOSE WHO LOVE CHILDREN

Throughout this book, we've stressed that praying with your children can become the springboard for developing your own prayer life. That's why we think it is important not only to pray *with* your children, but also to pray *for* them—on your own. If currently you do not pray on a regular basis, praying for your children can become the bridge to new habits, new patterns of mindfulness.

As much as we love our children, we're harried, fallible people who need to take time to reflect on the needs of these precious gifts. In the peace of prayer we have the opportunity to make explicit things that have been niggling at the backs of our minds. In prayer we can make resolutions to do better, and ask for the strength to carry out those resolutions.

Also, children, with their finely tuned spiritual sensor system, *know* that we are praying for them. In his memoir *Christ the Tiger,* Thomas Howard writes of his devout Protestant father, who would get up at dawn and pray for his family and a host of other people and needs, from local friends to far-flung missions around the globe. When Thomas came down for breakfast, his father would still be on his knees, and the feeling of his love would enfold him.

Few of us have the time and energy (and, let's face it, *devotion*) of Thomas Howard's father, but we can nevertheless set aside time to pray for our kids. We're not suggesting that you do so in some obvious way, as if to show off what you're doing; kids just *know*.

The circle of prayer need not be restricted to the nuclear family of parents and children. Members of the extended family—grandparents, aunts and uncles—have played vital roles in the moral and spiritual growth of children throughout the ages. In chapter 1 we wrote about Suzanne's grandfather, whose quiet example of reverence planted seeds in her heart that would not fully sprout until years later.

There are times when the *only* people praying for a child come from the extended family, because the child's parents don't pray. Should you let a grandchild, niece, or nephew know that you are praying for him or her, or even perhaps pray *with* one of them? These are obviously delicate matters that can only be addressed in specific contexts and with great prudence and tact. If prayer truly has an impact on the world, as we believe it does, then the grace it brings will become manifest in many quiet, unobtrusive ways.

The words of the prayers in this section, as elsewhere in the book, can be adapted to fit your relationship with the children you are praying for.

A Prayer for Children
We pray for children
   who give us sticky kisses,
   who hop rocks and chase butterflies,

who stomp in puddles and ruin their new pants,
who sneak Popsicles before supper,
who erase holes in math workbooks,
who can never find their shoes.
And we pray for those who stare at photographers
from behind barbed wire,
who've never squeaked across the floor in new
sneakers,
who've never "counted potatoes,"
who are born in places we wouldn't be caught
dead in,
who never go to the circus,
who live in an X-rated world.
We pray for children
who bring us fistfuls of dandelions and sing off-key,
who have goldfish funerals, build card-table forts,
who slurp their cereal on purpose,
who get gum in their hair, put sugar in their milk,
who spit toothpaste all over the sink,
who hug us for no reason, who bless us each night.
And we pray for those
who never get dessert,
who watch their parents watch them die,
who have no safe blanket to drag behind,
who can't find any bread to steal,
who don't have any rooms to clean up,
whose pictures aren't on anybody's dresser,
whose monsters are real.
We pray for children who spend all their allowance
before Tuesday,
who throw tantrums in the grocery store
and pick at their food,
who like ghost stories,
who shove dirty clothes under the bed

and never rinse out the tub,
who get quarters from the tooth fairy,
who don't like to be kissed in front of the car pool,
who squirm in church and scream in the phone,
whose tears we sometimes laugh at
and whose smiles can make us cry.
And we pray for those
whose nightmares come in the daytime,
who will eat anything,
who have never seen a dentist,
who aren't spoiled by anybody,
who go to bed hungry and cry themselves to sleep,
who live and move, but have no being.
We pray for children who want to be carried
and for those who must,
for those we never give up on
and for those who don't have a chance,
for those we smother
and for those who will grab the hand of anybody
kind enough to offer.

INA HUGHS

...

Then hear thou from heaven thy dwelling place, and
forgive, and render unto every man according unto all
his ways, whose heart thou knowest; (for thou only
knowest the hearts of the children of men:)
That they may fear thee, to walk in thy ways, so long
as they live in the land. . . .
2 CHRONICLES 6:30–31

...

Lord our God, you watch over us with the anxious
care of a mother and the protective pride of a father;
help us not only to nurture the spiritual lives of our

children, but also to learn from their innocence, wonder, and trust, so that we may grow together as a family united in your love. Amen.

GREGORY WOLFE

...

God, help us to be like bamboo, which bends and bows and sways in the winds of change but never breaks.

MARIAN WRIGHT EDELMAN

Prayer of a Single Parent

My Lord and Holy Companion,
    I am alone in the awesome task of making a home.
I ask Your holy help
    to show me how to take on the responsibilities
    of both mother and father.
Direct my heart
    so that I may dispense the qualities of both parents,
    of gentle compassion on one hand,
    of firm discipline on the other;
    may I transmit true tenderness coupled with true
      strength.

These twin talents of the masculine and feminine
    are both within me,
    but it is difficult, Lord,
    to balance their daily expression in our home.

The days are long and the nights lonely,
    yet, with Your divine support,
    the impossible will unfold as possible,
    and our home will be more than a house.

My efforts to be two persons
    find my time directed to a great degree

toward the needs of others;
yet I, as well, am in need of comfort and love.
Let my prayer,
my Lord and Secret One,
renew my energy
and remind me that I am not alone.
For you, my Lord, are with me!

The pathway of tomorrow is hidden from me;
perhaps it is just as well.
May the unknown future
only cast me into deeper trust and love of You
and fill my heart
with love enough for two. Amen.

EDWARD HAYS

...

O Lord my God, shed the light of your love on my child. Keep her safe from all illness and injury. Enter her tiny soul, and comfort her with your peace and joy. She is too young to speak to me, and to my ears her cries and gurgles are meaningless nonsense. But to your ears they are prayers. Her cries are cries for your blessing. Her gurgles are of delight at your grace. Let her as a child learn the way of your commandments. As an adult let her live the full span of life, serving your kingdom on earth. And finally in her old age let her die in the sure and certain knowledge of your salvation. I do not ask that she be wealthy, powerful or famous. Rather I ask that she be poor in spirit, humble in action, and devout in worship. Dear Lord, smile upon her.

after JOHANN STARCK

...

...

Sweet dreams, form a shade
O'er my lovely infant's head;
Sweet dreams of pleasant streams
By happy, silent, moony beams.

Sweet sleep, with soft down
Weave thy brows an infant crown.
Sweet sleep, Angel mild,
Hover o'er my happy child.

Sweet smiles, in the night
Hover over my delight;
Sweet smiles, Mother's smiles,
All the livelong night beguiles.

Sweet moans, dovelike sighs,
Chase not slumber from thy eyes.
Sweet moans, sweeter smiles,
All the dovelike moans beguiles.

Sleep, sleep, happy child,
All creation slept and smil'd;
Sleep, sleep, happy sleep,
While o'er thee thy mother weep.

Sweet babe, in thy face
Holy image I can trace.
Sweet babe, once like thee,
Thy maker lay and wept for me,

Wept for me, for thee, for all,
When he was an infant small.
Thou his image ever see,
Heavenly face that smiles on thee,

Smiles on thee, on me, on all;
Who became an infant small.

Infant smiles are his own smiles;
Heaven & earth to peace beguiles.
WILLIAM BLAKE, "A CRADLE SONG"

...

Starting forth on life's rough way,
    Father, guide them;
O! We know not what of harm
    May betide them;
'Neath the shadow of Thy wing,
    Father, hide them;
Waking, sleeping, Lord, we pray,
    God beside them.

When in prayer they cry to Thee,
    Do Thou hear them;
From the stains of sin and shame
    Do Thou clear them;
'Mid the quicksands and the rocks,
    Do Thou steer them;
In Temptation, trial, grief,
    Be Thou near them.

Unto Thee we give them up,
    Lord, receive them;
In the world we know must be
    Much to grieve them—
Many striving oft and strong
    To deceive them.
Trustful in Thy hands of love
    We must leave them.

WILLIAM CULLEN BRYANT, "A MOTHER'S PRAYER"

Prayer of Intercession for Children

Reader: God is just and merciful. Let us bring our needs and the needs of children and families before God.

For all children, especially the young children who are imperiled by the violence in their homes, neighborhoods, and schools, that they will be comforted and that we will work to make them safe.

All: O God, hear our prayer. Let justice roll down like waters, and righteousness like an ever flowing stream.

Reader: For all teenagers, especially the teenagers who are victims and perpetrators of violence, that they are guided safely toward a future of promise and opportunity.

All: O God, hear our prayer. Let justice roll down like waters, and righteousness like an everflowing stream.

Reader: For all parents, especially the parents who struggle in situations of domestic violence and child abuse, that they receive the strength and support they need to protect and nurture their children.

All: O God, hear our prayer. Let justice roll down like waters, and righteousness like an everflowing stream.

Reader: For our elected leaders, that they guide our nation toward a greater manifestation of Your justice, mercy, and peace.

All: O God, hear our prayer. Let justice roll down like waters, and righteousness like an ever-flowing stream.

Reader: For our nation, that we work to keep our children secure, our families strong, and our neighborhoods safe and leave no child behind.

All: O God, hear our prayer. Let justice roll down like waters, and righteousness like an ever-flowing stream.

MARIAN WRIGHT EDELMAN

Chapter 9

MAKE US MINDFUL OF THE
NEEDS OF OTHERS

During the news coverage of Mother Teresa's funeral, a tremendous outpouring of praise and love for her was recorded. A steady stream of passionate, deeply personal tributes to the inspiration provided by this tiny Albanian nun arose from an entire spectrum of people—from heads of state to the poorest of India's "untouchables." But in the midst of these testimonies to Mother Teresa's life of service a number of dissenting voices were heard. These critics claimed that Mother Teresa's ministries were a drop in the bucket compared to the needs of India and the world as a whole. Furthermore, they charged, Mother Teresa's faith in a transcendent God induced people to be passive and not work actively for justice and equity at the highest political and governmental levels, where large-scale social changes could be effected.

Criticisms similar to those made about Mother Teresa have been heard throughout human history. There have always been skeptics who look on faith and prayer as little more than a withdrawal into a private realm where people substitute pious sentiments and pleasant thoughts for real action.

No doubt arguments like these contain more than a grain of truth. Terrible injustices, such as slavery, have had defenders who invoked a higher spiritual authority to support their positions.

But chances are that most people instinctively side with Mother Teresa's vision. In the long run, our common sense tells us, the power of governments to alleviate social problems will mean little unless human hearts and minds are changed first. How many of the great social reformers have grounded their efforts in prayer and spiritual disciplines? In the twentieth century alone, one could point to Mohandas Gandhi and Martin Luther King Jr., to Pope John Paul II's impact on the collapse of Communism in Eastern Europe and Archbishop Desmond Tutu's efforts to end apartheid in South Africa.

A society should be judged not by its wealth or even its achievements in art and science, but by the way it treats its weakest and most vulnerable members. Throughout the Gospels, Jesus preaches the paradox that the first shall be last and the last shall be first; that the meek shall inherit the earth; that love, which grows out of the inwardness of prayer, is more powerful than empires. He also had a special place in his heart for children, the least powerful of creatures. When the disciples tried to block the people from having their children blessed by Jesus, he rebuked them. "Let the children come to me, do not hinder them; for to such belongs the kingdom of God. Truly, I say to you, whoever does not receive the kingdom of God like a child shall not enter it."

The vulnerability, openness, and wonder of a child are not characteristics that are highly valued by the world we live in today. Yet each of these qualities is essential to the life of prayer.

True prayer, according to most of the great spiritual masters, has three basic movements. First, prayer calls us to step back and move inward so that we can find the quietness and peace needed to put things into perspective. Second, prayer invites us to look upward, to seek God's help and comfort. Finally, buoyed by God's grace and love, we move outward, praying— and working—for the needs of others.

A child's perception of the larger world beyond neighborhood, school, and family may take years to develop. But at any stage of a child's development, his or her love reaches out to embrace the world the child knows. So much depends on how we raise our children. If we allow them to succumb to our materialistic culture, which urges them to seek the greatest amount of personal pleasure, then the natural generosity of childhood will be snuffed out. If, however, we give them the opportunity to reach outward in prayer, their hearts will swell with compassion. Precisely because children have little real power, prayer provides an outlet for their love and concern.

Perhaps one reason that so many people loved Mother Teresa was that, despite her multitude of wrinkles and her stooping posture, there was something radiantly childlike about her. The photographs of her holding a tiny, wizened newborn, rescued from some Calcutta gutter, depict the same delight we observed on our older children's faces when they held Benedict, our youngest, in their arms. Mother Teresa's stubbornness and persistence, her capacity for joy, her indifference to the trappings of worldly power and authority—all of these dimensions of her personality were childlike. Perhaps Mother Teresa's secret was that, thanks to a life of prayer, she never grew up.

The prayers in this section will help your child follow his or her generous impulses outward, to the world that lies beyond the front door. To be able to nurture and watch those impulses grow into habits of the heart is an honor and a privilege. For out of such impulses, revolutions are born.

All of the prayers in this chapter can be accompanied by corresponding activities—activities that will in turn temper and give a hard edge of realism to these prayers for the needs of others.

THE SPIRIT OF SERVICE

Prayer has been called "love in action," but authentic prayer impels us to move into the realm of deeds. As Richard Foster has put it, "To pray is to change." This change will inevitably cause us to seek to bring constructive change to the world around us. And that is the basis for service. One of the twentieth century's greatest servants, Martin Luther King Jr., once said:

> Everybody can be great. Because anybody can serve. You don't have to have a college degree to serve. You don't have to make your subject and your verb agree to serve. You don't have to know about Plato and Aristotle to serve. You don't have to know Einstein's theory of relativity to serve. . . . You only need a heart full of grace. A soul generated by love.

At the national summit on volunteerism that took place in 1997, leaders from all walks of life called on Americans to achieve a new commitment to service. Indeed, various organizations and governmental agencies have been working hard to instill in our young people a willingness to serve, perhaps as an antidote to the selfishness of our consumerist society.

The issue of service is a knotty one for our own family, one that we often struggle with. As full-time writers, we find it almost impossible to consider any of our time truly "free," since we are constantly working under the pressure of deadlines. With four children to raise, it just isn't possible for us to devote ourselves to the many worthwhile volunteer projects taking place in our community. We also don't have much, in a monetary sense, to give away to good causes. But despite all these fine excuses, our consciences do nag us: are we really doing as much as we can to serve others?

What we *have* tried to do, from time to time, is offer our home to individuals who are going through difficult times—more often than not, times of emotional distress and painful transition. Though it is always a challenge to fit another adult into our home and its routines, we've found ways to make room for an "extended family."

It would be wrong to depict these efforts at hospitality as totally stress-free. After all, our guests have often had to work through a lot of anguish and uncertainty. We've learned that if you respond to the biblical injunction that we "bear one another's burdens," you have to be prepared for a process that can frequently be messy and uncomfortable as well as joyful and healing.

The most startling revelation that has emerged from these episodes with visitors has to do with our children. When we began to bring people into our home, we worried about the potential impact on the kids. Would they be *too* burdened by these invasions of their privacy? As it turns out, we shouldn't have worried. Children who receive love themselves have an acute intuition about the emotional needs of others, and they can express love in ways that provide balm to battered souls. It's not just that playing with children has therapeutic value for people in distress. There's more to it than that. Children have remarkable powers of empathy and can fine-tune their responses to the people around them. They can also demonstrate unconditional love.

Our kids have adopted every one of our guests, treating them all as honorary aunts and uncles. They've learned that the ultimate meaning of service grows out of direct relationships—the concrete experience of one person helping another—rather than abstract idealism. And they include these visitors in their prayers. Watching them render this sort of service has filled us with awe, and with a great deal of pride. It's not hard to imagine these children bringing the same spirit to any form of service we asked of them.

As we wrote in chapter 4, there are innumerable opportunities to link prayer with service to society. Whether it is volunteering in a soup kitchen, visiting the elderly, or holding a fund-raising event in your community for a worthy cause, there are tremendous emotional and spiritual rewards when families render service together.

O God, take our tiny acorns of service and turn them
into towering oak trees of hope.
MARIAN WRIGHT EDELMAN

...

How shall I not give you
all that I have,
when you, in your great goodness,
give me all that you are?
ANONYMOUS

...

Dearest Lord, teach me to be generous.
Teach me to serve You as You deserve;
To give and not to count the cost;
To fight and not to heed the wounds;
To toil and not to seek reward,
Save that of knowing that
I do Your will, O God.
ST. IGNATIUS OF LOYOLA

...

Christ has no body now on earth but yours;
yours are the only hands with which he can do his
    work,
yours are the only feet with which he can go about
    the world,
yours are the only eyes through which his compassion
can shine forth upon a troubled world.
Christ has no body on earth now but yours.
ST. TERESA OF ÁVILA

...

O Lord our God, give us by thy Holy Spirit
a willing heart and a ready hand

to use all thy gifts to thy praise and glory;
through Jesus Christ our Lord.

ARCHBISHOP THOMAS CRANMER

...

Heavenly Father, whose blessed Son came not to be
served but to serve: Bless all who, following in his
steps, give themselves to the service of others; that
with wisdom, patience, and courage, they may minister in his Name to the suffering, the friendless, and the
needy; for the love of him who laid down his life for
us, your Son our Savior Jesus Christ, who lives and
reigns with you and the Holy Spirit, one God, for ever
and ever. Amen.

BOOK OF COMMON PRAYER

CELEBRATING DIVERSITY

When we were house-hunting for a move to the Philadelphia area a few years ago, we immediately fell in
love with the little town of Kennett Square in historic
Chester County. Kennett, as it's known to locals, is
situated in the lush, rolling hills of the Brandywine Valley, with its historic battlefields, ancient farmhouses,
and long association with the arts. Andrew Wyeth,
perhaps America's most beloved living painter, works
in the next town over from us, Chadds Ford. Kennett's origins date back to the early eighteenth century, and its downtown is full of quaint shops and
restaurants.

But Kennett's main claim to fame is that it is the
"Mushroom Capital of the World." The mushroom
industry, which got its start in the Kennett area a hundred years ago, employs a large number of Hispanic

workers, most of them immigrants from Mexico. Be-cause mushrooms are grown indoors, they are har-vested all year round. That means that the Hispanic workers are not migrants, and many of them have set-tled permanently in the community. Every day at the post office, men stand in line to get money orders, which will be sent back to family members in Mexico.

There is also a small but significant black commu-nity in Kennett. Some of the black families have lived in Kennett for over a century. The house we bought was built in 1862, just after the railroad line came through town. During the Civil War it was used as a staging post on the Underground Railway, and a few years after the war, it was the first home in the com-munity to be owned by a black family. There's some-thing wonderful about being able to live in a house which has truly been a part of history.

What struck us about Kennett, then, was that it seemed to be a microcosm of America as a whole—a multicultural community that is struggling to adjust to a diverse and changing population. Kennett seemed like a real place to us, not just another chic suburb of Philadelphia.

While the vast majority of people in the area get along very well, we've heard an occasional racist com-ment. One story we heard recently was of a Mexican immigrant who had spent ten years working on a mushroom farm to be able to buy a home. But when he and members of his extended family moved in to the newly purchased home, the white neighbors com-plained. The Hispanic culture, with its traditional em-phasis on frequent socializing on the front steps of the home, didn't please his uptight neighbors. It pained us to hear that story.

Our kids have experienced the best—and worst—aspects of living in such a community. On the local school bus a black girl taunted our daughter Helena about her new coat. We were tempted to dismiss the incident, thinking that it was just a mild case of children bickering after a long day at school, until Helena went on to tell me that the girl had hit her. The girl, it seems, had taken exception to Helena's attempts to make peace and had lashed out. But it wasn't only her actions that disturbed us, it was her words. "It's a black thing," the girl had told our daughter. "That's what my mom says, and she says you whites are part of the problem." Helena was not only hurt by the girl's outburst, she was also confused. We asked her if she had ever done or said anything to give offense to the girl. Helena said no, why should she? We then explained as best we could that her new coat might have made the girl jealous, that she might have resented what she perceived as the greater wealth and status of Helena's white family, and that the girl had expressed her frustration in anger. We asked Helena to try and understand the girl's situation and to try not to judge her. It wasn't easy for Helena to comprehend these issues, but when we offered the incident up in prayer Helena finally achieved some level of comfort.

On the more positive side, our son Charles's best friend is John Rodriguez, who lives just a few doors down the street. Charles and John go to the same parochial school and share the same ten-year-old's fascination for action heroes and the martial arts. Charles knows that John's dad doesn't speak English very well, but with the wise innocence of childhood, he doesn't know or care about things like ethnicity. If he and John continue to kneel together in prayer, at school and at church on Sunday, then Charles should grow into manhood with the same glorious—and holy—indifference.

One practical way to make the relationship between prayer and a loving celebration of diversity more tangible might be to have your family visit a church or a synagogue that is different from your own place of worship, perhaps in the company of a family you know. This kind of interfaith worship experience can do wonders to expand your children's horizons—and your own.

Lord our God, who created the rainbow to remind us that all colors are contained in the radiance of your divine light, help us to overcome our fears and prejudices and learn to see your face in the cultures and peoples of the world, so that we might deepen our compassion and expand our knowledge of the human heart, through the One Spirit who binds us all together in love.
GREGORY WOLFE

...

God our Father, Creator of the world,
please help us to love one another.
Make nations friendly with other nations;
make all of us love one another like a family.
Help us to do our part to bring peace in the world
and happiness to all people.
PRAYER FROM JAPAN

...

Grant me to recognize in other men, Lord God, the radiance of your own face.
TEILHARD DE CHARDIN

If anyone has hurt me or harmed me
knowingly or unknowingly in thought, word, or
   deed,
I freely forgive them.
And I too ask forgiveness if I have hurt anyone or
   harmed anyone
knowingly or unknowingly in thought, word, or deed.

May I be happy
May I be peaceful
May I be free

May my friends be happy
May my friends be peaceful
May my friends be free

May my enemies be happy
May my enemies be peaceful
May my enemies be free

May all things be happy
May all things be peaceful
May all things be free.

BUDDHIST PRAYER

...

We thank you, Lord, that we are citizens of a world
made up of different races. Your grace touches us all,
whatever our race and color. We rejoice in the richness
of our cultures, our music and dance, our folklore and
legends. We thank you for all these gifts. We delight in
the joy they bring to our lives.

ADAPTED FROM WOMEN OF BRAZIL

...

Living beings are without number:
I vow to row them to the other shore.

Defilements are without number:
I vow to remove them from myself.
The teachings are immeasurable:
I vow to study and practice them.
The way is very long:
I vow to arrive at the end.
FOUR VOWS OF THE BODDHISATTVA

...

Grandfather,
Look at our brokenness.

We know that in all creation
Only the human family
Has strayed from the Sacred Way.

We know that we are the ones
Who are divided
And we are the ones
Who must come back together
To walk in the Sacred Way.

Grandfather,
Sacred One,
Teach us love, compassion, and honor
That we may heal the earth
And heal each other.
OJIBWA PRAYER

...

May all beings have happiness, and the causes of
    happiness;
May all be free of sorrow, and the causes of sorrow . . .
And may all live in equanimity . . .
And live believing in the equality of all that lives.
FROM A BUDDHIST PRAYER

O God, you have bound us together in a common life.
Help us in the midst of our struggles
to confront one another without hatred or bitterness,
and to work together with mutual forbearance and
    respect.
We ask this through Jesus Christ our Lord. Amen.
CATHOLIC HOUSEHOLD BLESSINGS AND PRAYERS

THE POOR AND THE HOMELESS

When our daughter Magdalen turned seven she started
taking catechism classes in preparation for her First
Holy Communion. A few weeks into the classes, she
came up to Suzanne and asked whether Christ's injunction to give alms was the same thing as giving a blanket
to an old man on a cold winter's night. Suzanne was as-
tonished. "You can't possibly remember that," she said.
"You were only two years old!"

After Suzanne had answered Magdalen's question, a
vivid memory of that night came back to her. It was a
bitterly cold January night and Suzanne was returning
from visiting a friend. Magdalen was sleeping, bundled
up in her snow-suit, and Suzanne had spread a blanket
over her car seat to keep her warm. The car was old and
the heating didn't work. Suzanne remembered praying
at the time that the car wouldn't break down in the
middle of nowhere.

Suddenly a figure stumbled into the middle of the
road. Suzanne braked hard to avoid hitting him, went
into a skid, and came to a shuddering halt. Cursing
more because the jolt of the car had wakened Magdalen (she was a light sleeper and Suzanne had been
looking forward to carrying her straight from her car

seat to her bed) than that they had been in any serious danger, Suzanne got out of the car, prepared to give the man a piece of her mind.

It was then that Suzanne saw how old the man was and that he was wearing the most threadbare jacket she had ever seen. Instead of angry words, Suzanne found herself blurting out, "What do you think you're doing wandering about on a night like this?" He just stared at her vacantly and mumbled incoherently. Suzanne suddenly smelled alcohol on his breath.

She wondered what to do. Any money Suzanne might give the man would almost certainly be spent on drink. On the other hand, he was in desperate need. He was visibly shivering and his hands, when Suzanne touched them, felt like ice. Suzanne realized that it was the cold, as much as the booze, that made the man mumble. Suzanne went back to the car where Magdalen was bawling. "Mummy needs to borrow your blanket, sweetheart," she coaxed, stripping it off her, "to give to the cold man out there." At her words, Magdalen stopped crying and peered out of the window. Suzanne walked back to the man and pressed twenty dollars—all the money she had in her possession—into his hand. He looked at her vacantly for a few moments, then his eyes seemed to clear. "God bless you," he said. Then, before Suzanne could offer to drive him to wherever he was going, he shambled off into the darkness and disappeared.

Suzanne returned to the car and found that she was trembling. She had been reading some stories about angels and had the irrational thought that this old drunk might be a heavenly visitor in disguise. But she quickly shook off the thought as mere sentimentality. Still, there was something uncanny about how Magdalen had stopped crying, as if she had understood something Suzanne hadn't. Suzanne glanced back in the rear-view mirror. Magdalen was smiling and patting the place where her blanket had been. "Nice man," she kept saying. "Nice man."

Somehow, after all those years, Magdalen had remembered the incident and linked it to her faith in God.

Perhaps there is something sentimental in the notion that a drunk in the middle of the road might be an angel. But Mother Teresa often spoke in somewhat similar terms, when she said that in the faces of the poor one could see Christ in his "distressing disguise." Even if your family can't make time to do volunteer work at a soup kitchen or some other form of service to the poor, you can encourage your children to look into the eyes of the poor with a smile of love.

O God, I thank You for my home. Show me how to do all I can to make it a happy place, and how to help the boys and girls who have no homes.
CATHERINE BAIRD

...

Help all the children everywhere
Who hungry are and cold,
And people who have lost their homes,
And people who are old.
ELFRIDA VIPONT

...

Save me, O Lord, from selfishness—especially when I am saying my prayers. When I ask something for myself, may I remember all the others who want it as well, and never let me forget the boys and girls of other lands as well as at home who are hungry and lonely and unhappy. So I pray now: God bless all children everywhere.

DONALD O. SOPER

...

Blessed are the poor in spirit:
for theirs is the kingdom of heaven.

MATTHEW 5:3

...

O Merciful god, who answerest the poor,
Answer us.
O Merciful God, who answerest the lowly in spirit,
Answer us.
O Merciful God, who answerest the broken of heart,
Answer us.
O Merciful God,
Answer us.
O Merciful God,
Have compassion.
O Merciful God,
Redeem.
O Merciful God, have pity upon us,
Now,
Speedily,
And at a near time.

JEWISH PRAYER FOR THE DAY OF ATONEMENT

...

Praise the Lord! Praise, O servants of the Lord;
praise the name of the Lord.
Blessed be the name of the Lord
from this time on and forevermore. . . .
He raises the poor from the dust,

and lifts the needy from the ash heap,
to make them sit with princes,
with the princes of his people.
PSALM 113:1–2, 7–8

...

God, our sustainer,
You have called out your people into
the wilderness
to travel your unknown ways.
Make us strong to leave behind false
security and comfort,
and give us new hope in our calling;
that the desert may blossom as a
rose,
and your promises may be fulfilled in us.
In the name of Jesus Christ. Amen.
JANET MORLEY

...

Make us worthy, Lord, to serve our fellow men
throughout the world who live and die in poverty and
hunger. Give them through our hands this day their
daily bread, and by our understanding love, give peace
and joy.
MOTHER TERESA

...

I have no house . . . and I have houses. Amen.
I have no ground . . . and I have ground. Amen.
I have no temple . . . and I have temples. Amen.
If you look at me . . . I will be a lamp. Amen.
If you see me . . . I will be a mirror. Amen.
If you knock on me . . . I will be a door. Amen.
THE ACTS OF JOHN

Lord, I am grateful to You
that in your mysterious love
You have taken away from me
all earthly wealth,
and that You now clothe and feed me
through the kindness of others.
MECHTILD OF MAGDEBURG

VICTIMS OF WAR AND POLITICAL PERSECUTION

In their book *Parenting for Peace and Justice,* Kathleen and James McGinnis tell the story of a "home liturgy" in which several families gathered together to pray and learn more about their faith. The theme of the liturgy was to be the saints, and in preparation for the evening they discussed with their children the "saints" they had been named after. The first two children didn't prove difficult to talk with: their daughter was named after Mother Teresa and their eldest son was named after David Darst, a relative who had been a Vietnam War protestor.

But their youngest son, Tommy, proved a little more resistant. He immediately informed them that he did not want to talk about the disciple of Jesus known as "Doubting Thomas," because he was "the only one, after Jesus rose from the dead, who didn't come to the meeting!" Apparently, the McGinnises reflected, to miss a meeting was a grave sin in their family.

So they went on to talk about St. Thomas More, who had been executed by King Henry VIII of England for refusing to support Henry's divorce from Catherine of Aragon. Tommy seemed to be entranced by the story, particularly the part about chopping More's head off and displaying it for a month on the top of a pike. But Tommy clearly did not approve of Thomas More's choices. The next night, when the service was held, Tommy recounted the story of More's life but concluded: "But I wouldn't have done it!"

Younger children can't be expected to have a grasp of the political and ethical conflicts that are raging around the world. But as a child's awareness of the world expands, the nightly news can be filled with disturbing images—of famine and war and civil conflict—with which they must come to terms.

Despite the fact that modern media have made the world into a "global village," there is the constant danger that our children can become desensitized to the sufferings and joys of distant places. During and after the Persian Gulf War there were many comments about the footage from aircraft—and even from the tips of bombs themselves—making the conflict into a "Nintendo war." In our image-saturated society, where public events become made-for-TV movies in a matter of months, the line between fact and fiction can become blurred, and the process of desensitization begins.

One suggestion the McGinnises make in their book is that children be encouraged to clip an article from the newspaper and incorporate it into a family "litany" where each family member shares a story that is either distressing or hopeful. Then the family member prays about the situation mentioned in the story. The rest of the family can respond with a phrase like "Lord, hear my prayer." Whether the stories come from the newspaper (which our kids, for example, are just beginning to discover) or from the TV evening news, we think the McGinnises have a good idea, one that would apply to any of the themes in this chapter.

Blessed are they which are persecuted for
    righteousness' sake:
for theirs is the kingdom of heaven.
MATTHEW 5:10

...

O Jesus, King of the poor,
shield today
those who are imprisoned without charge,
those who have 'disappeared.'
Cast a halo of your presence around those who groan
    in sorrow
    or in pain.
KATE MCILHAGGA (ADAPTED)

...

Uphold, O God, all those who are
persecuted or imprisoned for their beliefs.
Be to them a light showing the way ahead;
a rock giving them strength to stand;
a song singing of all things overcome.
RICHARD HARRIES

...

God did not wait till the world was ready,
till . . . nations were at peace.
God came when the Heavens were unsteady,
and prisoners cried out for release.
MADELEINE L'ENGLE

...

You, my God,
are eternal and all powerful: . . .
You restore the sick
and set the prisoners free.
JEWISH PRAYER, EXCERPTED FROM ONE OF THE
EIGHTEEN BENEDICTIONS THAT MAKE UP THE AMIDAH

...

O God . . .
Restore me to liberty,
And enable me so to live now
That I may answer before you and before me.
Lord, whatever this day may bring,
Your name be praised.
DIETRICH BONHOEFFER

...

O Lord, hear our cry
and have mercy on us.
Receive our prayer
and have pity on us.
Accept our supplication
and have compassion on us.
Almighty God,
Father of great and infinite love,
never have we prayed to you
in vain.
MEDIEVAL HEBREW PRAYER OF SUPPLICATION

...

Lord, I pray for my brothers and sisters
who are in prison because of their stand against injustice,
and for all the other people who have "disappeared."
I pray for those undergoing torture;
Lord, give them strength, and the sense that they are
    not alone.

In particular I hold before you
those who believe that the world has forgotten them.
May they know that there are people who care,
and who are praying for them.
Jesus, arrested and tortured yourself,
be with them now,
and hold them in your wounded hands.

ANGELA ASHWIN

...

O God, make us children of quietness
and heirs of peace.

SYRIAN LITURGY OF ST. CLEMENT OF ALEXANDRIA

...

Faith of our fathers, living still
In spite of dungeon, fire and sword,
O how our hearts beat high with joy
Whene'er we hear that glorious word!
Faith of our fathers, holy faith,
We will be true to thee till death.

Our fathers, chained in prisons dark,
Were still in heart and conscience free,
And blest would be their children's fate,
Though they, like him, should die for thee.
Faith of our fathers, holy faith,
We will be true to thee till death.

Faith of our fathers, faith and prayer,
Shall keep our country brave and free,
And through the truth that comes from God,
Our land shall then indeed be free.
Faith of our fathers, holy faith,
We will be true to thee till death.

...

Faith of our fathers, we will love
Both friend and foe in all our strife,
And preach thee, too, as love knows how
By kindly words and virtuous life.
Faith of our fathers, holy faith,
We will be true to thee till death.
FREDERICK WILLIAM FABER

...

O Brother Jesus, who as a child was carried into exile,
Remember all those who are deprived of their home
    or country,
Who groan under the burden of anguish and sorrow,
Enduring the burning heat of the sun,
The freezing cold of the sea, or the humid heat of
    the forest,
Searching for a place of refuge.
Cause these storms to cease, O Christ.
Move the hearts of those in power
That they may respect the men and women
Whom you have created in your own image;
That the grief of refugees may be turned into joy.
AFRICAN PRAYER FOR REFUGEES

...

Heavenly Father, the whole family of humanity is
    yours
and in your care.
So we remember in your presence
those who have been torn from their families,
those who have taken them away,
and those who are left. . . .
Help us today to be signs of your care for them.
BERNARD THOROGOOD

God, from whom all holy desires, all good counsels, and all just works do proceed; give unto Thy servants that peace which the world cannot give; that both our hearts may be set to obey Thy commandments, and also that by Thee we being defended from the fear of our enemies may pass our time in rest and quietness; through the merits of Jesus Christ, our Saviour.

BOOK OF COMMON PRAYER

...

Lord Jesus Christ, who once said "Blessed are the peacemakers," teach me how to be one. Take from me all shyness and unwillingness to make friends, as well as all thoughts which stir up strife and ill-feeling. Show me the way to love others as much as I love myself, so that Your Kingdom may come and Your will be done on earth as it is now being done in Heaven. Amen.

J. M. MACDOUGALL FERGUSON

...

Praise to you, O Faithful God!
You never fail those who trust in you,
but you allow them to share in your glory.
You fight for us against everything
that could attack us or do us harm.
You are our shepherd,
and you free us from the snare.
You protect us who honor you, O God;
great is the sweetness that you give.

NOTKER

...

O Lord our God, whose compassion fails not: Support, we entreat you, the peoples on whom the terrors of invasion have fallen; and if their liberty be lost to

327

the oppressor, let not their spirit and hope be broken,
but stayed upon your strength till the day of deliverance, through Jesus Christ our Lord.
ERIC MILNER-WHITE AND G. W. BRIGGS

...

Almighty God, ever-loving Father,
your care extends beyond the boundaries of race and
    nation
to the hearts of all who live.
May the walls, which prejudice raises between us,
crumble beneath the shadow of your outstretched arm.
We ask through Christ our Lord.
LITURGY OF THE HOURS

...

O God of earth and altar,
Bow down and hear our cry;
Our earthly rulers falter,
Our people drift and die;
The walls of gold entomb us,
The swords of scorn divide;
Take not thy thunder from us,
But take away our pride.

From all that terror teaches,
From lies of tongue and pen,
From all the easy speeches
That comfort cruel men,
From sale and profanation
Of honor and the sword,
From sleep and from damnation,
Deliver us, good Lord.

G. K. CHESTERTON

...

Have mercy, O God,
on all who are sorrowful,
those who weep and those in exile.
Have pity on the persecuted and the homeless
who are without hope;
those who are scattered
in remote corners of this world;
those who are in prison
and ruled by tyrants.
Have mercy on them
as is written in your holy law,
where your compassion
is exalted!

JEWISH PRAYER

...

I will extol thee, O Lord; for thou hast lifted me
up, and hast not made my foes to rejoice over me.
O Lord my God, I cried unto thee, and thou hast
    healed me.
O Lord, thou hast brought up my soul from the
    grave:
thou hast kept me alive, that I should not go down
    into the pit.
Sing unto the Lord, O ye saints of his, and give
thanks at the remembrance of his holiness.
For his anger endureth but a moment; in his favour is
    life:
weeping may endure for a night, but joy cometh in
    the morning.

PSALM 30:1–5

...

The Lord is my light and my salvation;
whom shall I fear?

The Lord is the strength of my life;
of whom shall I be afraid?
PSALM 27:1

...

O my God!
You who have pity on the poor,
hear us!
You who pity the oppressed,
hear us!
You who have pity on anguished hearts,
hear us!
JEWISH PRAYER, EXCERPTED FROM VARIOUS
SUPPLICATIONS IN THE MISHNAH

...

O God of the slave and slave owner
of the exploited and the exploiter
of the hated and the hater,
teach us to forgive and to love.
MARIAN WRIGHT EDELMAN

...

You will bear up the wretched
in your powerful hands.
You save the poor,
the needy and the oppressed
from the anger of violent men.
HYMN PROBABLY COMPOSED IN THE TALMUDIC PERIOD,
THIRD TO FIFTH CENTURY C.E.

...

Look upon us in our suffering,
And fight our struggles,
Redeem us speedily, for thy Name's sake,

...

For Thou art a mighty Redeemer.
Blessed art Thou, Lord, Redeemer of Israel.
"GEULAH," JEWISH BLESSING

...

The Lord neither slumbers nor sleeps;
He awakens those who sleep and arouses those who
  slumber,
He makes the mute talk,
He frees the captives, supports the falling, and
  straightens those who are bent down.
To Thee alone we give thanks.
"NISHMAT," PART OF A TRADITIONAL JEWISH BLESSING

...

God help us to change. To change ourselves and to
change our world. To know the need for it. To deal
with the pain of it. To feel the joy of it. To undertake
the journey without understanding the destination.
The art of gentle revolution.
MICHAEL LEUNIG

...

O Lord, help us who roam about. Help us who have
been placed in Africa and have no dwelling-place of
our own. Give us back our dwelling-place. O God, all
power is yours in heaven and earth.
PRAYER OF AN AFRICAN CHIEF

PEACE AND JUSTICE

Whenever adults get together to discuss such large-
scale social problems as drug use, violence, and teenage
pregnancy, one solution that is nearly always put forward is that of "better education." If only our children

...

hear the correct messages from an early age, the reasoning goes, they won't make such costly and tragic mistakes. And yet, even where such educational programs have been in place for years, the problems persist—and often get worse.

In attempting to account for the failure of such efforts, a growing number of parents and educators have come to the conclusion that they were based on false premises. The notion that children only need the right information—and perhaps some strong exhortations to "Just say no"—to make the right choices in life is now regarded by many as sentimental and dangerously naïve. Indeed, new research has bolstered a rather old-fashioned idea: that children need to internalize the habits and disciplines of the moral life in the home if they are to have the capacity to say no to bad things and actively embrace the good. The facts, messages, and exhortations conveyed at school tend to remain abstract because they are addressed primarily to the "head." But in the daily struggle in which family members must make sacrifices, tolerate differences, and accept responsibilities, these everyday habits give shape and form to the "heart."

Old illusions die hard, however. Take some recent attempts to counter the apathy of the MTV generation toward politics and public affairs. We've noticed a trend in recent years to encourage children to embrace political positions of various stripes. One of the more memorable episodes came when Madonna wrapped her naked body in an American flag and urged teenagers to "Rock the vote." This is admittedly an extreme example of the silliness to which pop culture can descend, but we wonder if it doesn't capture the spirit of the times. Rock stars and actors champion a variety of political causes and bandy about a lot of grand words—peace, justice, diversity, and so on. But in all their pronouncements we sense the telltale failure of head and heart to unite.

The real flaw with what has been called political correctness is not so much the prescribed stands on particular issues as the tendency to substitute facile opinions for profound and hard-won principles. There's also a smugness and self-righteousness to so much political posturing—a tone and a bearing that seem totally at odds with the tradition of compassion as "suffering with" someone else. Political ideas are now more like lifestyle and fashion "statements" than like commitments that will last a lifetime. And so, ironically, the MTV generation simply adds politics to clothes, hairstyles, and musical fads in its search for what's hip at the moment.

In the face of such ironies, many parents today wish that their children would come to know a peace that takes root in the heart, a spiritual peace "which passes all human understanding." But peace of that kind can't be found in the hyperactive fantasies of pop culture.

A better guide to the true meaning of peace is Zen master Thich Nhat Hanh. Nominated for the Nobel Peace Prize by Martin Luther King Jr., Nhat Hanh, a Vietnamese Buddhist monk, has written extensively about Buddhist spirituality and its relation to social action. He speaks of meditation as "the miracle of mindfulness"—the ability to live more intensely and alertly in the present moment. When we withdraw into meditation and become truly mindful, he writes, we discover in ourselves a vivid awareness of the interdependence of all things.

We have to strip away all the barriers in order to live as part of the universal life. A person isn't some private entity traveling unaffected through time and space as if sealed off from the rest of the world by a thick shell. . . . Perhaps one can say that we are only alive when we live the life of the world, and so live the sufferings and joys of others.

To meditate on the interdependence of all things, says Nhat Hanh, gives rise to compassion and a sense of personal responsibility for others.

In the Judeo-Christian tradition, the attempt to deny our interdependence is the cause of all our woes. When Adam and Eve break faith with God and try to live on their own, selfishness and discord replace the peace of Eden.

Prayer is the means by which we seek to regain our connectedness to God and to our neighbors. Prayer employs a language of the heart that is at once more intimate and more concrete than the often windy rhetoric of politics. It also provides the contemplative space which can serve as the seedbed for authentic social action.

Ultimately, peace and justice are rooted in compassion for our neighbors, in a transcendent love that restores the web of human interdependence. Since the first neighbors we encounter in life are our own family members, it's not hard to see why someone once said: "Charity begins at home."

Blessed are the peacemakers: for they shall be called the children of God.
MATTHEW 5:9

Blessed are they which do hunger and thirst after righteousness: for they shall be filled.
MATTHEW 5:10

...

Lord, make me an instrument of your peace.
Where there is hatred, let me sow love;
Where there is injury, pardon;
Where there is doubt, faith;
Where there is despair, hope;
Where there is darkness, light;
And where there is sadness, joy.

O, Divine Master, grant that I may not so much
seek to be consoled as to console,
to be understood as to understand,
to be loved, as to love.

For it is in giving that we receive,
it is in pardoning that we are pardoned,
and it is in dying that we are born to eternal life.
ST. FRANCIS OF ASSISI

...

Peace of the running waves to you,
Deep peace of the flowing air to you,
Deep peace of the quiet earth to you,
Deep peace of the shining stars to you,
Deep peace of the shades of night to you,
Moon and stars always giving light to you,
Deep peace of Christ, the Son of Peace, to you.
TRADITIONAL GAELIC BLESSING

...

Lord, think Your thoughts in me
do Your work through me

build Your peace in me
share Your love through me.
MARIAN WRIGHT EDELMAN

...

God, grant us peace and goodness, blessing and grace,
kindness and mercy.
TRADITIONAL HEBREW PRAYER FOR PEACE

...

I will be truthful.
I will suffer no injustice.
I will be free from fear.
I will not use force.
I will be of good will to all men.
MOHANDAS GANDHI

...

O God, the Lord of all,
your Son commanded us to love our enemies
and to pray for them.
Lead us from prejudice to truth;
deliver us from hatred, cruelty, and revenge;
and enable us to stand before you,
reconciled through your Son, Jesus Christ our Lord.
    Amen.
CATHOLIC HOUSEHOLD BLESSINGS AND PRAYERS

...

The peace of God
which passes all understanding,
keep our hearts and minds
in the knowledge and love of Jesus Christ our Lord;
and the blessing of God Almighty,
the Father, the Son and the Holy Spirit,
be upon us and remain with us always.
ADAPTED FROM PHILIPPIANS 4:7

We pray for world peace,
that ways of aggression and violence against fellow-
    humans
and against God's creation may be renounced,
and that world leaders may lessen the threat of
    nuclear destruction;
we pray especially for our leaders
and all others who strive to bring peace.
Let there now be light for all, Light of all creation.
ADAPTED FROM *WORSHIP IN AN INDIAN CONTEXT*

...

O Lord Jesus,
stretch forth your wounded hands in blessing over
    your people,
to heal and restore,
and to draw them to yourself and to one another in
    love.
PRAYER FROM THE MIDDLE EAST

...

May there be peace in the higher regions, may there
    be peace in the firmament;
may there be peace on earth.
May the waters flow peacefully; may the herbs and
    plants grow peacefully;
may all the divine powers bring us unto peace.
The Supreme Lord is peace.
May we all be in peace, peace, and only peace;
and may peace come unto each of us.
THE VEDAS

...

Great Spirit, Great Spirit, my Grandfather,
all over the earth the faces of living things are all alike.
With tenderness have these come up out of the ground.

Look upon these faces of children without number
and with children in their arms,
that they may face the winds
and walk the good road to the day of quiet.

BLACK ELK

...

Peace between neighbors,
Peace between kindred,
Peace between lovers,
In the love of the King of life.

Peace between person and person,
Peace between wife and husband,
Peace between women and children,
The peace of Christ above all peace.

Bless, O Christ, my face.
Let my face bless everything;
Bless, O Christ, mine eye,
Let mine eye bless all it sees.

TRADITIONAL GAELIC PRAYER

THE ENVIRONMENT

One of the best family vacations we ever had was a two-week holiday on an island off the coast of Maine. Even though the island was barely a quarter of a mile from the mainland, it was still quite an adventure for land-lubbers like us. Living in a small cottage only a few feet from the water's edge, we were the sole possessors of the island, which is a little over thirty acres in size.

Very quickly we realized that this island could be seen as a microcosm: man and nature existing in a delicate balance. Little things could mar the beauty and

pristine freshness of the place. Some previous (and obviously irresponsible) occupants of the cottage, for example, had broken some bottles on the beach, so our
kids had to have shoes on at all times. We would even
find ourselves almost physically recoiling every time
we'd see some trash floating in the water. It took only a
few days for our children to learn new rules of respect—
and even reverence—for the environment.

In the last thirty years, people have become more
concerned with the health of the environment than
ever before. But in this same period we humans have
continued to place greater and greater strains on the
natural world from which we spring.

Many of us have turned to Native American lore to
gain a deeper reverence for the natural realm. Native
Americans have always understood the interdependence of all living things. Perhaps Chief Seattle of the
Suquamish people put it most succinctly:

> This we know. The earth does not belong to
> man; man belongs to the earth. This we know. All
> things are connected. Whatever befalls the earth
> befalls the sons of the earth. Man did not weave the
> web of life. He is merely a strand in it. Whatever he
> does to the web, he does to himself.

The Judeo-Christian tradition, on the other hand,
has come in for heavy criticism by certain environ-
mental activists for allegedly fostering a view of man as
the rapacious conqueror of nature. In the story of the
garden of Eden, the Bible speaks of humanity as having "dominion" over the created order, and there's little doubt that some arrogant souls in Western history
have taken that to mean "domination." But the real

meaning of the word "dominion" is closer to what we call stewardship, the solemn responsibility of caring for the natural world.

Children need no encouragement to revel in the beauty and grandeur of nature. With every hop, skip, and jump across a backyard or park they pronounce their benediction on the goodness of creation.

God who made the earth, the air, the sky, the sea,
Who gave the light its birth, careth for me.

God who made the grass, the flower, the fruit, the tree,
The day and night to pass, careth for me.

God who made the sun, the moon, the stars,
is he who, when life's clouds come on, careth for me.
ANONYMOUS

...

Each little flower that opens,
Each little bird that sings,
He made their glowing colors,
He made their tiny wings.

Refrain: All things bright and beautiful,
      All creatures great and small,
      All things wise and wonderful,
      The Lord God made them all.

The purple-headed mountain,
The river running by,
The sunset, and the morning
That brightens up the sky. *Refrain*

The cold wind in the winter,
The pleasant summer sun,

The ripe fruits in the garden,
He made them ev'ry one. *Refrain*

He gave us eyes to see them,
And lips that we might tell
How great is God Almighty,
Who has made all things well. *Refrain*

HYMN, "ALL THINGS BRIGHT AND BEAUTIFUL," BY
CECIL FRANCES ALEXANDER

...

Dear Father, let the beasts and birds
Be sheltered, safe and fed,
And let me ne'er forget to share
With them my daily bread.

ELFRIDA VIPONT

...

The lark's on the wing;
The snail's on the thorn:
God's in his Heaven—
All's right with the world!

...

ROBERT BROWNING

Praised be our Lord for the wind and the rain,
For clouds, for dew and the air;
For the rainbow set in the sky above
Most precious and kind and fair.
For all these things tell the love of our Lord,
The love that is everywhere.

ELIZABETH GOUDGE

...

O God, I thank You for this day of life
for eyes to see the sky
for ears to hear the birds

...

for feet to walk amidst the trees
for hands to pick the flowers from the earth
for a sense of smell to breathe in the sweet perfumes
 of nature
for a mind to think about and appreciate the magic of
 everyday miracles
for a spirit to swell in joy at Your mighty presence
 everywhere.
MARIAN WRIGHT EDELMAN

...

I find you, Lord, in all Things
and in all
my fellow creatures, pulsing with
your life;
as a tiny seed you sleep in what is
small
and in the vast you vastly yield
yourself.
RAINER MARIA RILKE, *THE BOOK OF HOURS*

...

The whole earth is full of God's glory.
ISAIAH 6:3

...

O God the Father of us all, we thank Thee for Thy
 gift of harvest.
Bless all who sowed and all who reaped: and make us
 glad to share
Thy gifts with all Thy children. For Jesus' sake. Amen.
G. W. BRIGGS

The Prayer of the Cricket
O God,
I am little and very black,

but I thank You
for having shed
Your warm sun
and the quivering of Your golden corn
on my humble life.
Then take—but be forbearing, Lord—
this little impulse of my love:
this note of music
You have set thrilling in my heart. Amen.
CARMEN BERNOS DE GASZTOLD (TRANSLATED BY
RUMER GODDEN)

...

Most high, most powerful, good Lord, to you
  belong praise,
glory, honor and all blessing!
Praised be my Lord God with all his creatures, and
  especially our
brother the sun, who brings us the day and brings us
  the light;
fair is he and shines with a great splendor.
O Lord, he signifies you.
Praised be my Lord for our sister the moon, and for
  the stars,
which he has set clear and lovely in the heavens.
Praised be my Lord for our brother the wind, and for
  air and
cloud, calms and all weather, by which you uphold
  life in all creatures.
Praised be my Lord for our sister water, who is very
  serviceable
unto us and humble and precious and pure.
Praised be my Lord for our brother fire, through
  whom you give

light in the darkness; and he is bright and pleasant
and very mighty and strong.
Praised be my Lord for our mother the earth, who
sustains us and
keeps us, and brings forth various fruits and flowers
of many colors.
Praise and bless the Lord, and give thanks to him,
and serve him
with great humility.
ST. FRANCIS OF ASSISI

...

The earth has been laid down, the earth has been
laid down
The earth has been laid down, it has been made.
The earth spirit has been laid down
It is covered over with growing things, it has been
laid down.
The earth has been laid down, it has been made.
The sky has been set up, the sky has been set up
The sky has been set up, it has been made.
The mountains have been laid down, the mountains
have been laid down
The mountains have been laid down, they have
been made.
The waters have been laid down, the waters have
been laid down
The waters have been laid down, they have been made.
The clouds have been set up, the clouds have been
set up
The clouds have been set up, they have been made.
NAVAJO SWEATHOUSE CHANT

...

Blessed are You, our God, Ruler of the universe, Who made the wonders of creation.

Blessed are You, our God, Ruler of the universe. Your strength and power fill our world. [On seeing lightning and hearing thunder.]

Blessed are You, our God, Ruler of the universe, Who made the big and beautiful sea.

Blessed are You, our God, Ruler of the universe, Who created the fruit of the tree.

Blessed are You, our God, Ruler of the universe. Thank you for creating our world with beauty big and small everywhere.

TRADITIONAL HEBREW PRAYERS OF THANKSGIVING FOR NATURE

...

The earth is full of your goodness,
your greatness and understanding,
your wisdom and harmony.
How wonderful
are the lights that you created.
You formed them
with love, knowledge and understanding.
You endowed them
with strength and power,
and they shine very wonderfully on the world,
magnificent in their splendour.
They arise in radiance
and go down in joy.
Reverently
they fulfill your divine will.

They are tributes to your name
as they exalt your sovereign rule
in song.
JEWISH HYMN, PROBABLY COMPOSED IN ONE OF THE
GROUPS OF MYSTICS THAT SPRANG UP AT THE TIME OF
THE SECOND TEMPLE

...

Be a gardener.
Dig a ditch,
toil and sweat,
and turn the earth upside down
and seek the deepness
and water the plants in time.
Continue this labor
and make sweet floods to run
and noble and abundant fruits to spring.
Take this food and drink
and carry it to God
as your true worship.
JULIAN OF NORWICH

...

With your feet I walk
I walk with your limbs
I carry forth your body
For me your mind thinks
Your voice speaks for me
Beauty is before me
And beauty is behind me
Above and below me hovers the beautiful
I am surrounded by it
I am immersed in it
In my youth I am aware of it

And in old age I shall walk quietly
The beautiful trail.

NAVAJO PRAYER

...

Bless the Lord, O my soul. O Lord my God, thou
art very great; thou art clothed with honour and
majesty.

Who coverest thyself with light as with a garment:
who stretchest out the heavens like a curtain:

Who layeth the beams of his chambers in the waters:
who maketh the clouds his chariot: who walketh
upon the wings of the wind:

Who maketh his angels spirits; his ministers a flam-
ing fire:

Who laid the foundations of the earth, that it should
not be removed for ever.

Thou coveredst it with the deep as with a garment: the
waters stood above the mountains.

At thy rebuke they fled; at the voice of thy thunder
they hasted away.

They go up by the mountains; they go down by the valleys unto the place which thou has founded for them.

Thou hast set a bound that they may not pass over;
that they turn not again to cover the earth.

He sendeth the springs into the valleys, which run
among the hills.

They give drink to every beast of the field: the wild
asses quench their thirst.

By them shall the fowls of the heaven have their habi-
tation, which sing among the branches.

He watereth the hills from his chambers: the earth is
satisfied with the fruit of thy works.

...

He causeth the grass to grow for the cattle, and herb
for the service of man: that he may bring forth food
out of the earth.

And wine that maketh glad the heart of man, and oil
to make his face to shine, and bread which strength-
enest man's heart.

The trees of the Lord are full of sap: the cedars of
Lebanon, which he hath planted;

Where the birds make their nests: as for the stork, the
fir trees are her house.

The high hills are a refuge for the wild goats; and the
rocks for the conies.

He appointed the moon for seasons: the sun knoweth
his going down.

Thou makest darkness, and it is night: wherein all the
beasts of the forest creep forth.

The young lions roar after their prey, and seek their
meat from God.

The sun ariseth, they gather themselves together, and
lay them down in their dens.

Man goeth forth unto his work and to his labour until
the evening.

O Lord, how manifold are thy works! in wisdom hast
thou made them all: the earth is full of thy riches.

So is this great and wide sea, wherein are things creeping innumerable, both small and great beasts.

There go the ships: there is that leviathan, whom thou
hast made to play therein.

These wait all upon thee; that thou mayest give them
their meat in due season.

That thou givest them they gather; thou openest thine
hand, they are filled with good.

Thou hidest thy face, they are troubled: thou takest
away their breath, they die, and return to their dust.

Thou sendest forth thy spirit, they are created: and
thou renewest the face of the earth.

The glory of the Lord shall endure for ever: the Lord
shall rejoice in his works.

He looketh on the earth, and it trembleth: he toucheth
the hills, and they smoke.

I will sing unto the Lord as long as I live: I will sing
praise to my God while I have my being.

My meditation of him shall be sweet: I will be glad in
the Lord. . . .

PSALM 104

...

It is lovely indeed, it is lovely indeed.
I, I am the spirit within the earth . . .
The feet of the earth are my feet . . .
The legs of the earth are my legs . . .
The bodily strength of the earth is my strength . . .
The thoughts of the earth are my thoughts . . .
The voice of the earth is my voice . . .
The feather of the earth is my feather . . .
All that belongs to the earth belongs to me . . .
All that surrounds the earth surrounds me . . .
I, I am the sacred words of the earth . . .
It is lovely indeed, it is lovely indeed.

NAVAJO SONG

...

Heaven is His head
Earth is His feet.
Four compass points are His hands.
Sun and moon are His eyes.
Ether is His breath.
Fire is His mouth.
Teaching is His breast.

Non-teaching is His back.
Grass and plants are His hair.
Mountains are His bones.
Sea is His bladder.
Rivers are His veins.
LAURETANIAN LITANY

...

The world is charged with the grandeur of God.
It will flame out, like shining from shook foil;
It gathers to a greatness, like the ooze of oil
Crushed. Why do men then now not reck his rod?
Generations have trod, have trod, have trod;
And all is seared with trade; bleared, smeared with
    toil;
And wears man's smudge and shares man's smell:
    the soil
Is bare now, nor can foot feel, being shod.

And for all this, nature is never spent;
There lives the dearest freshness deep down things;
And though the last lights off the black West went
Oh, morning, at the brown brink eastward, springs—
Because the Holy Ghost over the bent
World broods with warm breast and with ah! bright
    wings.
GERARD MANLEY HOPKINS, "God's Grandeur"

...

Earth teach me stillness as the grasses are stilled with
    light.
Earth teach me suffering as old stones suffer with
    memory.
Earth teach me humility as blossoms are humble
    with beginning.

Earth teach me caring as the mother who secures her
young.
Earth teach me courage as the tree which stands all
alone.
Earth teach me limitation as the ant which crawls on
the ground.
Earth teach me freedom as the eagle which soars in
the sky.
Earth teach me resignation as the leaves which die in
the fall.
Earth teach me regeneration as the seed which rises
in the spring.
Earth teach me to forget myself as melted snow
forgets its life.
Earth teach me to remember kindness as dry fields
weep with rain.

UTE PRAYER

...

O our Mother the Earth, O our Father the Sky,
Your children are we, and with tired backs
We bring you the gifts you love.
Then weave for us a garment of brightness;
May the warp be the white light of morning,
May the weft be the red light of evening,
May the fringes be the falling rain,
May the border be the standing rainbow.
Thus weave for us a garment of brightness,
That we may walk fittingly where birds sing,
That we may walk fittingly where grass is green,
O our Mother the Earth, O our Father the Sky.

TEWA PRAYER, "SONG OF THE SKY LOOM"

Going Further In:
Resources for Family Prayer

Select Bibliography

This bibliography only scratches the surface of the enormous number of books on prayer and spirituality that are currently available. (A recent search of the Library of Congress online database for books on "children and prayer" yielded the maximum number of "hits": five hundred.) The following selection focuses on books that may be of some immediate practical use for parents—collections of prayers, meditations on the spirituality of children, introductions to several of the world's great religious traditions. Nearly all of these books are currently in print and are thus readily available. Since prayer and spiritual reading are such good companions, we hope you will continue to discover new books that will nourish your family's spiritual life.

Abramowitz, Yosef, and Rabbi Susan Silverman. *Jewish Family and Life: Traditions, Holidays, and Values for Today's Parents and Children*. New York: Golden Books, 1997. Created by the editors of the first-rate online magazine *Jewishfamily.com*, this book is a lively, well-written, and comprehensive guide to incorporating Jewish traditions into modern family life. As the subtitle suggests, the book is divided into three sections: traditions, holidays, and values. The main body of the text is complemented by many illustrations, sidebars, and practical suggestions for activities. While prayer is only one emphasis, this book is firmly situated within the larger experience of Jewish life. A truly outstanding resource.

Ashwin, Angela. *The Book of a Thousand Prayers*. London: Marshall Pickering, 1996. One of the best all-around collections of prayers, comprehensive in scope but containing a great deal of material that is accessible and relevant to family life.

Balthasar, Hans Urs von. *Prayer*. Translated by Graham Harrison. San Francisco: Ignatius Press, 1986. This book isn't what you would call light reading. It is a serious work of theology by the late Swiss Catholic thinker—well written, but extremely dense with ideas. Those who feel ready to plunge into it will find that the book is filled with richly rewarding insights.

Benson, Robert. *Living Prayer*. New York: Jeremy P. Tarcher/Putnam, 1998. There is no simple way to describe this book. Benson has written a very personal account of his growth in prayer, but for all its subjectivity, the book can speak to everyone's experience. We can think of few better books for those who are beginning to take their first steps into a life of prayer.

Catholic Household Blessings and Prayers. Washington, D.C.: United States Catholic Conference, 1989. Though this book is published by the American Catholic bishops, there is none of the stiffness and stuffiness that one tends to expect from "official" church publications. From the handsome layout and graceful illustrations to the range and selection of prayers and blessings, this collection has something for every Catholic family. Much of the book deals with the feasts and memorials of the Church year, including seasonal graces and family prayers. Also included are some of the most traditional Catholic prayers, including litanies and the Rosary.

Chesto, Kathleen O'Connell. *Family Prayer for Family Times*. Mystic, Conn.: Twenty-Third Publications, 1995. Kathleen Chesto has spent nearly thirty years thinking and writing about family prayer and ritual for Roman Catholics. What makes this particular book of hers so valuable is not simply its excellent collection of prayers but the inclusion of many rituals that give prayer a rich cultural context. For example, we discovered here that pretzels were made in the Middle Ages as a Lenten food; they were made without butter or animal fat, and their shape depicts praying arms. As a friend of ours says, "If family prayer can involve as many of the senses as possible, I believe it will prove more life-giving and sustaining." Kathleen Chesto understands that thought and makes it a part of her book.

Cloyd, Betty Shannon. *Children and Prayer: A Shared Pilgrimage.* Nashville: Upper Room Books, 1997. Betty Cloyd is a deaconal minister in the United Methodist Church and has served as a consultant in prayer and spiritual formation. She is also the mother of four children. All of these things make Cloyd a highly qualified writer on the subject of children and prayer. But one of the best things about this book is that in preparing to write it Cloyd conducted a series of interviews with children between the ages of three and thirteen—interviews that provided her with many insights directly from the mouths of babes.

Coles, Robert. *The Spiritual Life of Children.* Boston: Houghton Mifflin, 1990. Pulitzer Prize–winning author Robert Coles is one of America's most widely respected experts on child psychology. He also brings to his writings a deep knowledge of literature and the experience of many years as a professor of psychiatry and medical humanities at Harvard University. *The Spiritual Life of Children* sums up nearly forty years of fieldwork in which he interviewed countless children in this country and abroad. The stories that these children tell—stories emerging out of Jewish, Christian, and Islamic backgrounds—will leave you profoundly moved. Despite his scholarly credentials, Coles writes with clarity as well as passion. He is also the author of such books as *The Moral Life of Children* and *The Political Life of Children.*

Donin, Hayim Halevy. *To Pray as a Jew: A Guide to the Prayer Book and the Synagogue Service.* New York: Basic Books, 1980. Rabbi Donin's book is a comprehensive source of information on Jewish prayer. Precisely because it is so comprehensive, so packed with detail and information, it might prove daunting to the beginning student of Jewish prayer. But read in conjunction with other, more accessible books, it will prove to be an invaluable resource.

Edelman, Marian Wright. *Guide My Feet: Prayers and Meditations on Loving and Working for Children.* Boston: Beacon Press, 1995. Marian Wright Edelman began writing a book on public policy relating to children and ended by writing a book of prayers and meditations. There is something profoundly right about the intuition that motivated her, because the only way we can ensure that our society treats children justly is to first love and care for them—and prayer gives shape and meaning to our love. In addition to the beautiful prayers and quotations Edelman gathers here, there are several memorable passages that recount the rich life she was privileged to have growing up in an African-American family with a father who was a minister.

Edwards, Michelle. *Blessed Are You: Traditional Everyday Hebrew Prayers.* New York: Lothrop, Lee & Shepard Books, 1993. Here is one of the rare illustrated books for young children that truly illuminate the *nature* of prayer rather than merely furnishing cute images to accompany prayer. Geared for younger children, this book combines large-format illustrations with the classic Jewish blessings, including the "*Modeh Ani,*" the "*Ha-motzi,*" and the "*Sh'ma,*" or Shema. The prayers are printed in English, Hebrew, and a transliteration of the Hebrew. Edwards states that "the children in this book are not shown praying because remembering God is part of their everyday lives." Her illustrations depict characters she created—the twins, David and Devrah, along with their baby brother, Jacob—sharing simple pleasures, from swimming and camping out to baking bread and picking apples. Prayer, according to Edwards, should be the companion of the ordinary.

Foster, Richard J. *Prayer: Finding the Heart's True Home.* San Francisco: HarperSanFrancisco, 1992. Richard Foster is one of America's leading spiritual writers. In this book he draws on extensive research into the rich diversity of spiritual traditions within the Judeo-Christian heritage. He has distilled all this knowledge into an extremely readable and well organized introduction to the subject of prayer. The warm and inviting spirit that suffuses Foster's writing makes *Prayer* one of the best, most accessible books on this subject for contemporary readers.

Foster, Richard J. *Prayers from the Heart.* San Francisco: HarperSanFrancisco, 1994. This collection of prayers is based on Foster's best-selling book *Prayer.* Its three sections correspond to the "three aspects of the human journey: looking *inward* to the heart, reaching *upward* toward God, and moving *outward* to care for others."

Griffin, Emilie. *Clinging: The Experience of Prayer.* San Francisco: Harper & Row, 1984; New York: McCracken Press, 1994. *Clinging* is considered by many notable teachers of prayer (Eugene Peterson, Richard Foster, and the late Henri Nouwen, among others) to be a fine introduction to the life of prayer. Written in simple, contemporary language, with a sense both of the poetic and the practical, the book describes seven different moods in prayer-life: beginning, yielding, darkness, transparency, hoops of steel (spiritual friendship), fear of heights (advancing in prayer), and the central idea of unitive prayer, which is described as God's embracing, or "clinging." Griffin came to the contemplative life in the midst of raising a young family. Her book is sprinkled with many "childhood" insights and comparisons.

Griffin, William. *Jesus for Children: Read-Aloud Gospel Stories.* Mystic, Conn.: Twenty-Third Publications, 1994.

To help his own children draw closer to the story of Jesus as told in the four Gospels, William Griffin took the biblical passages and turned them into brief, colorful vignettes. The result, here shared with the world, is thoroughly delightful, full of wit and wisdom. The opening story, that of the angel Gabriel's "annunciation" of the Good News to the virgin Mary, begins: " 'Stay where you are,' said the young girl, 'or I'll scream!' " The small liberties Griffin takes in expanding the biblical texts are often funny, but they are always reverent.

Guiley, Rosemary Ellen, ed. *Blessings: Prayers for the Home and Family.* New York: Pocket Books, 1996. This collection of prayers focuses on the rhythms of family life, with prayers for morning and evening, table and home, school and work, friends and pets.

Hammer, Reuven, *Entering the High Holy Days: A Guide to the Origins, Themes, and Prayers.* Jewish Publication Society, 1998. A well-written and authoritative guide to the Jewish High Holy Days, which begin with Rosh Hashanah and end with Yom Kippur, the Day of Atonement.

Hays, Edward, *Prayers for the Domestic Church.* Leavenworth, Kans.: Forest of Peace Publishing, 1979. The "domestic church" of this book's title is, of course, the family. According to the author, it is vital that we think of the idea of "church" as something that goes beyond the buildings we enter on the Sabbath. The roots of spirituality begin in the home, with the moments of praise, thanksgiving, and petition we offer up in the context of daily life. Fr. Hays, a Catholic priest and an expert on prayer, storytelling, and ecumenism, has written and collected here dozens of prayers to mark every aspect of family life—from prayers on buying a new car to blessings for births, graces for all occasions, daily prayer services, and much, much more. Though there are some Catholic-specific prayers in this collection, most of the prayers can be said by any Christian. Perhaps the most wonderful thing about the book is that it has the ability to inspire you to create your own prayers and family rituals. (It certainly inspired us to do just this!) We cannot praise this book highly enough.

How to Be a Perfect Stranger: A Guide to Etiquette in Other People's Religious Ceremonies. Volume 1, *America's Largest Faiths,* edited by Arthur J. Magida; Volume 2, *Other Faiths in America,* edited by Stuart M. Matlins and Arthur J. Magida. Woodstock, Vt.: Jewish Lights Publishing, 1996. The titles of these books pretty much spell out their intentions. For those who wish not only to know more about the worship experiences of other religious traditions but also to enter into those experiences directly, these books provide the knowledge needed to be a respectful visitor.

Hughs, Ina. *A Prayer for Children.* New York: William Morrow, 1995; Fireside Books, 1997. This isn't really a book *about* prayer, but it did grow out of a prayer for children that Ina Hughs wrote, and which became a poem beloved by millions (we've included it in the section on prayers for parents, grandparents, and others who love children). In this book Hughs, a longtime newspaper columnist, offers a series of amusing and wise vignettes about parents and children. She is so observant and so honest that as you read these stories you find yourself nodding and smiling (and occasionally wincing) through them all.

Karenga, Maulana. *Kwanzaa: A Celebration of Family, Community and Culture.* Los Angeles: University of Sankore Press, 1998. The author of this book is the founder of the Kwanzaa celebration. Here he provides a concise overview of the history, values, symbols, and activities of Kwanzaa.

Kilpatrick, William, and Gregory and Suzanne M. Wolfe. *Books That Build Character: A Guide to Teaching Your Children Moral Values through Stories.* New York: Touchstone/Simon & Schuster, 1994. Prayer and reading aloud are the perfect bedtime activities for children. Of course, it goes without saying that the great children's books need not have any overt spiritual messages in order to nurture a child's heart. In this parents' guide, we begin with several chapters outlining the relationship between storytelling and a child's moral development. The rest of the book consists of an annotated bibliography of more than three hundred classic and contemporary books for children. The bibliography is divided into a wide variety of genres and subdivided by appropriate age groups.

Kilpatrick, William, and Gregory and Suzanne M. Wolfe. *The Family New Media Guide: A Guide to Teaching Your Children Moral Values through Videos and Other Multimedia Products.* New York: Touchstone/Simon & Schuster, 1997. Parents can't be blamed for worrying about the moral implications of the new media—the Internet is like the real world: parts of it aren't for children. At the same time, Hollywood, digital media, and the Internet aren't going to go away, so it is vital that parents seek out the best content for their children, especially when the children are very young. This guide opens with chapters about the moral issues raised by movies and the new electronic media, including computer games and the Internet. The second part of the book consists of an annotated guide to the best films, spoken word audiotapes, CD-ROMs, and Internet websites for children.

Kopciowski, Elias, comp. *Praying with the Jewish Tradition.* Grand Rapids, Mich.: Eerdmans, 1997. In the introduction to this book of prayers, Rabbi Lionel Blue writes: "Jewish prayers take the form of blessings. They ask little and are God-centered. God is like this or like that they say (or both), and the world which he fashioned is so, and this is the way a wise and good man should journey through it." These prayers, Rabbi Blue continues, often come in pairs, forming a dialectic— between optimism and a sense of human vanity, between God's relationship with the Jews and with all the people of the world. This dialectic is important "in an age when spirituality is easily confused with sentimentalism and feeling with faith." We couldn't agree more. This collection includes prayers of praise, thanksgiving, mercy, and daily living.

Lamott, Anne. *Traveling Mercies: Some Thoughts on Faith.* New York: Pantheon, 1999. Anne Lamott's writing—whether it be in her novels or personal narratives—is hilarious and poignant in equal measure. Her earthy language may shock some readers, but her honesty and insight are undeniable. In this book Lamott tells the story of her return to the Christian faith after years of self-destructive behavior. Her story will resonate with anyone who is seeking, with a fair amount of nervousness and insecurity, to learn more about the ancient Christian faith and the way people are living it out today.

L'Engle, Madeleine. *Ladder of Angels.* New York: Harper & Row, 1988. Twenty years ago, one of our most imaginative children's writers, Madeleine L'Engle, was asked to judge a "Children of the World Illustrate the Old Testament" contest. L'Engle, the author of *A Wrinkle in Time* and numerous other novels as well as spiritual meditations, wrote a series of short poems and meditations to accompany the sixty-five best pictures. The result is this marvelous book. The intersection of L'Engle's childlike wisdom and these youthful encounters with the Bible is irresistible. The real revelation in the book, however, is not L'Engle's text but the colorful creations in pastel, crayon, and Magic Marker made by the children. They remind us how easy—and how wrong—it is for us to underestimate the spiritual and emotional depth of a child's heart and the capacity of that heart to respond to the ancient stories of faith.

Lewis, C. S. *Letters to Malcolm: Chiefly on Prayer.* New York: Harcourt Brace, 1964. The ever-popular author of *The Chronicles of Narnia,* one of the greatest series of children's books ever written, was just as accomplished as a Christian apologist. Compared to many of his books on religious faith, *Letters to Malcolm* is more informal and more personal. Penned near the end of Lewis's life, it contains a lifetime's worth of insight into the life of prayer.

McGinnis, James and Kathleen. *Parenting for Peace and Justice: Ten Years Later.* Maryknoll, N.Y.: Orbis Books, 1990. You will probably not be comfortable with this book unless you think of yourself as being left of the political center. Nonetheless, Catholic social activists Kathleen and James McGinnis have written a thoughtful book on how parents and children alike can link their spiritual lives to the need for compassionate action in the world. Among the subjects of this book are ways to help children deal with violence, racism, and sexism.

Nhat Hanh, Thich. *The Miracle of Mindfulness: A Manual on Meditation.* Boston: Beacon Press, 1975. Thich Nhat Hanh is one of the world's most admired spiritual writers. A Zen master, he is also a poet and peace activist who was nominated for the Nobel Peace Prize by Martin Luther King Jr. in 1967. This short book is an illuminating guide to the heart of Buddhist meditation, which fosters a growing mindfulness about the world around us. Included are stories, advice, and a series of exercises that unite body and mind in meditation. While this book was not written with children in mind, many of the insights and exercises can be adapted for use in family life. Nhat Hanh is also the author of the classic *Living Buddha, Living Christ.*

Norris, Kathleen. *Amazing Grace: A Vocabulary of Faith.* New York: Riverhead Books, 1998. The genesis of this book, according to best-selling writer Kathleen Norris, was the experience she had on returning, as an adult, to her childhood Christian faith: as she came back into a church atmosphere, she encountered a bewildering variety of Christian terms, symbols, and theological concepts that meant very little to her. Her brief, engaging meditations on many of these terms and symbols help readers to see beyond what can appear to be intimidating abstractions into the heart of the Christian worldview.

Norris, Kathleen. *The Cloister Walk*. New York: Riverhead Books, 1996. Though she is a Presbyterian, poet, and spiritual writer Kathleen Norris found herself becoming deeply attracted to Catholic monasticism, and in particular the Benedictine tradition. In this collection of reflections, stories, and essays, Norris explores the ancient habits of Benedictine monks, including their prayer life, their emphasis on community, and their attitude toward work. What she discovers is a spirituality that has a thousand applications to everyday life.

Riley, Dorothy Winbush. *The Complete Kwanzaa: Celebrating Our Cultural Harvest*. New York: Harperperennial, 1996. One of the most popular and comprehensive books on the subject, *The Complete Kwanzaa* explains the traditional ceremonies, foods, clothing, and history of this African American holiday. It also contains poems and other texts to help celebrants reflect on the seven principles that lie at the heart of Kwanzaa.

Tutu, Desmond. *An African Prayer Book*. New York: Doubleday, 1995. In this collection, the Nobel Peace Prize–winner and former Anglican archbishop of Johannesburg, Desmond Tutu—one of the world's great crusaders for peace and justice—offers the richness of his continent's spirituality.

Wangerin, Walter, Jr. *Whole Prayer: Speaking and Listening to God*. Grand Rapids, Mich.: Zondervan, 1998. Walter Wangerin Jr. is well known for his award-winning novels *The Book of the Dun Cow* and *The Book of Sorrows*. But he is also a best-selling spiritual writer who comes out of the Lutheran tradition. This book is a wonderful introduction to prayer within a Christian context. The stress here is on prayer as *conversation*—speaking with God rather than merely to him. Many of the insights found in this book will apply directly to family prayers. Highly recommended.

Wolfe, Gregory, and Suzanne M. Wolfe. *Climb High, Climb Far: Inspiration for Life's Challenges from the World's*

Great Moral Traditions. New York: Fireside Books, 1996. In spite of all the violence and discord in the world, there are millions of people who exhibit a re- markable degree of generosity and love. The truth is that many of these contemporary individuals are mo- tivated by their belief in ancient moral and spiritual traditions. In this book we go back to these traditions to find moral inspiration in quotations from the world's great religions. We also provide quotes and stories that demonstrate just how vital these ancient tradi- tions are in the lives of people today. The book is or- ganized into fifteen sections, including childhood, friendship, work, service, nature, citizenship, the el- derly, and death.

Magazines and Devotional Publications for Children and Families

Despite the wealth of books and prayer collections available today, one of the chief concerns that any parent will have about family prayer life is that it not fall into a routine and become stale and boring. One of the best ways to introduce variety into family prayer is to subscribe to magazines or subscription-based prayer guides that include specific devo- tions, scriptures, and many other features for every day of the year. The following selection is by no means exhaustive, but it does contain some of the most reputable and reliable publications available.

Devo'Zine. The Upper Room, P.O. Box 37146, Boone, IA 50037-0146. (Six issues per year; $16.95; 1-800-925- 6847.) A devotional magazine written by youth and youth leaders and published by The Upper Room, a Methodist organization that has become one of America's leading publishers on the subject of prayer and Christian spirituality, *Devo'Zine* is designed to link teens to their peers and to help strengthen their faith. Each issue contains meditations, prayers, feature articles, reflection questions, full-color art, and more. It is also available in a Lutheran edition.

Guideposts for Kids. Guideposts, 39 Seminary Hill Road, Carmel, NY 10512. (Six issues per year; $15.95; 1-800-431-2344.) An offshoot of the enormously popular devotional magazine *Guideposts,* this magazine is perfect for younger children who want a spiritual guide all their own. Each issue contains feature stories, comics, fiction, puzzles, and articles with moral and spiritual guidance.

Guideposts for Teens. Guideposts, 39 Seminary Hill Road, Carmel, NY 10512. (Six issues per year; $19.95; 1-800-431-2344.) The latest devotional publication from *Guideposts*—for teens.

Magnificat. Magnificat, P.O. Box 91, Spencerville, MD 20868-9978. (Twelve monthly issues plus supplements for Lent/Easter and Advent/Christmas; $39.95; 301-853-6600.) *Magnificat* is not geared to young children, so it won't be helpful for children under the age of about eight, but for anyone older it is one of the best Catholic devotional publications on the market. Each issue contains morning and evening prayers, along with the specific readings for Mass, for every day of the year. In addition, there are articles on spirituality, brief paragraphs on the lives of the saints, and many other rewarding features. We use *Magnificat* for evening prayers most nights of the week.

Pockets. The Upper Room, P.O. Box 37146, Boone, IA 50037-0146. (Eleven issues per year; $16.95; 1-800-925-6847.) *Pockets* is a forty-eight-page devotional magazine targeted to elementary school age children (ages six to twelve) and intended for their personal use. It includes full-color illustrations, stories, poems, games, activities, daily scripture readings, recipes, and contributions from children.

ABOUT THE AUTHORS

GREGORY and SUZANNE M. WOLFE are the parents of four children. With William Kilpatrick, they have written *The Family New Media Guide* and *Books That Build Character*. Gregory seves as Writer in Residence at Seattle Pacific University. He is the publisher and editor of *Image: A Journal of the Arts and Religion*, one of America's leading quarterlies, and is the author of several books, including *Malcolm Mugggeridge: A Biography*. Suzanne teaches English literature at Seattle Pacific University and is currently working on her first novel. Both Gregory and Suzanne hold degrees from Oxford University. They live in Seattle, Washington.

To learn more about prayer and spirituality in family life, visit the Wolfes' Web site: www.circleofgrace.com.

Credits

369

Credits